Reader's Guide
to
LORD ALFRED TENNYSON

Reader's Guide to LORD ALFRED TENNYSON

W. Cormier

CENTRUM PRESS
NEW DELHI-110002 (INDIA)

CENTRUM PRESS
H.O.: 4360/4, Ansari Road, Daryaganj,
New Delhi-110 002 (India)
Ph.: 23278000, 23261597

B.O.: No. 1015, Ist Main Road, BSK IIIrd Stage
IIIrd Phase, IIIrd Block,
Bangalore - 560 085 (India)
Tel.: 080-41723429
Visit us at: www.centrumpress.com

Reader's Guide to Lord Alfred Tennyson

First Edition, 2009

ISBN 978-93-80106-78-6

PRINTED IN INDIA

Printed at Balaji Offset, Delhi.

Contents

Preface

Alfred Tennyson was born August 6th, 1809, at Somersby, Lincolnshire, fourth of twelve children of George and Elizabeth Tennyson. The poet's grandfather had violated tradition by making his younger son, Charles, his heir, and arranging for the poet's father to enter the ministry. The contrast of his own family's relatively straitened circumstances to the great wealth of his aunt Elizabeth Russell and Uncle Charles Tennyson made Tennyson feel particularly impoverished and led him to worry about money all his life.

He also had a lifelong fear of mental illness, for several men in his family had a mild form of epilepsy, which was then thought a shameful disease. His father and brother Arthur made their cases worse by excessive drinking. His brother Edward had to be confined in a mental institution after 1833, and he himself spent a few weeks under doctors' care in 1843.

Since Tennyson was always sensitive to criticism, the mixed reception of his 1832 Poems hurt him greatly. Critics in those days delighted in the harshness of their reviews: the Quarterly Review was known as the "Hang, draw, and quarterly." John Wilson Croker's harsh criticisms of some of the poems in our anthology kept Tennyson from publishing again for another nine years. Late in the 1830s Tennyson grew concerned about his mental health and visited a sanitarium run by Dr. Matthew Allen, with whom he later invested his inheritance and some of his family's money.

Author

Chapter 1

Introduction

Alfred Tennyson, 1st Baron Tennyson (6 August 1809 – 6 October 1892) was Poet Laureate of the United Kingdom and remains one of the most popular English poets. Tennyson excelled at penning short lyrics, including "In the valley of Cauteretz," "Break, break, break", "The Charge of the Light Brigade", "Tears, idle tears" and "Crossing the Bar". Much of his verse was based on classical mythological themes, although *In Memoriam A.H.H.* was written to commemorate his best friend Arthur Hallam, a fellow poet and classmate at Trinity College, Cambridge, who was engaged to Tennyson's sister, but died from a cerebral hemorrhage before they were married.

Tennyson also wrote some notable blank verse including Idylls of the King, Ulysses, and Tithonus. During his career, Tennyson attempted drama, but his plays enjoyed little success in his lifetime. Tennyson wrote a number of phrases that have become commonplaces of the English language, including: "nature, red in tooth and claw", "better to have loved and lost", "Theirs not to reason why, / Theirs but to do and die", and "My strength is as the strength of ten, / Because my heart is pure". He is the second most frequently quoted writer in *The Oxford Dictionary of Quotations,* after Shakespeare.

EARLY LIFE

Tennyson was born in Somersby, Lincolnshire, a rector's son and fourth of 12 children. He was one of the descendants of King Edward III of England. Reportedly, "the pedigree of his grandfather, George Tennyson, is traced back to the middle-class line of the Tennysons, and through Elizabeth

Clayton ten generations back to Edmund, Duke of Somerset, and farther back to Edward III." His father, George Clayton Tennyson (1778–1831), was a rector for Somersby (1807–1831), also rector of Benniworth and Bag Enderby, and vicar of Grimsby (1815).

The reverend was the elder of two sons, but was disinherited at an early age by his own father, the landowner George Tennyson (who belonged to the Lincolnshire gentry as the owner of Bayons Manor and Usselby Hall), in favour of his younger brother Charles, who later took the name Charles Tennyson d'Eyncourt. Rev. George Clayton Tennyson raised a large family and "was a man of superior abilities and varied attainments, who tried his hand with fair success in architecture, painting, music, and poetry."

Rev. Tennyson was "comfortably well off for a country clergyman and his shrewd money management enabled the family to spend summers at Mablethorpe and Skegness, on the eastern coast of England." His mother, Elizabeth Fytche was the daughter of Stephen Fytche, vicar of St. James Church, Louth (1764) and rector of Withcall (1780), a small village between Horncastle and Louth.

Tennyson's father "carefully attended to the education and training of his children." Tennyson and two of his elder sisters were writing poetry in their teens, and a collection of poems by all three was published locally when Alfred was only 17. One of those brothers, Charles Tennyson Turner later married Louisa Sellwood, the younger sister of Alfred's future wife; the other poet brother was Frederick Tennyson. One of Tennyson's other brothers, Edward Tennyson, was institutionalised at a private mental asylum, where he later died.

EDUCATION AND FIRST PUBLICATION

Tennyson was first a student of Louth Grammar School for four years (1816–1820) and then attended Scaitcliffe School, Englefield Green and King Edward VI Grammar School, Louth. He entered Trinity College, Cambridge in 1828, where he joined a secret society called the Cambridge Apostles. At

Cambridge Tennyson met Arthur Henry Hallam, who became his best friend. His first publication was a collection of "his boyish rhymes and those of his elder brother Charles" entitled *Poems by Two Brothers* published in 1827. In 1829 he was awarded the Chancellor's Gold Medal at Cambridge for one of his first pieces, "*Timbuctoo*".

Reportedly, "it was thought to be no slight honour for a young man of twenty to win the chancellor's gold medal." He published his first solo collection of poems, *Poems Chiefly Lyrical* in 1830. "Claribel" and "Mariana", which later took their place among Tennyson's most celebrated poems, were included in this volume. Although decried by some critics as overly sentimental, his verse soon proved popular and brought Tennyson to the attention of well-known writers of the day, including Samuel Taylor Coleridge.

RETURN TO LINCOLNSHIRE

Tennyson with his wife Emily and his sons Hallam and Lionel. In the spring of 1831, Tennyson's father died, requiring him to leave Cambridge before taking his degree. He returned to the rectory, where he was permitted to live for another six years, and shared responsibility for his widowed mother and the family. Arthur Hallam came to stay with his family during the summer and became engaged to Tennyson's sister, Emilia Tennyson.

In 1833, Tennyson published his second book of poetry, which included his well-known poem, *The Lady of Shalott*. The volume met heavy criticism, which so discouraged Tennyson that he did not publish again for 10 more years, although he continued to write. That same year, Hallam died suddenly and unexpectedly after suffering a cerebral hemorrhage while on vacation in Vienna.

Though scholars are mostly of the view that Tennyson's friendship with Hallam was close but platonic rather than homosexual, some have questioned the nature of the relationship. There is no dispute, however, that Hallam's sudden death in 1833 had a profound impact on Tennyson, and inspired several masterpieces, including In Memoriam

A.H.H., a long poem detailing the 'Way of the Soul'. Tennyson and his family were allowed to stay in the rectory for some time, but later moved to Essex. An unwise investment in an ecclesiastical wood-carving enterprise soon led to the loss of much of the family fortune. He then moved to London.

RECOGNITION

In 1842, while living modestly in London, Tennyson published two volumes of *Poems,* the first of which included works already published and the second of which was made up almost entirely of new poems. They met with immediate success. Poems from this collection, such as *Locksley Hall,* "Tithonus", and "Ulysses" have met enduring fame. *The Princess: A Medley,* a satire of women's education, which came out in 1847, was also popular.

W. S. Gilbert later adapted and parodied the piece twice: in *The Princess* (1870) and in *Princess Ida* (1884). It was in 1850 that Tennyson reached the pinnacle of his career, finally publishing his masterpiece, *In Memoriam A.H.H.,* dedicated to Hallam. Later the same year he was appointed Poet Laureate in succession to William Wordsworth. In the same year (13 June), Tennyson married Emily Sellwood, whom he had known since childhood, in the village of Shiplake. They had two sons, Hallam Tennyson — named after his friend — and Lionel.

THE POET LAUREATE

After William Wordsworth's death in 1850, Tennyson succeeded to the position of Poet Laureate, which he held until his own death in 1892. He fulfilled the requirements of this position by turning out appropriate but often uninspired verse, such as a poem of greeting to Alexandra of Denmark when she arrived in Britain to marry the future King Edward VII. In 1855, Tennyson produced one of his best known works, "The Charge of the Light Brigade," a dramatic tribute to the British cavalrymen involved in an ill-advised charge on 25 October 1854, during the Crimean War.

Other esteemed works written in the post of Poet Laureate

include *Ode on the Death of the Duke of Wellington* and *Ode Sung at the Opening of the International Exhibition*.

Queen Victoria was an ardent admirer of Tennyson's work, and in 1884 created him Baron Tennyson, of Aldworth in the County of Sussex and of Freshwater in the Isle of Wight. Tennyson initially declined a baronetcy in 1865 and 1868 (when tendered by Disraeli), finally accepting a peerage in 1883 at Gladstone's earnest solicitation. He took his seat in the House of Lords on 11 March 1884. Tennyson's life at Freshwater features in Virginia Woolf's play of the same name, in which Tennyson mingles with his friend Julia Margaret Cameron and G.F. Watts. He was the first English writer raised to the Peerage. A passionate man with some peculiarities of nature, he was never particularly comfortable as a peer, and it is widely held that he took the peerage in order to secure a future for his son Hallam.

Recordings exist of Tennyson declaiming his own poetry, which were made by Thomas Edison, but they are of understandably poor quality. These were made in the last few years of Tennyson's life and include recordings of The Charge of the Light Brigade, and excerpts from "The splendour falls" (from The Princess), "Come into the garden" (from Maud), "Ask me no more," "Ode on the death of the Duke of Wellington," "Charge of the Heavy Brigade", and "Lancelot and Elaine".

Towards the end of his life Tennyson revealed that his "religious beliefs also defied convention, leaning towards agnosticism and pandeism": Famously, he wrote in *In Memoriam*: "There lives more faith in honest doubt, believe me, than in half the creeds." In *Maud*, 1855, he wrote: "The churches have killed their Christ." In "Locksley Hall Sixty Years After," Tennyson wrote: "Christian love among the churches look'd the twin of heathen hate."

In his play, *Becket*, he wrote: "We are self-uncertain creatures, and we may, Yea, even when we know not, mix our spites and private hates with our defence of Heaven." Tennyson recorded in his *Diary*: "I believe in Pantheism of a sort." His son's biography confirms that Tennyson was not

Christian, noting that Tennyson praised Giordano Bruno and Spinoza on his deathbed, saying of Bruno: "His view of God is in some ways mine." D. 1892.

Tennyson continued writing into his eighties, and died on 6 October 1892, aged 83. He was buried at Westminster Abbey. A memorial was erected in All Saints' Church, Freshwater. He was succeeded as 2nd Baron Tennyson by his son, Hallam, who produced an authorised biography of his father in 1897, and was later the second Governor-General of Australia. Throughout his career some anthologists have noted subtle anti-American undertones in his work. Tennyson never denied the underlying themes when questioned about them.

THE ART OF TENNYSON'S POETRY

Tennyson used a wide range of subject matter, ranging from medieval legends to classical myths and from domestic situations to observations of nature, as source material for his poetry. The influence of John Keats and other Romantic poets published before and during his childhood is evident from the richness of his imagery and descriptive writing. He also handled rhythm masterfully. The insistent beat of *Break, Break, Break* emphasizes the sadness and relentlessness of the subject matter. Tennyson's use of the musical qualities of words to emphasize his rhythms and meanings is sensitive. The language of "I come from haunts of coot and hern" lilts and ripples like the brook in the poem and the last two lines of "Come down O maid from yonder mountain height" illustrate his telling combination of onomatopoeia, alliteration and assonance:

The moan of doves in immemorial elms
And murmuring of innumerable bees.

Tennyson was a craftsman who polished and revised his manuscripts extensively. Few poets have used such a variety of styles with such an exact understanding of metre. He reflects the Victorian period of his maturity in his feeling for order and his tendency towards moralizing and self-indulgent melancholy. He also reflects a concern common among Victorian writers in being troubled by the conflict between religious faith and expanding scientific knowledge. Like many writers who write a great deal over a long time, he can be pompous or banal, but his personality rings throughout all his works—work that reflects a grand and special variability in its quality.

Tennyson possessed the strongest poetic power; he put great length into many works, most famous of which are *Maud* and *Idylls of the King*, the latter one of literature's greatest treatments of the legend of King Arthur and The Knights of the Round Table.

PARTIAL LIST OF WORKS

- From *Poems, Chiefly Lyrical* (1830):
- *The Dying Swan*
- *The Kraken*
- *Mariana*
- *Lady Clara Vere de Vere* (1832)
- From *Poems* (1833): *The Lotos-Eaters*
- *The Lady of Shalott* (1832, 1842)
- From *Poems* (1842): *Locksley Hall*
- *Tithonus*
- *Vision of Sin*
- *The Two Voices* (1834)
- "Ulysses" (1833)
- *The Princess* (1847)
- "Tears, Idle Tears"
- *In Memoriam A.H.H.* (1849)
- *Ring Out, Wild Bells* (1850)
- *The Eagle* (1851)
- *The Sister's Shame*
- *The Charge of the Light Brigade* (1854) - an early recording exists of Tennyson reading this
- *Maud* (1855/1856)
- *Enoch Arden* (1862/1864)
- *Flower in the crannied wall* (1869)
- *The Window* - Song cycle with Arthur Sullivan. (1871)
- *Harold* (1876) - began a revival of interest in King Harold

- *Idylls of the King* (composed 1833-1874)
- *Locksley Hall Sixty Years After* (1886)
- *Crossing the Bar* (1889)
- *The Foresters* - a play with incidental music by Arthur Sullivan (1891)
- *Now Sleeps the Crimson Petal* - it appeared as a song in the film Vanity Fair, with musical arrangement by Mychael Danna.

Chapter 2

Medievalism and Tragedy

While bringing Irish Iseult to King Mark at the beginning of Tristram of Lyonesse, Swinburne's hero introduces Iseult (and the unfamiliar reader as well) to the whole body of Arthurian myth that surrounds Tristram and Iseult's story. The two are sailing aboard the Swallow when

the soft speech between them grew again
With questionings and records of what men
Rose mightiest, and what names of love or fight
Shone starriest overhead of queen or knight. [Poems, IV, 27]

Among these "records," Tristram recounts the experiences of the knight Balen, whose legend Swinburne took up thirteen years after the publication of Tristram in his second grand poem on Arthurian themes, The Tale of Balen (published in 1896). Tristram's brief description of Balen's life serves as a virtual precis of the later work, revealing how little Swinburne's essential conception of the heroic character and fate of Balen changed during almost two decades. Swinburne summarizes Tristram's view of "the toil of Balen," who, for all his labor and virtue and for "all his days," reaped

but thorns for fruit and tears for praise,
Whose hap was evil as his heart was good,
And all his works and ways by wold and wood
Led through much pain to one last labouring day
When blood for tears washed grief with life away. [Poems, IV, 29]

The emphasis here, as in the Tale itself, is upon Balen's deeds and his innocence. In this last truly important Victorian medievalist poem, the good knight's various attempts to cleanse and regenerate an irretrievably corrupt world are ineffectual. The omission of Balen from most critical considerations of Swinburne's accomplishment is surprising since his Tale is a dense and extraordinarily energetic work. As is typical of Swinburne, this long narrative poem is self-consciously innovative, if not revolutionary.

Indeed, because of its unique form and unusual prosody as well as its energy and poignancy, the work was much admired by its initial reviewers and early critics. As Clyde Hyder recalls, "The Times suggests that [Balen] is not 'unworthy of comparison with the efforts of the late Poet Laureate.'The Saturday Review more justly reflects that Swinburne's version is truer to the spirit of the old story".

Hyder reinforces such commentaries, insisting that "the skillful use of the nine-line stanza for narrative purposes could not fail to excite admiration." Comments by significant early ciritics support his contention. T. Earle Welby describes Balen as "the freshest, most human, most lucid, least straining long poem of Swinburne's last twenty years ... full of its own youth and of the clean sharp air of his native Northumberland".

The poem is, for Welby, one of Swinburne's "masterpieces on the great scale." Georges Lafourcade insists that Balen is a "subtle and powerful" poem. Even more forcefully, Samuel Chew asserts that it "is certainly the finest achievement of Swinburne's later life, an extraordinarily fresh evocation of the spirit of adventure, of chivalry, and of the wild northern country". Regarding Swinburne's "metrical feat," Chew observes, "the stanza is varied in tone and color to suit the sense, now light and dancing, now swift, trenchant and severe."

However, the only recent critic to concur with these early evaluations is Jerome McGann, who argues that Balen "is graced with a richness and artistic ease which only come when a poet's mind and crafthave reached maturity". In contrast, McSweeney's enthusiasm for Balen is minimal. Despite McGann's often incisive discussion of the poem and despite the visibly rapid growth of interest in Swinburne's works and their remarkable influence on his contemporaries as well as on subsequent generations of writers, however, no thorough and sympathetic analysis of Balen has yet appeared. Such an analysis not only helps to refute the gradually dissolving commonplace among Victorianists that Swinburne entered his dotage after 1879.

It also demonstrates the extent to which the poet continued until the end of the century to be a major force in the extremely complex and persistent developments of Victorian medievalism. In The Tale of Balen, Swinburne once again confronts and overturns the typically Victorian idealization of medieval times, particularly the "Golden Age" of Arthur.

In his conception of history as essentially cyclical, this age, like any other, is characterized by the agonies of disappointed love, by travail and Empedoclean strife, by the futile battle against evil, by dissimulation of all kinds and, perhaps most significantly, by a hopeless tangle of moral uncertainties and ambiguities that always frustrate and eventually destroy the stalwart and ingenuous heart.

As McGann carefully points out in his treatment of the Tale, the world of Camelot is thoroughly corrupt. Unlike its depiction in the early books of Tennyson's Idylls of the King, the image of Arthur's realm and the forces that control it in Swinburne's poem is a morally bleak one: "In the world ruled by Arthur nothing is innocent or even what it seems: all pleasures are delusive joys or entirely illusory, while all pain is cruelty and viciousness developed through forms of deception or cowardice or self-indulgence".

Through his inversion of Victorian preconceptions about the medieval world, but also by means of other radically innovative procedures and techniques, Swinburne constructs a remarkable poem, one whose central thematic concerns are Love and Fate, as is the case with his other major works set in medieval times. But here Swinburne extends his previous uses of medieval sources and a medieval atmosphere by thoroughly Hellenizing his subject matter.

Although much of the poem's starkly compressed narrative is taken up with intense descriptions of chivalric warfare, the events described are not fundamentally romantic. Balen's martial successes (like Oedipus' apparent accomplishments) only lead Balen closer to the malignant fate that Merlin continually reminds us is inevitable for him. Similarly, the love focused on here is always fraternal or filial (appropriate to the feudal context) rather than erotic, and Balen's dedication to his fellow man always turns out badly, if not tragically, for those he seeks to aid and for himself.

As a result, the poem is fraught with dramatic ironies and with highly realistic moral ambiguities. Both depend, in large part, upon Swinburne's careful depiction of his hero as an ingenuous, exuberant, and stoical knight. Swinburne's "Balen the Wild" is not, like the antihero of Tennyson's idyll, an irrepressibly savage man. He is, instead, a vital and morally pure primitive. He is quintessential Romantic man, but his energies and admirable moral inclinations serve only tragic and therefore dolorously unromantic ends.

Essential to Swinburne's endeavor in Balen are its form, its prosody, and its image patterns, all of which prove to be obstacles to readers' enjoyment of the Tale but which themselves constitute crucial archaisms reinforcing the poem's medieval atmosphere as well as its tragic view of the human condition. In the Dedicatory Epistle to his collected Poems, Swinburne explains:

> The form ... was chosen as a test of the truth of my conviction that such a work could be done better on the straitest and strictest principles of verse than on the looser and more slippery lines of mediaeval or modern improvisation. The impulsive and irregular verse which had been held sufficient for the stanza selected or accepted by Thornton and by Tennyson seemed capable of improvement and invigoration as a vehicle or a medium for poetic narrative. And I think it has not been found unfit to give something of the dignity as well as facility to a narrative which recasts in modern English verse one of the noblest and loveliest old English legends. [Hyder (ed.), Swinburne Replies.]

Yet Swinburne himself at first had reservations about the poem's form and prosody, as he implies in a letter to Theodore

Watts six months before Balen's publication. Visiting his ailing mother, Swinburne recounts that "I have just had a very pleasant interview with her and read her part of the tale of Balen in Mallory [sic] and the first fytte of my poem, which she seems much pleased with-metre and all".

Like Swinburne's mother, early readers of The Tale of Balen seemed to find its prosody no barrier to enjoyment, though modern critics seem daunted by the highly alliterative and densely rhymed nine-line stanzas. Philip Henderson observes that "the poem has been highly praised, but a metre resembling 'The Lady of Shalott' becomes almost unendurable when spun out to such a length". The resemblance between Swinburne's iambic tetrameter stanzas and those of Tennyson's poem is immediately apparent to every reader and seems with the same immediacy to be appropriately "medieval."

Although few readers pursue the reasons for this nearly subliminal perception, they are quite clear. The use of frequent repetition, of short lines, and of predominantly monosyllabic words results in the appearance of an almost balladic simplicity that, because of entrenched literary prejudices, we at once associate with the "primitive" past, i.e., with medieval times. Yet for Swinburne, as for Tennyson, these deceptively unsophisticated stanzas that evoke a medieval atmosphere can be used to achieve complex, sometimes sublime effects. In Balen they do suggest a return to natural primitivism, which is reinforced by abundant nature imagery; they allow for the extremely compressed depiction of intense action (especially in battle scenes); and they enable the poet repeatedly to underscore his tragic world view by means of simple understatement and frequent ironies.

In his attempt to generate a medieval atmosphere, Swinburne employs nature imagery copiously. Like Tennyson's Idylls, The Tale of Balen is organized seasonally. Its seven sections begin with an evocative description of springtime, and its final "fytte" starts with a philosophical depiction of winter, which for "northern men" inspires "Music that bids the spirit sing / And day give thanks for night."

Between the seasonal frames, the poem is dense with similes and metaphors from nature, reinforcing our identification of Balen as primitive man. Much like Tristram, he is a virtuous extension of nature, which is throughout the poem a benevolent force, though it has no control over any heroic individual's inevitably tragic fate.

Stanza one of the first section typifies Swinburne's use of nature imagery and simple langauge to create an exuberant mood and to achieve transcendental thematic effects.

In hawthorn-time the heart grows light,
The world is sweet in sound and sight,
Glad thoughts and birds take flower and flight,
The heather kindles toward the light,
The whin is frankincense and flame.
And be it for strife or be it for love
The falcon quickens as the dove
When earth is touched from heaven above
With joythatknowsnoname. [Poems, IV, 157]

Swinburne presents us here with the Empedoclean world of his poem governed by Mars and Venus, the falcon and the dove, strife and love. It is a world that is nonetheless innocent-indeed, intractably regenerate (perpetually quickened "When ... touched from heaven"), at least as far as nature land Balen) are concerned. In the next stanza we find that the "northern child" Balen

glad in spirit and sad in soul
With dream and doubt of days that roll
As waves that race and find no goal
Rode on by bush and brake and bole. [Poems, IV, 157]

The simple diction and imagery in this passage underscore Balen's oneness with the seminal benevolent and destructive forces of nature. He is a medieval brother, not only to Balan, but also to Swinburne's Chastelard, Meleager, Thalassius, and Tristram. Throughout Balen, Swinburne uses these images to suggest a return to nature that Victorians such as Ruskin and Morris continually associated with medieval times. (For instance, the pun on the word nature in Ruskin's famous chapter "The Nature of Gothic" has to my knowledge not yet been mentioned by his critics.) He also employs images from nature to enhance the medieval atmosphere. Pre-Raphaelite effects periodically suspend the poem's intense action and provide tableaux, as in a Gothic tapestry. Our eyes are drawn from the activity of man to the significant stasis of nature, which reflects the benevolent generative forces always at work in the world:

And down a dim deep woodland way
They rode between the boughs asway
With flickering winds whose flash and play
Made sunlight sunnier where the day
Laughed, leapt, and fluttered like a bird
Caught in a light loose leafy net
That earth for amorous heaven had set
To hold and see the sundawn yet
And hear what morning heard. [Poems, IV, 201]

This is a striking example of a Pre-Raphaelite "special moment" in which, as Jeffrey Prince has observed, characters "often half mad with the acute deliquescence of their world ... tend to dwell on isolated moments of intense sensation which lend meaning to their thwarted lives". Beyond the nature imagery that evokes a primitive atmosphere and the static qualities typical of medieval art, the versification in Balen enables Swinburne to compress action in balladic fashion.

The most expert and prolific of Victorian ballad writers, Swinburne enunciates in his essay "The Poems of Dante Gabriel Rossetti" his central ideas about the ballad as a literary form: The highest form of ballad requires from a poet at once narrative power, lyrical, and dramatic; it must hold in fusion these three faculties at once, or fail of its mark: it must condense the large loose fluency of romantic taletelling into tight and intense brevity; it must give as in summary the result and extract of events and emotions, without the exhibition of their gradual change and growth which a romance of the older type or the newer must lay open to us in order; it must be swifter to step and sharper of stroke than any other form of poetry.

The writer of a first-rate tragic ballad must be yet more select in his matter and terse in his treatment of what he selects from the heap of possible incident, than Chaucer in the compilation of his "Knight's Tale" from the epic romance of Boccaccio, or Morris in the sculpture of his noble master-poem, "The Lovers of Gudrun," from the unhewn rock of a half-formed history or a half-grown legend. Ballads have been cut out of such poems as these, even as they were carven out of shapeless chronicles. There can be no pause in a ballad, and no excess; nothing that flags, nothing that overflows; there must be no waste of a word or a minute in the course of its rapid and fiery motion.

Two passages in which Swinburne exploits the potential effects of balladic compression are especially instructive. For instance, when Balen and his brother successfully confront the forces of King Ryons, Arthur's Welsh foe, they

smote their strong king down, ere yet
His hurrying horde of spears might get
Fierce vantage of them. Then the fight
Grew great and joyous as it grew,
For left and right those brethren slew,
Till all the lawn waxed red with dew
More deep than dews of night. [Poems, IV, 187]

The extreme telescoping of action here contributes to the medieval atmosphere by suggesting a historical distance that Swinburne confirms in the next stanza: "And ere the full fierce tale was read / Full forty lay before them dead." The tumultuous events just described have immediately become petrified as a tale. Events and the hero's response to them are similarly compressed early in the fourth section of the poem when Balen confronts Launceor. He pursued Balen with Arthur's sanction after Balen had rashly beheaded his own enemy but Arthur's friend, the Lady of the Lake, and fled Camelot (fytte three).

Balen's spear through Launceor's shield
Clove as a ploughshare cleaves the field
And pierced the hauberk triple-steeled,
That horse with horseman stricken reeled,
And as a storm-breached rock falls, fell
And Balen turned his horse again

And wist not yet his foe lay slain,
And saw him dead that sought his bane
And wrought and fared not well. [Poems, IV, 177]

Here, besides achieving remarkable compression and explosive energy, we find Swinburne making careful use of his stanza's ninth, trimeter line to force upon us, through the kind of ironic understatement typical of Malory and Chaucer, an awareness of Balen's pervasively tragic world view. Immediately afterwards, musing "in manyminded mood / If life or death were evil or good," Balen watches helplessly as Launceor's distraught "maiden flower-like white" appears suddenly from the woods and kills herself — she "struck one swift and bitter stroke / That healed her, and she died." Such unanticipated tragedies punctuate the Tale and reinforce its fatalism. Swinburne in fact throughout the poem associates his medieval subject and the work's medievalist form and atmosphere with specifically Greek conceptions of the tragic human condition, a procedure that is neither illogical nor unprecedented.

Associations of the medieval with the Hellenic and specifically with Homer, though lost to most of Swinburne's contemporaries, have their roots in the eighteenth century. Alice Chandler cites such an association in the works of both Richard Hurd (who published Letters on Chivalry and Romance in 1760) and Thomas Warton: "Hurd wrote in a passage that seems to mark the ending of an exclusively neoclassic ideal that Homer would have preferred the Middle Ages to his own times 'for the improved gallantry of the feudal limes and the superior solemnity of their superstitions.' This idea was echoed in The History of English Poetry by Thomas Warton who claimed that medieval manners had 'the same common merit with the pictures in Homer, that of being founded in truth and reality'".

Those Arthurian and Trojan themes are two of the central sources of subject matter for medieval romanceurs reveals how natural the connection between them is, but it was one seldom made during the nineteenth century. However, Swinburne, conscious in his usual scholarly fashion of his place in literary tradition, revives the historical association between Greek and Arthurian mythology. Discussing The Tale of Balen in the Dedicatory Epistle to his collected Poems, Swinburne observes:

The age when these [Arthurian] romances actually lived side by side with the reviving legends of Thebes and Troy, not in the crude and bloodless forms of Celtic and archaic fancy but in the ampler and manlier developments of Teutonic and medieval imagination, was the age of Dante and Chaucer....

There is no episode in the cycle of Arthurian romance more genuinely Homeric in its sublime simplicity of submission to the masterdom of fate than that which I have rather reproduced than recast in "The Tale of Balen": and impossible as it is to render the text or express the spirit of the lliad in prose or rhyme — above all, in English blank verse-it is possible in such a metre as was chosen and refashioned for this poem, to give some sense of the rage and rapture of battle for which Homer himself could only find fit and full expression by similitudes drawn like mine from ... the sea.

The identification of the Hellenic and the medieval depends, of course, on the intense fatalism Swinburne perceives at the heart of both cultures' mythologies. Significantly, it is a perception that only a few of his contemporaries, including Hardy and Arnold, would have shared, but it is one with which Georges Lafourcade concurs. He explains that in Balen, Swinburne has "returned to the more sober style and monotonous metre of his early poems; with unfailing instinct he has recaptured the essential features of the medieval theme — he sense of unjust oppressive doom heroically endured." Appropriately, Lafourcade concludes his discussion of the poem with a deft observation: "Balen is to Tristram what Erechtheus is to Atalanta". Swinburne would certainly have approved this juxtaposition of medieval narrative and Greek tragedy.

The tragic implications of Balen's life and the fatalistic world view that this poem propounds are monitored throughout the Tale by the narrator as well as by Merlin, who functions virtually as a symbol of Fate. The narrator, too, continually reminds us that his hero's "hap was evil as his heart was good." In the course of the poem's events Balen is motivated principally by filial and feudal ties-by his remarkable, entirely democratic loyalty to all men and women who are not clearly enemies and by his unshakable loyalty to Arthur, who in Swinburne's poem lacks both wisdom and vision. Like nearly all of Balen's characters including the hero himself, Arthur repeatedly acts in rash, uninformed ways. Surrounding every event in the tale, moreover, is an atmosphere of moral ambiguity that, as in all tragedies, lends force to the poem's fatalism.

The omnipresence of "doom" is articulated in the first stanzas of each section of the poem, and it is always described with metaphors from nature. These descriptions help to define the poem's symmetrical structure and emphasize its fundamental concern with mutability and with the inseparability of all contraries in the cycles of nature, history, and every man's life-generation and destruction, triumph and defeat, joy and grief. In the poem's third stanza we are introduced to a constitutionally ebullient Balen, whose "blood and breath / Sang out within him" and for whom "time and death / Were even as words a dreamer saith." Balen is a monist, a pantheist, and a stoic, as are all Swinburne's unequivocal heroes. For him

light and life and spring were one.
The steed between his knees that sprang,
The moors and woods that shone and sang,
The hours where through the spring's breath rang,
Seemed ageless as the sun.

But we learn immediately that despite his exultant, Words worthian communion with the objects and spirit of nature,

His soul forfelt a shadow of doom,
His heart foreknew a gloomier gloom
Than closes all men's equal ways. [Poems, IV, 157-58]

At every turn in the poem we are reminded of that "shadow of doom," sometimes with a heavy-handedness that becomes oppressive. The narrator serves, in one role, as a fatalistic choral voice, as does Merlin throughout the poem. At the beginning of section seven, parallel to the opening of every other section, the entirely sympathetic narrator repeats that

Aloud and dark as hell or hate
Round salen s head the wind of fate
slew storm and cloud from death's wide gate:
sut joy as grief in him was great
To face God's doom and live or die,
sorrowing for ill wrought unaware,
Rejoicing in desire to dare
All ill that innocence might bear
With changeless heart and eye. [Poems, IV, 214]

Despite alarming prophecies and events that confirm them, Balen maintains an irrepressible spirit. His autonomy, stoicism, and tenacity are subtly but ingeniously defined in this passage by Swinburne's pun on bear. Balen simultaneously endures evil, unwittingly conveys it to others, and exposes it in the Arthurian world. One evil that Balen quite literally bears throughout the poem is the sword Malison, which he wins from the distressed maiden captive to it in the first fytte. As the central symbol of fate, it is the vehicle for all Balen's unwitting "evil" deeds, which include his killing the Lady of the Lake, Launceor, Garlon, and his own brother Balan. Each sword stroke for Balen is increasingly dolorous. But two additional and sub ordinate emblems of fate's malignancy also appear, each presiding over approximately half the poem. The first is Arthur; the second, Balen's foe Garlon.

Arthur is himself a victim of inscrutable forces but also the indirect cause of Balen's fate, insofar as Balen is continually trying either to placate or to please his monarch. Digressing from the legend as it appears in Malory, Swinburne periodically in the first half of his narrative allows the forbidding shadow of Arthur's incestuous relationship with Morgause and its fatal consequence (Mordred) to interrupt and dominate his hero's own experiences.

Morgause appears first at Camelot, just before Balen releases the maiden from Malison's spell, and then at the funeral of her husband, King Lot, who unsuccessfully attempts to rescue King Ryons, his brother whom Balen has captured.

During both of Morgause's appearances Swinburne makes ironic use of eye imagery to remind us of fate's inevitability and to suggest the ominous interaction throughout the Arthurian saga between Arthur's blind rashness and Merlin's futile vision.

At Camelot in the poem's second fytte, Morgause is described, significantly, sitting between two other ill-fated Arthurian beauties, Iseult and Guenevere, but Morgause is "darklier doomed than they whose cheer / Foreshadowed not yet the deadlier year / That bids the queenliest head bow down" (Poems, IV, 163). As Morgause views vain attempts by various knights to liberate the maiden from the power of Malison, her "eyes / That dwelt on days afar," alternating "bright and dark,... / Shone strange as fate" (Poems, IV, 166). Shortly, in a striking instance of foreshadowing after Lamoracke fails to draw the mysterious sword, Morgause's eyes meet Arthur's,

And one in blood and one in sin
Their hearts caught fire of pain within
And knew no goal for them to sin
But death that guerdons guilt. [Poems, IV, 164]

The inevitability of continued suffering and corruption, of ruined dreams, and of evil's ultimate dominion in the world is affirmed once more with eye imagery at the end of the poem's fifth section when Morgause mourns Lot's death:

The splendour of her sovereign eyes
Flashed darkness deeper than the skies [144/145]
Feel or fear when the sunset dies
On his that felt as midnight rise
Their doom upon them, there undone
By faith in fear ere thought could yield
A shadowy sense of days revealed,
The ravin of the final field,
The terror of their son.
For Arthur's, as they caught the light
That sought and durst not seek his sight,
Darkened, and all his spirit's might
Withered within him even as night

Withers when sunrise thrills the sea.
But Mordred's lightened as with fire
That smote his mother and his sire
With darkling doom and deep desire
That bade its darkness be. [Poems, IV, 195]

Deftly, Swinburne here reveals that Arthur and the ideals he represents are not sovereign in the world of Camelot. In league with Mordred, Morgause presides over events while her ruthlessly destructive son by Arthur is a functionary of "darkling doom." Thus, both occasions on which the larger Arthurian myth is introduced during the first half of Balen serve to reinforce the poem's tragedy and to enhance the significance of Balen's traditionally subordinate tale and our response to it.

Through much of the second half of the narrative, Garlon, King Pellam's brother who is repeatedly described as "the invisible evil," symbolizes Fate, just as Arthur is an emblem of its power in the world during the first half. Early in the sixth section (the poem's last two fyttes are half the work), Balen encounters the first of Garlon's victims that we hear of, an anonymous wayfaring knight accompanied by a maiden.

At Arthur's request, Balen pursues him. In his usual fraternal manner Balen, knowing nothing at all of the knight's background, spontaneously agrees to be his protector: "I / Will be your warrant or will die" (Poems, IV, 200). Then at Arthur's very doorstep a symbolic challenge to the establishment of any dreams of order or the survival of goodness in the world unexpectedly occurs:

Suddenly fell the strange knight, slain
By one that came and went again
And none might see him; but his spear
Clove through the body, swift as fire. [Poems, IV, 200) [145/146]

This victim of Garlon is significantly like Balen in being "one that death held dear," a "man whose doom" is "forefelt as dire." But he is unlike Balen because his premonitions "Had darkened all his life's desire." Balen never fears Garlon while pursuing him after this event, nor ultimately does he fear death itself. In the Tale's last scene, unknowingly about to fight his own brother, Balen demonstrates the stoic resignation that is, throughout the narrative, the counterpart of his indefatigable zest for life. He says,

"Be it life or death, my change I take,
se it lifews to build or deathts to break:
And fall what may, me lists not make
Moan for sad life's or death's sad sake."
Then looked he on his armour, glad
And high of heart, and found it strong. [Poems, IV, 22425]

It is finally this irrepressible gusto and Balen's impulsive determination to combat all apparent evils that result in his own and Balan's destruction. But all this is predetermined, as Merlin continually reminds us and as the symbol of Garlon suggests.

Balen and the maiden encounter the third victim of "the invisible evil" in section six when they come upon the grief-stricken father of a boy seriously wounded by Garlon. The father's description of Garlon makes clear the extent to which he symbolizes all men's doom. Almost an allegorical figure, Garlon resembles Death in Chaucer's "Pardoner's Tale":

"Invisible as the spirit of night
That heaven and earth in depth and height
May see not by the mild moon's light
Nor even when the star would grant them sight,
He walks and slays as plaguets blind breath
Slays." [Poems. IV, 206]

The Chaucerian atmosphere is blatant in this passage, with its allusions to astrology and the plague. But unlike Chaucer's Death, which is the traditional wages of sin, death in Balen overshadows the lives of all heroic men. It threatens to and always does undermine good works and ideals. Moreover, premonitions of its inevitability darken "all [the] life's desire" of those singled out as special targets of Fate.

By means of these emblematic victims whose tragedies are grand and poignant, Fate's power is revealed to the world. Balen and Arthur are, of course, two such victims, and Merlin is the monitory spokesman against Fate in the case of each hero. But, as in all tragedies, Merlin's prophetic wisdom ironically brings on "all the latter woe" rather than retarding it. Early in section six of the Tale we learn that, just before the first appearance of Garlon, Merlin had "shown the king / The doom that songs unborn should sing." As a result, "on the king for fear's sake fell / Sickness, and sorrow deep as hell." Like the role of the seer in many Greek tragedies, the role of Merlin as an unwilling functionary of Fate in The Tale of Balen intensifies the poem's ironies and our emotional responses to them.

Throughout the poem Merlin serves as a self-appointed liaison between Arthur and Balen. Formally, he mediates between the Tale's Arthurian materials and those concerned exclusively with Balen. He thus becomes an extension of the narrator iout, like the chorus in a Greek tragedy, remains indirectly involved in events and emotionally engaged with them. Thus, after explaining to Arthur why the king was wrong to banish Balen for slaying the Lady of the Lake, and after recounting the conspiracy between Lady Lyle and the maiden who bore Malison to Camelot, he can lament,

"grief it is to think how he
That won it, being of heart so free
And perfect found in chivalry,
Shall by that sword be slain." [Poems, IV, 173]

Similarly, after Launceor's death at Balen's hands and the suicide of Launceor's beloved, Merlin addresses Balen despairingly:

"My heart is wrung for this deed's sake,
To know thee therefore doomed to take
Upon thine hand a curse, and make
Three kingdoms pine through twelve years change,
In want and woe: for thou shalt smite
The man most noble and truest knight
That looks upon the live world's light
A dolorous stroke and strange." [Poems, IV, 184]

The whole world of Balen is indeed dolorous and strange not only because of the catastrophic fate its heroes suffer but also because the morality of actions taken by them is persistently indeterminate. Although Balen's filial values and heroic virtues never become suspect in the course of the poem, his impetuous behavior does. Like the greatest heroes in Homer and in Greek tragedy, Balen suffers from both hamarfia and hubris. The poem's first fytte recounts Balen's origins and his first rash actions that tarnished the honor his knightly deeds had brought to "the strange north strand / That sent him south so goodly a knight".

Insulted by one of Arthur's kinsmen, Balen "Swift from his place leapt" and "wrote / His wrath in blood upon the bloat / Brute cheek" of the "king-born knave". In this encounter Balen is defending Northumberland as well as his own pride, but the morality of his actions and the justification for them remain equivocal. For his rash violence in killing the slanderous knight, Balen is imprisoned by Arthur for six months, and the present action of the poem begins in its second fytte with the arrival of the maiden captive to Malison's spell. She appears just as Balen's own captivity ends.

In almost all Balen's subsequent deeds the morality of his behavior is similarly indeterminate, because in the world of Camelot as realistically depicted by Swinburne, moral certainties are impossible, and even the most apparently virtuous actions affect Balen and his world in unanticipated, adverse ways. As Balen himself realizes at his death, "here / Light is as darkness, hope as fear / And love as hate". Ultimately, the reader is led to sympathize with every character in the Tale who is not totally flat.

No matter how ostensibly "evil," each is, like Balen and like Arthur, a victim of Fate in a perversely amoral world. Such is the case with King Lot and King Pellam, each of whom in his assault upon Balen (or Arthur) acts from filial motives. As a result, we do not know, for instance, how to construe Balen's sudden murder of the Lady of the Lake in fytte two, even though the narrator informs us that by "her fell craft his mother died." Our first response to Balen's impetuous deed is like Arthur's:

"Alas for shame," the high king said,
"That one found once my friend lies dead;

Alas for all our shame!" [Poems, IV, 169]

The implication of Arthur's last words here is, significantly, that any of us might have done precisely as Balen did, but our actions, like his, would have been misguided. Despite all monitions, impulse tragically governs all men's behavior, as it has done in Arthur's relations with Morgause and as it does Balen's throughout his Tale.

Balen's character itself therefore often seems only equivocally virtuous. His usually admirable ebullience and vitality appear as mere unwarranted capriciousness when he refuses to return Malison to the maiden who bore it to Camelot. Despite her clear warning that

"with it thou shalt surely slay
Of all that look upon the day
The man best loved of thee, and lay
Thine own life down for his,"

Balen perversely responds, "God's will ... it is, we know, / Wherewith our lives are bound" (Poems, IV, 166). What in other circumstances we would describe as tenacity, here seems to be simple stubbornness. Later in the poem, commenting on the martial valor of Balen and his brother during the battle between Arthur's forces and those of King Lot, the narrator reinforces the moral uncertaintites that pervade the Tale when he observes that

Strong wonder smote the souls of men
If heavenws own host or hellSs deep den
Had sent them forth to slay. [Poems, IV, 191]

But as in Blake's Marriage of Heaven and Hell, facile moral tags are in this poem mere stultifying fictions. In Swinburne's pessimistic adaptation of Blake's optimistic epistemology, such terms as heaven and hell are inadequate to the tragic conception of human experience projected by this poem.

Throughout The Tale of Balen moral ambiguity alternates with transparent irony in conveying Swinburne's world view. No matter how virtuous Balen's motives initially appear, his actions inevitably generate suffering, if not calamity. His keeping Malison, of course, provides the vehicle for the poem's framing tragedy, but many subordinate tragedies intervene. His killing of Launceor in self-defense results in the suicide of that knight's beloved. His capture of King Ryons and Lot's attempt to rescue his brother end with Lot's death and the slaughter of "many a mother's son". Balen's killing of Garlon, as prophesied, "Brought sorrow down for many a year / On many a man in many a land". Afeer Pellam's death and the de struction of his castle, Balen travels aimlessly, seeing that "on either hand" in

Bright fields and cities built to stand
Till time should break them, dead men lay;
And loud and long from all their folk
Living, one cry that cursed him broke;
Three countries had his dolorous stroke
Slain, or should surely slay. [Poems, IV, 213]

And, in his penultimate adventure, Balen is responsible for three other deaths. Bringing the knight Garnysshe to a garden in which his adulterous beloved lies with another, Balen watches Garnysshe impetuously behead the false lovers. When Garnysshe repents, he rebukes Balen: "ere this my life was glad. / Thou hast done this deed." He explains: "I had lived my sorrow down, hadst thou / Not shown me what I saw but now". Balen's well-intentioned strategy has failed, but he enunciates it nonetheless:

"God knows,
I did, to set a bondman free,
sut as I would thou hadst done by me,
That seeing what love must die to see
Lovets end might well be woe's." [Poems, IV, 220]

With the suicide of Garnysshe, Balen himself is ready for death. Soon hearing merrymakers in the neighborhood blowing a horn, he says, "That blast is blown for me ... / The prize am I who am yet not dead".

Balen, of course, dies, ironically, at the hands (and virtually in the arms) of his brother, an appropriate culmination to a moving legend. Swinburne surely chose this subject for his last major Arthurian work because of its tragic poignancy and because it allowed him to extend and complete his poetic discussion of Love. In previous works his focus had been primarily on the tragedy of erotic love and the comedy of pantheistic spiritual passion that serves throughout Swinburne's poems as a consolatory counterpoint to eros.

Among the optimistic poems, for example, that dwell on joyous intercourse with nature, see, for example, "Thalassius," "On the Cliffs," "A Nympholept," "The Lake of Gaube," and "The Garden of Cymodoce." Also, in works such as Atalanfa in Calydon, "Phaedra," and his novels he had dealt with perverse examples of filial love. However, in The Tale of Balen, Swinburne is able to represent in tragic fashion the whole spectrum of filial and fraternal love relationships.

The medieval setting of Balen is especially appropriate because the poet can make use of nineteenth-century idealizations of medieval society as pervasively altruistic and harmonious. Such portrayals appear from Scott through Carlyle, Ruskin, Arnold, Marx, and Morris. Alice Chandler correctly observes that "feudalism was seen as fatherhood, and the medieval world-to adopt Carlyle's phrase-was thought to be 'godlike and my Father's", The extended implication here is that all God's children are bound by unbreakable filial ties.

Such is unequivocally the case in Swinburne's poem (though populated by several feudal families hostile to one another), and he fully exploits the tragic ironies that arise because of these ties. The work is significantly, dedicated to his mother and recounts events in the lives of at least three pairs of actual brothers.

In his dedication Swinburne alerts us to the emphasis upon filial "Love that holds life and death in fee, / Deep as the clear unsounded sea" (Poems, IV, 155), and in the Tale itself we are repeatedly reminded that familial ties, like erotic ones, are sublime but inevitably tragic. Apart from continual narrative reminders that Balen and Balan are doomed, we are given the examples of King Lot's devotion to his brother, Ryons, and of Pellam's fatal dedication-"For love of this my brother slain" (Poems, IV, 210) — to avenging Garlon's death. Such blood ties between brothers exemplify but are ultimately subsumed under larger secular, religious, and aesthetic systems of reciprocal filial allegiance appropriate to the feudal context.

In the poem, brothers who vainly sacrifice themselves for one another become types, respectively, of Arthur, the worldly king whose filial dedication to humanity is doomed; of Christ, the spiritual king whose symbols are preserved in Pellam's castle and whose self-sacrifice for mankind (from the evidence of the radically fallen world of this poem) was equally futile; and of the poet whose attempt in verse at least to memorialize tragedies of human allegiance is fated to enjoy at best only cyclical and therefore limited success.

The poem "needs must live a springtide space, / While April suns grow strong" (Poems, IV, 155). These larger exemplars of sublime devotion to the human community serve as a chronological frame and thematic groundwork for the more extended particular treatments of doomed brotherly love in the poem.

Among the framing filial relationships the most significant and the one treated in the greatest detail is Balen's with Arthur. In a passage from the poem's sixth fytte, immediately after Arthur defeats Lot's forces, Swinburne's proverbial hero worship appears in service to the poem's essential theme. Balen alights from his horse before the king

In reverence made for love's sake bright
With joy that set his face alight
As theirs who see, alive, above,
The sovereign of their souls, whose name
To them is even as love's own flame
To enkindle hope that heeds not fame
And knows no lord but love. [Poems, IV, 198]

Arthur's paternalism inspires in Balen transcendent emotions that generate selfless behavior.

The same is also true of all relationships in the poem that are characterized by brotherly love. Selfless generosity and devotion, even to others who have no familial claims, appear repeatedly. For instance, just after the deaths of Launceor and his beloved, King Mark appears, "whose name the sweet south-west / Held high in honour" (Poems, IV, 181).

Resembling the poet dedicated to memoralizing tragic lovers in Tristram of Lyonesse and in this poem, Mark "made moan to hear their doom," and

for their sorrow's sake he sware
To seek in all the marches there
The church that man might find most fair
And build therein their tomb. [Poems, IV, 182]

Like those who survive the victims of fraternal or erotic love in this poem (at least those not immediately bent on revenge), Mark is sorrowful but resigned to events, rather than rancorous toward Balen, who is directly responsible for the lovers' deaths. Acceptance like Mark's reflects the fatalistic world view held by almost all the characters in the poem.

An episode in the sixth fytte also reveals the extent to which spontaneous love of one's fellows (along with its contrary, strife between feudal camps) governs the world of Balen.

Accompanied by his maiden, Balen discovers a castle occupied by a "lady stricken" who, to be healed, requires a bowl of blood from "a maiden clean and whole / In virgin body and virgin soul / Whose name was writ on Royal roll." Spontaneously, the maiden insists upon making whatever sacrifice is necessary: "'Good knight of mine, good will have I /To help this healing though I die.'" Predictably, Balen adds, "'Nay ... but love may try /What help in living love may lie'" (Poems, IV, 203-205). Although this attempt fails, the lady is later saved by sisterly self-sacrifice. "Another maid in later Mays / Won with her life" the "woful praise" of healing her.

The numerous instances of self-sacrificial devotion to one's fellows that are recounted in The Tale of Balen serve primarily to enhance the tragic example of Balen himself, who is the model of brotherly love (except, of course, in his behavior to those who directly threaten him, his family, and his king).

As in the case of the "lady stricken," Balen at every turn devotes himself spontaneously to the welfare of others. He does so with the first of Garlon's viceims and the father of the third, whose son Garlon has unexpectedly assauleed and wounded, "even ere love might fear / That hate were strong as death" (Poems, IV, 206). Balen commiserates, explaining that Garlon has already killed "'two knights of mine, / Two cornrades, sealed by faith's bright sign'" (Poems, IV, 206).

When Balen soon finds and impetuously kills Garlon, however, the repercussions are catastrophic, just as they are almost every time Balen tries to serve his king, protect the reputation of his homeland, or assist a fellow knight. As I have observed, such is the case with Garnysshe, whom Balen strives to aid immediately after he has killed Garlon along with his brother, Pellam, and realized the dreadful truth of Merlin's prophecies concerning the dolorous stroke. Balen is renewed at first by his encounter with Garnysshe-his "face as dawn's grew bright, / For hope to help a happier man" (Poems, IV, 218). But Garnysshe falls on his own sword after killing his faithless beloved and the knight beside her.

The culmination of all Balen's frustrated, misguided, and doomed exercises in fraternal devotion is, of course, his fatal encounter with his real brother, an encounter steeped in dramatic irony. Balen does battle with the "good knight" guarding the island simply because of external circumstances and pressures, not because of any significant internal motivation.

The extent to which the Tale's final calamity is inevitable and compulsory becomes clear when the merrymakers instruct Balen that "all for whom these halls make cheer" must fight the knight on the island who "guards ... I Against all swords that chance brings near." Tragically disheartened by the dolorous reslilts of all his previous experiences, Balen proceeds to the island, even though he decries the "evil custom" that allows "none whom chance hath led / Hither, if knighthood crown his head, / To pass unstirred to strife" (Poems, IV, 222). Apparently Balen, like the reader, by now sees the "evil custom" as a symbol of the whole tragic and fatal enterprise of life itself. He is therefore resigned to the inevitability of his participation.

The tragedy of the heroic brothers' combat at the end of the Tale is fully prepared for early on. In fact, all Balen's fraternal overtures, his doomed attempts to assist fellow knights, reflect Balen's determination to extend to the rest of the world his sublime relationship with Balan, which is detailed early in the narrative. The extraordinary sense of identity between the brothers encompasses more than their names. Balan is first described as the

Twin flower of bright Northumberland,
Twin sea-bird of their loud sea-strand,
Twinsong-birdoftheirmorn. [Poems, IV, 179}

The narrator celebrates "The likeness graven of face and face" when the two "kissed and wept upon each other / For joy and pity ... / And love engraffed by sire and mother" (Poems, IV, 180). The striking term engraffed suggests the extent to which Balen and Balen are virtually twin parts of a single organism. Alone each is, by implication, deficient and the world disharmonious. Balen's exuberance and nostalgia at their reunion is, thus, in every sense natural:

the might of joy in love
Brake forth within him as a fire,
And deep delight in deep desire
Of far-flown days whose full-souled quire
Rang round from the air above. [Poems, IV, 179]

After the two knights part, it is understandable that Balen tries repeatedly but without success to complete and fulfill himself in relationships based upon the fraternal pattern that must be the basis of all wholesome social intercourse and of any potentially ideal human community in the world of this poem. Unique to Swinburne's version of the legend, this fact geometrically amplifies the ironic significance of Balen's final battle.

As in all great tragedies, fate in Balen operates as a force that is both internal and external, impelling and compelling. No external threats alone-including the Lady of the Lake, King Ryons' soldiers, Garlon, Pellam, or even the atmosphere of Christian sanctification that protects Pellam-can destroy Balen.

This monarch among knights, heroic in his strength, his filial virtues, his tenacity, endurance, and stoicism, can succumb only to his own best powers symbolized by his brother, Balan. At the same time, however, in his last fight

Balen finally liberates himself from an irretrievably corrupt and grievous world, one for which his heart is too high, his spirit too pure. Swinburne describes the last moments of the brothers' battle in appropriately ironic terms. By the end of it, "With blood that either spilt and bled / Was all the ground they fought on red." Each knight "umnailed and marked" from the fight "poured and drank the draught of death, / Till fate was full at last" (Poems, IV, 227) in a parody communion, a metaphorical celebration of the supreme tragedy of fraternal love. At the end they make "a mutual moan" that defines their tragedy:

"Both we came out of one tomb, One star-crossed motherts woful womb, And so within one grave pitws gloom Untimely shall we lie." [Poems, IV, 230]

Thus, "the last blind battle broke / The consummated spell" that has surrounded the lives of these brothers. But using the mode of correspondences, in the way Swinburne has by now taught us to read his narrative, we realize that more is revealed here than the tragedy of two heroic medieval knights. Balen's career, based on thwarted filial and fraternal ideals, is by extension the tragedy of mankind whose pitiable fate it is to strive for fulfillment through filial, erotic, and fraternal love, but, in doing so, to generate only strife and be freed from frustration and suffering only in death.

Chpater 3

Idylls of the King

Tennyson is often regarded as the most skilled stylist and most representative poet of the Victorian period, and *Idylls of the King* is his magnum opus. Throughout his tenure as poet laureate he repeatedly revised the volume, and its themes concerned him for most of his life. *Idylls* addresses what Tennyson considered to be a growing tendency toward hedonism in Victorian society and an attendant rejection of spiritual values.

While many critics have since found his idylls excessively moralistic, *Idylls of the King* attests to Tennyson's remarkable lyrical skill and his place as one of the greatest poets in the English language. As a child, Tennyson's reading of Sir Thomas Malory's *Morte d'Arthur* sparked his interest in Arthurian myth. As this interest developed, so did Tennyson's concern those ancient English ideals, as well as society's sense of common decency, were being desecrated by the gradual corruption of accepted morality. Drafts of Arthurian poems from Tennyson's youth still exist, and he would later write his friends that he had mentally "composed" a number of other Arthurian poems for inclusion in an envisioned monumental achievement.

The first full-length idyll that Tennyson wrote and that would later be included in the finished *Idylls* was "Morte d'Arthur," which was written at the same time as *In Memoriam* (1850); fragments of each appear in the same notebook. *In Memoriam* was written in 1833 at the time of the death of Arthur Henry Hallam, Tennyson's closest friend. Meanwhile, Tennyson, still convinced of the degeneration of Victorianism, continued work on his visionary masterpiece. He read most of the available sources on Arthurian legend and even learned sufficient Welsh to read some of the original documents. He also visited Wales and the west country of England to view the actual sites connected with Arthur: Bude, Tintagel (King Mark's Castle), Land's End at the tip of Cornwall (where Lancelot is said to have been), and Glastonbury.

TEXTUAL HISTORY

The extensive and intricate publication history of *Idylls of the King* reflects Tennyson's lifelong preoccupation. "Morte d'Arthur" was published in a two-volume collection of Tennyson's poetry in 1842, but was later wholly incorporated into "The Passing of Arthur" (the very last idyll), which did not appear in the *Idylls* until 1870. In the intervening period, Tennyson privately printed a "trial book" of four idylls—"Enid," "Vivien," "Elaine," and "Guinevere"—with the title *The True and the False. Four Idylls of the King.* He later changed the title to *Idylls of the King* when it was published in 1859; this version contained only four of the eventual twelve idylls. After the 1859 edition, however, Tennyson continued to produce material that would find its way into later editions.

"A Dedication," in honor of Prince Albert, an admirer who died in 1861, was published as a pamphlet in 1862. In December of 1869 Tennyson published *The Holy Grail, and Other Poems,* which, along with a selection of other poems, includes "The Holy Grail" and three other idylls—"The Coming of Arthur," "Pelleas and Ettarre," and "The Passing of Arthur." The "Dedication" and the four Arthurian idylls from *The Holy Grail* were included in *Idylls of the King* of January 1870, which also contained renamed versions of the four original idylls. In 1871 Tennyson published "The Last Tournament" in a periodical, and a year later republished it together with "Gareth and Lynette" in a book called *Gareth and Lynette,* along with notes locating their places in the *Idylls.* In 1885 "Balin and Balan" appeared in *Tiresias and Other Poems,* with a note that it would introduce "Merlin and Vivien." The poetry of *Idylls of the King* is comprised of poetry written over an extended period of Tennyson's life, and even when the twelve idylls had been assembled, Tennyson continued to make small changes to the volume; the final state of the *Idylls* did not appear until 1899, after the author's death, when Hallam Tennyson, on his father's verbal instruction, inserted a line into the epilogue.

PLOT AND MAJOR CHARACTERS

Framed by "The Coming of Arthur" and "The Passing of Arthur," *Idylls of the King* portrays the rise and fall of Arthur's kingdom, and coextensively, the decline of the Arthurian ideal. At the beginning of the book, Arthur becomes leader not because of birthright, but because of his extraordinary military skill and leadership. He subsequently surrounds himself with a group of dedicated knights who vow to uphold a standard of sexual purity: the knights restrict themselves to monogamous sexual relationships, holding themselves to the same standards to which women had traditionally been held. In the springtime of Arthur's reign, his knights are inspired to extraordinary feats of bravery; in "Gareth and Lynette," for example, the "kitchen-knave" Gareth overcomes three knights and even Death itself.

But the Arthurian pledge begins to deteriorate when rumors of Guinevere's (the king's wife) affair with Lancelot are spread by Vivien, the emissary of Arthur's enemy King Mark. Guinevere's deed and Vivien's word attack the code of purity that had held the kingdom together. Among other things, the disillusionment with the destruction of the civilized pact in favor of animalistic passions hastens Merlin's pitiful demise.

Arthurian society dissolves, precipitated by the transgression of its moral code. In an effort to bolster Arthur's waning ideal, the knights seek out the Holy Grail, but only a few return from the quest. Without his young knights, Arthur and his remaining forces must then face an attack by Mordred (rumored to be Arthur's bastard son) and the Saxons. On the way to the battle, Arthur visits Guinevere in the nunnery to which she has confined herself; Guinevere repents, but too late to save the dying Arthurian ideal. Arthur defeats and kills Mordred, but is also mortally wounded. Guinevere's adulterous affair with Lancelot has led to the downfall of the Arthurian moral code and to Arthur's own death.

MAJOR THEMES

Although Tennyson always thought of the idylls as allegorical (his word was "parabolic"), he refused to make literal identifications between incidents, characters, or situations in the poems and what they stood for, except to indicate generally that by King Arthur he meant the soul, and that the disintegration of the court and the Round Table revealed the disruptive effect of the passions. Indeed, the decay of the Round Table came increasingly to seem to him an apt symbol for the decay of nineteenth-century England. *Idylls of the King* expresses his ideal of the British Empire as an exemplar of moral and social order: the "Table Round / A glorious company" would "serve as a model for the mighty world."

However, when individual acts of betrayal and corruption result from adultery committed by Guinevere and Lancelot, the ensuing disorder destroys the unity of the Round Table, symbolizing the effects of moral decay that were Tennyson's chief contemporary concern. Although Malory's *Morte d'Arthur* pictures Mordred—the alleged product of Arthur's incestuous relationship with his half-sister—as the cause of Arthur's downfall, Tennyson instead concentrates on Guinevere's adultery with Lancelot. This moralizing of Arthurian legend led many, particularly William Gladstone, to expect in the *Idylls* a national, Christian epic comparable to that of John Milton's *Paradise Lost* in terms of its moral vision; Tennyson wrote, "I tried in my *Idylls* to teach men the need of an ideal"—a moralistic, Victorian standard of proper conduct.

CRITICAL RECEPTION

Critical reception varied with the different editions of *Idylls of the King,* and many critics regretted its piecemeal publication and complained that the separately created idylls resist treatment as a cohesive whole. Furthermore, although they almost universally applauded Tennyson's style and particularly his use of blank verse, critics were divided between those who thought it a worthy companion to Malory and those who found it more play-acting than drama, with the costumes failing to disguise Tennyson's contemporaries and their concerns.

According to many critics, *Idylls of the King* fails to generate tragic interest in the characters: characters like Vivien, Ettarre, and King Mark are despicable; Guinevere and the rest of the women are generally too weak; and, for nineteenth-century poet and critic Algernon Swinburne, Arthur is no more than an uninspiring cuckold. A clear moral distinction and didactic undercurrent also drain the volume of significant dramatic interest, some critics have noted, while others contend that Tennyson's vision of a spiritually elevated world was betrayed by his concessions to a smug and materialistic Victorian ethic.

Recently, however, a growing number of critics have dismissed such generalizations, and *Idylls* has come to be viewed as the embodiment of the Victorian period and of a poet who reflected both the thoughts and feelings of his generation.

Chapter 4

The Two Voices

Throughout his life Tennyson was subject to trance-like fits of abstraction in which the veil of sensory appearances seemed to draw aside and the inner life of things to stand revealed. It was largely on the testimony of such fleeting intuitions that the poet based his faith in spiritual being as the ultimate reality. A friend, Mrs. Marian Bradley, wrote that Tennyson remarked, after reading the Grail Idyll aloud: "Yes, it is true.

There are moments when this flesh is nothing to me, when I feel and know the flesh to be the vision, God and the spiritual the only real and true-depend upon it, the spiritual is the real, it belongs to one more than the hand and the foot." The records of the poet's life contain many statements of a like nature; for instance, near the end of his life Tennyson told an acquaintance: "Sometimes as I sit here alone in this great room I get carried away out of sense and body, and rapt into mere existence, till the accidental touch or movement of one of my own fingers is like a great shock and blow and brings the body back with a terrible start."

Yet Tennyson had inherited his full measure of the family's black blood with its susceptibility to prolonged periods of moroseness and depression. When these were on him, he distrusted all irrational promptings from the beyond as delusory snares, and tended to fall back for support on more conventional religious ideas.

Since Tennyson's temperament was at all times and to an unusual extent characterized by a variability between the extremes of exaltation and despair, it is small wonder that the enigma of human consciousness with its conflicting intuitions should from the outset appear as a dominant motif in his poetry. Already in his earliest writing a polarity is observable, represented by two kinds of poetry, one showing morbid preoccupation with the artist's subjection to his times the other marked by a refusal to accept any such restriction.

Thus, among Tennyson's Juvenilia one group of poems, prevailingly pessimistic and low-spirited in tone, exhibits a paralyzing sense of insecurity with regard to the outside world. The opening lines of the rejected "Perdidi Diem" sound a typical note:

I must needs pore upon the mysteries
Of my own infinite Nature and torment
My Spirit with a fruitless discontent ...

More explicit is the "Supposed Confessions" of a "Second-rate Sensitive Mind" in which the poet reproaches himself for having abandoned the "common faith" bequeathed by his mother. He speaks of his "gloomed fancy" and makes significant reference to his "damned vacillating state" and to "our double nature." As if in guilty acknowledgment of the penalty attached to denial of God, he cries: "I am void,/ Dark, formless, utterly destroyed."

In a contrary mood, however, Tennyson is aggressively disposed to repudiate the world and to seek immunity from its disturbances in the depths of his own imaginative being. The most arresting early example of such self-withdrawal is the poem entitled "The Mystic," omitted after the 1830 volume. Possession of the visionary power has set the central figure apart from his fellows: "How could ye know him? Ye were yet within/ The narrower circle." While one hesitates to make out a case for Tennyson as in any sense a true mystic, this poem written before he was twenty-one is penetrated with strange insights and shows a remarkable grasp of the experiences which it purports to describe. In his condition of "still serene abstraction" the mystic transcends the boundaries of normal being and stands outside the limitations of time and space:

He often lying broad awake, and yet
Remaining from the body, and apart

In intellect and power and will, hath heard
Time flowing in the middle of the night,
And all things creeping to a day of doom.

It may be noted in this connection, however, that the levels of intuitive awareness in Tennyson's poetry, as identified in the third section of the present chapter, very closely conform to the categories of mystical experience analyzed by William James in his Varieties of Religious Experience. Likewise, the four characteristics of the mystical habit of mind listed in Bertrand Russell's essay, "Mysticism and Logic", might be illustrated by innumerable passages from Tennyson.

Another poem, published in 1830 but not thereafter, ascribes equal authority to the revelations of the individual imagination. This is [Greek title], based, as its title indicates, on the Heraclitean doctrine of flux:

All thoughts, all creeds, all dreams are true,
All visions wild and strange;
Man is the measure of all truth
Unto himself. All truth is change.
All men do walk in sleep, and all
Have faith in that they dream:
For all things arc as they seem to all,
And all things flow like a stream.
There is no rest, no calm, no pause,
Nor good nor ill, nor light nor shade,
Nor essence nor eternal laws:
For nothing is, but all is made.
But if I dream that all these are,
They are to me for that I dream;
For all,things are as they seem to all,
And all things flow like a stream.

That the youthful Tennyson lived more intensely in his dreams than in the world around him is apparent from such a work as the prize poem "Timbuctoo," which incorporates material from a still earlier poem, "Armageddon." Here the imaginative faculty is symbolized by the Seraph, whose function it is to "visit his eyes with visions." And to the vision of the fabled city thus vouchsafed the poet ecstatically gives himself up, deliberately postponing until the end of the poem any recognition of discrepancy between the actual and the ideal.

The most remarkable passage in "Timbuctoo," however, is the following in which Tennyson again undertakes to present a version of the mystical experience, but now in such a way as to infer that the seer and the poet have a common source of inspiration:

I felt my soul grow mighty, and my spirit
With supernatural excitation bound
Within me, and my mental eye grew large
With such a vast circumference of thought,
That in my vanity I seemd to stand
Upon the outward verge and bound alone
Of full beatitude. Each failing sense,
As with a momentary flash of light,
Grew thrillingly distinct and keen. I saw
The smallest grain that dappled the dark earth,
The indistinctest atom in deep air,
The Moon's white cities, and the opal width
Of her small glowing lakes, her silver heights
Unvisited with dew of vagrant cloud,
And the unsounded, undescended depth
Of her black hollows. The clear galaxy
Shorn of its hoary lustre, wonderful,
Distinct and vivid with sharp points of light,
Blaze within blaze, an unimagind depth
And harmony of planet-girded suns
And moon-encircled planets, wheel in wheel,
Arch'd the wan sapphire. Nay — the hum of men,
Or other things talking in unknown tongues,
And notes of busy life in distant worlds
Beat like a far wave on my anxious ear.
A maze of piercing, trackless, thrilling thoughts,
Involving and embracing each with each,
Rapid as fire, inextricably link'd,
Expanding momently with every sight
And sound which struck the palpitating sense,

The issue of strong impulse, hurried through
The riven rapt brain...

The volume of poetry published in 1832 affords grounds for a still clearer differentiation between the two opposing tendencies manifested in the tentative compositions of extreme youth. Thus, Tennyson's lapses into self-doubt provide the theme of "The Two Voices" with its dramatic representation of a "divided will."

Although the voice of faith eventually carries the day, it is the voice of doubt which may well seem the more persuasive to modern readers. The poet's awareness of the interdependence between state of mind and artistic productivity underlies the whole debate. Because be has lost religious conviction, he feels that he can no longer devote his talent to the services of mankind as in other days, "When, wide in soul and bold of tongue,/ Among the tents I paused and sung." The first voice, denoting the materialism which has laid waste the human spirit, mocks the quest for spiritual absolutes:

Much less this dreamer, deaf and blind,
Named man, may hope some truth to find,
That bears relation to the mind.

Playing on Tennyson's uncertainty about the mysterious ways of the mind, the Mephistophelean voice continues:

If straight thy track, or if oblique,
Thou know'st not. Shadows thou dost strike,
Embracing cloud, Ixion-like...

In the shadow of suicidal despair the poet tries to controvert the tempter by appealing to the "mystic gleams" which, despite the inherent "baseness in his blood," have from time to time brought intimations of a controlling and beneficent purpose in life. But evidently Tennyson himself was not sufficiently convinced by this argument to make it the basis for affirmation. The poet quite simply has no internal resources equal to the task of vanquishing doubt.

This is accomplished for him by the voice from outside which speaks for conventional Christian faith. Through intuitive sympathy with the pious church-bound family, as well as with the beauty of the natural world, the poet discovers a need to identify himself with the life around him. And in this way hope is reborn under sanctions which have traditionally given the individual release from a too oppressive sense of his limitations. The artistic success of the 1832 volume, however, derives from poems which celebrate the life of the imagination.

In the greater objectivity of these compositions and in the skill with which their creator has mastered new and complex techniques for the projection of theme, we can measure Tennyson's progress towards a clearer realization of his genius. There is present, for example, an increased complexity of meaning, conveyed not by explicit statement, but through structural and textural devices of considerable subtlety.

The poet conceives many of his poems on a centrifugal or wheel-like principle, the crux of the situation being the hub around which, like spokes, the contributory actions are in constant rotation.

Paradoxically, it is the apparent immobility of this hub in contrast to the encircling play of circumstances which holds the reader's attention focussed on the center. Tennyson began to experiment with this method as early as "Recollections of the Arabian Nights," where we follow the poet into the heart of Haroun Alraschid's enchanted garden, led on by the song of the nightingale, or rather

Not he, but something which possess'd
The darkness of the world, delight,
Life, anguish, death, immortal love,
Ceasing not, mingled, unrepress'd,
Apart from place, withholding time...

A similar contrast between an outer, temporal, and shifting sphere of activity and an inner, timeless, and fixed core of apprehension is developed in other early poems, such as "The Hesperides and The Sea Fairies." In its aesthetic implications this technique approximates very closely the concept of art as stasis.

Tennyson's increasing control over the formal elements in his poetry is observable in such a poem as "The Lady of Shalott" (text) where structure supplies the key to meaning.

A spell has entranced the lady and confined her to one room in her remote and silent castle.

As if to emphasize her isolation from all human affairs, we are made conscious of the unceasing flow of life around the island of Shalott. The road runs by, the aspens quiver, the waves run, the slow horses trail the heavy barges, the shallop flitteth. The condition of the lady's enchantment is that she shall sit all day weaving into a tapestry similitudes of the life of this outer world as reflected in a mirror. Her dedication to this unworldly task is brought into vivid contrast with the multifarious concerns of the wayfarers on the road to Camelot — the village-churls, the market girls, the troop of damsels, the abbot, the shepherd-lad, and the knights.

Her web is the shadow of a shadow, presenting an idealized version of the actuality which will destroy her when she meets it face to face. For everything is changed by the arrival within the mirror of Lancelot's image. No longer able to endure an existence of make-believe, the lady turns to the window and so invokes the curse. At once the web floats free and the mirror cracks; these are, we realize, metaphors for the creative imagination which has been shattered by the intrusion of direct experience. Appropriately, the world which the lady enters has been drained of the color and animation lent by fancy; and the manner of her dying symbolizes the extinction of the vitalizing imagination within her.

The discrimination between two ways of life, the one of artistic detachment, the other of emotional involvement, is construed in more general terms in "The Lotos-Eaters." Again the poet makes brilliantly effective use of contrast. The restless dark-blue sea which environs lotos-land reminds the mariners of their homes and families, of warfare, and of all the strenuous claims of social existence. Within the charmed circle, however, there is surcease from care.

For the lotos eaters, just as for the Mystic and the bewitched lady of Shalott, time and space have ceased to have any meaning; the mariners have come to "a land where all things always seem'd the same!" The fruit of the lotos induces a dreamlike state of irresponsibility in which "the inner spirit sings." The choric song itself is dramatic in conception. The odd stanzas, lyric and descriptive in quality, weave the spell of the lotos, while the even ones follow a rhetorical pattern suggestive stive of the conflict within the consciences of the speakers.

Furthermore, the successive stanzas (as rewritten for publication in 1842) tend to increase in length as if to imply a growing recognition of all that is at stake. Then, after the swooning magic of the seventh stanza has taken the senses captive, the meter of the last stanza changes (following the introductory invocation to the lotos) to express the final troubled moment of decision when the mariners make their choice not to return to the outside world.

Yet persuasively as Tennyson could present the ideal of individual self-fulfillment, it is apparent from other poems in the 1832 volume that he was not completely happy in this aesthetic position. Membership in the Cambridge "Apostles," and especially the selfless example of Hallam. had brought him into closer touch with the spiritual predicament of the Victorians. Did not his absorption in the beauties of literature and of the Somersby countryside amount to an egocentric evasion of the obligations which the age imposed on its promising young artists? Friends and critics were at one in their insistence that the imagination could not be allowed to remain a law unto itself, but must be submitted to a higher tribunal. The Paris of Enone is lost through hearkening to Aphrodite's invitation to sensual self-gratification rather than to Pallas Athene's grave exhortation:

Self-reverence, self-knowledge, self-control,
These three alone lead life to sovereign power.
Yet not for power (power of herself [10/11]
Would come uncall'd for) but to live by law,
Acting the law we live by without fear;
And, because right is right, to follow right
Were wisdom in the scorn of consequence.

The same voice sounds in "The Palace of Art" (text) so insistently as to suggest a revision of the creed exemplified in "The Lady of Shalott" and "The Lotos-Eaters." The dedication makes clear that this poem was intended to be a refutation of art for art's sake, though one can hardly fail to note that the attack on that concept is conducted in such equivocal terms as to leave some doubt about the poet's perfect good faith. Once again, as in "The Lady of Shalott," the focus of attention is an isolated consciousness; but in "The Palace of Art," unlike "The Lady of Shalott," the reader sympathizes with the external forces which break in on the soul's self-possession.

The soul's motive in alienating itself from the world is one of aristocratic disdain for humanity. This it frankly admits in such a way as to reveal a total absence of any sense of social responsibility:

O Godlike isolation which art mine,
I can but count thee perfect gain,
What time I watch the darkening droves of swine
That range on yonder plain.

The palace of art symbolizes the many-chambered life of the imagination, furnished with all the treasures of natural beauty, myth (including Christianity), the arts, literature, and the accumulated learning of scientists and philosophers. To the soul, seclusion among its hoarded possessions seems justifiable because of the artistic response which they evoke. It sings, but sings alone, untroubled by the fact that there is no one to hear its song:

No nightingale delighteth to prolong
Her low preamble all alone,
More than my soul to hear her echo'd song
Throb thro' the ribbed stone...

But after three years of unruffled self-absorption, disillusionment sets in. Despair brings on "deep dread and loathing of her solitude," and then the spectres of incipient madness, portrayed by a series of powerful and disturbing images. Driven at length to expiate its guilt, the chastened soul returns to the world and communion with its kind; but the end of the poem remains somewhat ambiguous in its implications. The palace of art is not destroyed, but remains intact against the time when the poet will return, bringing others to enjoy its felicities. Presumably, then, we are to believe that Tennyson would not altogether discredit the life of the imagination, but rather would insinuate that the artist must become aware of the responsibility to communicate his insights.

THE MASK OF CONFORMITY

With the collection of poems published in 1842 Tennyson begins to assume his familiar guise as Victorian prophet. The dilemma of the divided will persists, but has become so overlaid by other concerns as to be all but unrecognizable to the reader not familiar with poet's habits of mind in their germinal state. The protagonist of Locksley Hall undergoes the same crisis of doubt that found subjective expression in "Supposed Confessions of a Second-rate Sensitive Mind" and "The Two Voices"; but now larger social implications are involved.

To bring the theme home to his age, Tennyson embeds it in melodramatic narrative of a kind dear to his heart: namely, crossed love between lovers of unequal worldly station. Furthermore, the poem concludes on a very much more positive note than "The Two Voices." After rejecting the temptation to sink into sensuality on an Eastern island, the hero takes the more manly decision to join the army and fight for his country. [Tennyson habitually associated the East with laxity of will and self-indulgence. See, for example, "The Hesperides," "Tithonus," and "The Voyage."]

Such a poem as "Tithonus" indicates Tennyson's growing disposition to disguise his private thoughts under extrinsic layers of meaning. Although not published until 1860, "Tithonus" was contemporary in conception with "Ulysses" (text). This extraordinarily beautiful and moving treatment of classical myth is usually read as an utterance of its author's grief over Hallam's death; but, like "The Lady of Shalott," it is also almost certainly a symbolic representation of Tennyson's a aesthetic philosophy. Taken so, Eos stands for the Keatsian ideal of beauty which holds the poet in bondage. Tithonus remembers the first thrilling visitations of the creative impulse:

Ay me! ay me! with what another heart
In days far-off, and with what other eyes
I used to watch-if I be he that watchd
The lucid outline forming found thee; saw
The dim curls kindle into sunny rings;
Changed with thy mystic change, and felt my blood
Glow with the glow that slowly crimsond all
Thy presence and thy portals, while I lay,
Mouth, forehead, eyelids, growing dewy-warm
With kisses balmier than half-opening buds
Of April, and could hear the lips that kiss'd
Whispering I knew not what of wild and sweet,
Like that strange song I heard Apollo sing,
While Ilion like a mist rose into towers.

Now, weighed down by age (a metaphor, perhaps, for Tennyson is desolation over the loss of his friend), the speaker asks only that he be allowed to return to share the common lot of his fellowmen:

Let me go; take back thy gift.
Why should a man desire in any way
To vary from the kindly race of men,
Or pass beyond the goal of ordinance
Where all should pause, as is most meet for all?

The general run of new poems published in 1842, however, does not require, nor indeed call for, such probing after ulterior meanings. Tennyson had been less inattentive to criticisms of his previous work than be pretended; and in his desire for a wider measure of recognition he was beginning to court the public.

The direction in which he was tending is clear from new developments which now begin to manifest themselves in his writing. In the first place, whereas he bad before viewed contemporary life in the subjective and individualistic terms of "The Two Voices," he now made a determined effort to write poems of topical Interest, realistic in situation and conventional in tone. These are the so, called En lisb Idyls, sentimental narratives of domestic life. Along with "Locksley Hall," but more obviously addressed to Victorian tastes, the 1842 volumes included the following poems in this manner: "The Gardener's Daughter," "Dora," "Audley Court," "Walking to the Mail," "The Talking Oak," "Lady Clare," "Edward Gray" and "The Lord of Burleigh."

Although now and then the more sombre and moody streak in Tennyson's temperament cropped up, it was kept subservient to the controlling tone of bland tractability. In "Walking to the Mail," for instance, Sir Edward Head's spiritual malady, so similar to that portrayed in "Locksley Hall," provides matter for no more than a passing comment, and that of a moralizing kind:

No, sir, he,
Vext with a morbid devil in his blood
That veil'd the world with jaundice, hid his face
From all men, and commercing with himself, [14/15]
He lost the sense that handles daily life—
That keeps us all in order more or less—
And sick of home went overseas for change.

A like change takes place in the conduct of many of the poems derived from the author's reading. Tennyson's uneventful life made him more reliant than most English poets on literary sources of inspiration; but as we have seen in the cases of "The Lady of Shalott," "The Lotos-Eaters," and "Tithonus," his happiest use of myths or legends generally involved a reinterpretation of their original significance in terms of some private and highly personal insight. In the 1842 collection, however, the reworking is undertaken with a didactic intent.

As a result, the poet's handling of traditional stories frequently appears by modern standards overly explicit and rather offensively moralistic. The titles of these poems too often bring to mind the edifying tag-lines which incorporate their themes. Thus, for example: "Morte d'Arthur" ("The old order changeth, yielding place to new"), "Godiva" ("So the Powers, who wait/ On noble deeds, cancell'd a sense misused"), "Sir Galahad" ("My strength is as the strength of ten,/ Because my heart is pure").

In this body of poetry, too, we begin to recognize the

Tennyson who was to constitute himself the advocate and defender of so many of the Victorians' cherished shibboleths. In particular, that dream of progress towards an Utopia social order, which was so deeply ingrained in the age, keeps recurring throughout these poems: in "Morte d'Arthur," "Locksley Hall," "The Golden Year" (first published in 1846), "The Day-Dream," "The Poet's Song." Likewise, passing references to aesthetic matters (in "The Gardener's Daughter," "The DayDream," and "The Golden Year") show Tennyson moving towards the Ruskinian positions that art is incidental to life, that beauty only shines in use, and that the artist is a product of his society. In her description of the proper ends of poetry Princess Ida of "The Princess" endorses that commingling of ethics and aesthetics which made for the highest artistic accomplishment in the eyes of the age:

But great is song
Used to great ends; ourself have often tried
Valkyrian hymns, or into rhythm have dash'd
The passion of the prophetess; for song
Is duer unto freedom, force and growth
Of spirit, than to junketing and love.

Yet, as Tennyson drew closer to the laureateship and popular recognition as the official poetic voice of Victorian England, doubts lingered in his mind-if not so much the old ones of his capacity to fill this role, then new and equally grave ones occasioned by a clearer comprehension of the compromises necessary to fame. In a mood half humorous, half bitter, the speaker in "Will Waterproof's Lyrical Monologue" contrasts the conditions of literary success in the nineteenth century to those pertaining in previous periods:

Hours when the Poet's words and looks
Had yet their native glow,
Nor yet the fear of little books
Had made him talk for show;
But, all his vast heart sherris-warm'd,
He flash'd his random speeches,
Ere days that deal in ana swarm'd
His literary leeches.

More biting are the lines in "Walking to the Mail" which castigate society for its callous and blundering disregard for originality of mind:

Well—after all—
What know we of the secret of a man?
His nerves were wrong. What ails us who are sound,
That we should mimic this raw fool the world,
Which charts us all in its coarse blacks or whites,
As ruthless as a baby with a worm,
As cruel as a schoolboy ere he grows
To pity–more from ignorance than will.

The evolution of the poet's aesthetic theories between 1832 and 1850, his *annus mirabilis,* is best illustrated by In Memoriam. Anyone at all familiar with the poetry of Tennyson knows something of the history and influence of this elegy, which traces the author's progress from grief-stricken despair over Hallam's death to an ultimate affirmation of faith which all Victorian England, from the Queen down, accepted as meeting the needs of the modern spirit.

What is less generally recognized is that In Memoriam is also an intimate record of Tennyson's thinking about the nature and purpose of his poetry during the period of seventeen years in which the elegy from its start as a collection of random lyrics grew into a highly formalized apologia.

By 1850, the year when In Memoriam was published, Tennyson had relinquished for good and all the confessional tone that runs through so much of his youthful poetry, including the early sections of In Memoriam itself. In the Prologue to the poem, not written until 1849, the poet could say with the diffidence of hindsight: "Forgive these wild and wandering cries,/ Confusions of a wasted youth."

On this evaluation, In Memoriam is the best commentary. The author passes through four readily identifiable stages of development in clarifying his artistic intent; and these stages are roughly equivalent to his psychological advance from unrestrained grief through emotional numbness to hesitant hope and the eventual recognition that bereavement has provided a basis for religious certainty.

At the outset the poet is too overcome by Hallam's loss to use poetry as anything but a means of release, though he does pause to wonder over the vagaries of the imagination which can convert every emotion into grist for its mill:

What words are these have fallen from me?
Can calm despair and wild unrest
Be tenants of a single breast,
Or Sorrow such a changeling be?

He writes without forethought, speaking of himself as "that delirious man"

Whose fancy fuses old and new,
And flashes into false and true,
And mingles all without a plan.

By the nineteenth poem, however, a greater degree of objectivity has led to the discovery that the poetic impulse occurs only in moments of comparative detachment, such as follow on paroxysms of sorrow. As the artist regains control, he is increasingly reluctant to put his faculties at the disposal of undisciplined emotion. There is even a touch of scorn in the thirty-fourth poem with its reference to

Fantastic beauty; such as lurks
In some wild poet, when he works
Without a conscience or an aim.

Tennyson now enters a phase when, personal suffering somewhat alleviated, he can scrutinize his aesthetic motives more closely.

Hallam's death has opened up tragic depths within his consciousness and left a sense of inability to deal adequately in poetic terms with the profounder implications of the experience. He thinks of the Gospel story and concludes that the noblest expressions of spiritual truth are directly provocative of action:

Tho' truths in manhood darkly join,
Deep-seated in our mystic frame,
We yield all blessing to the name
Of Him that made them current coin;
For Wisdom dealt with mortal powers,
Where truth in closest words shall fail,

When truth embodied in a tale
Shall enter in at lowly doors.
And so the Word had breath, and wrought
With human hands the creed of creeds
In loveliness of perfect deeds,
More strong than all poetic thought...

By contrast his obsession with self in the name of art seems unworthy; he has "loiter'd in the master's field,/ And darkend sanctities with song." Yet there remains the indisputable fact that poetry assuages his stricken feelings as no other outlet can: "But in the songs I love to sing/ A doubtful gleam of solace lives." This being true, he will continue to think of his muse as the unpretending handmaiden of a private impulse:

If these brief lays, of Sorrow born,
Were taken to be such as closed
Grave doubts and answers here proposed,
Then these were such as men might scorn.
Her care is not to part and prove;
She takes, when harsher moods remit,
What slender shade of doubt may flit,
And makes it vassal unto love;
And hence, indeed, she sports with words,
And better serves a wholesome law,
And holds it sin and shame to draw
The deepest measure from the chords;
Nor dare she trust a larger lay,
But rather loosens from the lip
Short swallow-flights of song, that dip
Their wings in tears, and skim away.

For this self-imposed limitation in scope Tennyson presents in the seventy-seventh poem additional historical justification. Since the modern age offers no themes comparable to those which inspired the masterpieces of the past, the contemporary poet cannot hope for lasting fame and may as well confine his art to his own individual concerns. By the eighty-fifth poem, however, Tennyson has seen hope dawn; and concurrently he begins to wonder, though as yet without any great amount of confidence, whether his poetic insights are solely attributable to grief playing with symbols and "pining life" fed on fancies. The dream allegory of the one hundred and third poem, which has interesting affinities with "The Palace of Art," sounds a new and altogether more ambitious note. Here the poet first confesses that his suffering has been largely self-regarding.

He has made out of Hallam's memory an idol to be set up in the private shrine of the imagination and worshipped, with the poetic faculties, represented as maidens, presiding over the rites as votaries. But now to Tennyson, as to the hero in "Locksley Hall," has come "a summons from the sea," in response to which he has gone out into the world, there to be greeted by the living presence of his friend grown to heroic size.

As Tennyson boards the ship, so often for him a symbol of the active life Hallam likewise admits the maidens, who have "gather'd strength and grace/ And presence, lordlier than before" in preparation for the nobler demands henceforth to be made of them. After this it is not surprising in the one hundred and eighth poem to find the author renouncing the self-absorbed and inconclusive brooding of the earlier lyrics, and embracing in exchange that concept of participation in the common lot for which Tithonus had yearned:

I will not shut me from my kind,
And, lest I stiffen into stone,
I will not eat my heart alone,
Nor feed with sighs a passing wind.
What find I in the highest place,
But mine own phantom chanting hymns?
And on the depths of death there swims
The reflex of a human face.
I'll rather take what fruit may be
Of sorrow under human skies:
'T is held that sorrow makes us wise,
Whatever wisdom sleep with thee.

His doubts superseded by a firm faith in human destiny, Tennyson could look back as an artist and find that he had not undergone his spiritual ordeal in vain:

I trust I have not wasted breath:
I think we are not wholly brain,
Magnetic mockeries; not in vain,
Like Paul with beasts, I fought with Death...

Confident that he has attained self-mastery, the poet is ready — "I to go on to other things." The Epilogue to "In Memoriam" brings before us an emotionally mature Tennyson who has not only silenced the disputation of the two voices, but has also brought his poetry into tune with the spirit of the age— or so he chooses to believe. In this conviction he can pretend in retrospect to disown as either frivolous or ineffectual the promptings of an inner awareness so much at variance with what he now feels his poetic mission to be:

No longer caring to embalm
In dying songs a dead regret,
But like a statue solid-set,
And moulded in colossal calm.
Regret is dead, but love is more
Than in the summers that are flown,
For I myself with these have grown
To something greater than before;
Which makes appear the songs I made
As echoes out of weaker times,
As half but idle brawling rhymes,
The sport of random sun and shade.

Chapter 5

Shadow and Substance

We have now arrived at Tennyson's middle period, the time of the "Enoch Arden" volume and Idylls of the King, the time, in other words, when the poet produced the work for which the Victorians valued him most highly and by which the twentieth century judges him most harshly. For it has become the commonly accepted view that in order to establish his contemporary reputation Tennyson temporized with his age, sold, so to speak, his birthright for a mess of pottage. And certainly, as we have seen, he was not immune to the coercive pressures which Victorian society exerted on his artistic theory and practice. As early as 1834 an admiring friend, James Spedding, had observed with foreboding this hesitancy to stand on his own feet:

His frailty is that he has not faith enough in his own powers, which produces two faults, first that he does not give his genius full beat; and, secondly, that he seeks for strength not within but without, accusing the baseness of his lot in life and looking to outward circumstances for more than a great man ought to want of them, and certainly more than they will ever bring. Yet there are evidences enough that, even during the years of his greatest prestige as Victorian man of letters, Tennyson held aloof from his age and continued to live most intensely within the world of his own mind.

Since, however, the conscious artist took pains to sublimate any traces of his inner consciousness, the revelations of its operation must be sought not on the surface of his poetry, but rather in the modes of perception by which he illuminated subject-matter ostensibly selected for its popular appeal.

The thoughtful reader, who approaches the poetry of the 1850s and the 1860s by way of what came before, can hardly fail to observe in this later work the recurrence of certain themes and an habitual reliance on certain formal devices which are at variance with the expressed content of the material. It is as though there brooded in the background a mind constantly alert to strange and disturbing implications in the most commonplace circumstances. Thus, many of the poems which seem to be indisputably the products of Victorian literary convention have an extra dimension which, once recognized, relates them to the deeper sources of the author's poetic vision. One such manifestation of an ulterior purpose is the reappearance of the dream motif throughout Tennyson's poetry.

From biographical records it is ascertainable that the poet was at all times subject in his sleep to extraordinarily vivid and suggestive dreams, and that this trait became more pronounced with age. In his account of Tennyson's last years, his grandson writes: "He had strange dreams, too: 'Priam has appeared to me in the night,' he said one morning to Hallam. Sometimes his dreams were of fir woods, cliffs and temples; once of building a succession of gorgeous pagodas which reached right up to heaven; once that he was Pope of the world and had to bear all its sins and miseries on his shoulders."

Furthermore, the poems themselves show a knowledge of dream psychology unique in the period, and such as could only have been acquired through autoanalysis. Especially frequent and accurate are the notations relating to the intermediary processes between waking and sleeping. In "A Dream of Fair Women" the transition from idle musing to the world of dreams is described as follows:

And then, I know not how,
All those sharp fancies, by down-lapsing thought
Stream'd onward, lost their edges, and did creep
Roll'd on each other, rounded, smooth'd, and brought
Into the gulfs of sleep.
At last methought that I had wander'd far
In an old wood ...

And at the end of the same poem the writer describes his reluctant return to actuality in this way:

No memory labors longer from the deep
Gold-mines of thought to lift the hidden ore
That glimpses, moving up, than I from sleep
To gather and tell oer
Each little sound and sight. With what dull pain
Compass'd, how eagerly I sought to strike
Into that wondrous track of dreams again!
But no two dreams are alike.

"The Vision of Sin" suggests how the direction of a dream may be radically altered if the sleeper is partially aroused; and a line in "Mariana in the South" calls attention to the occasional phenomenon of self-consciousness in the dreaming mind: "Dreaming, she knew it was a dream." The following stanza from "The Two Voices" shows that Tennyson had likewise been impressed by the continuity of memory between dreams:

As here we find in trances, men
Forget the dream that happens then,
Until they fall in trance again...

The early sonnet "To"——, ("As when with downcast eyes"), derives from the common experience that memories, originating in dreams, may linger in waking thoughts as familiar but only partially recoverable intimations; and the same notion occurs in "The Two Voices":

Moreover, something is or seems,
That touches me with mystic gleams,
Like glimpses of forgotten dreams—

Tennyson's close attention to the dream state would be less arresting if it were not clear that he intermittently attached a good deal of importance to the activities of the sleeping mind. Might not its very passivity, at such times release the intuitive faculty and thus open up channels for the apprehension of truths of which the waking intellect is imperceptive? In "The Lover's Tale" the poet speaks of "delicious dreams, our other life"; and later in the same poem he writes, commenting on the interrelations between the hero's conscious view of his situation and the phantasmal dreams inspired by it:

Alway the inaudible, invisible thought,
Artificer and subject, lord and slave,
Shaped by the audible and visible,
Moulded the audible and visible.

"The Higher Pantheism" is still more explicit: "Dreams are true while they last, and do we not live in dreams?" But it was in In Memoriam that Tennyson explored most fully the implications of dreams as a means of attaining to spiritual truths lying beyond the ken of ratiocination.

As early as the fourth poem of In Memoriam the poet introduces a concept of sleep as the sponsor of emotive being in contrast to the activities of the purposive mind. Full realization of Hallam's loss comes to him when he has given his "powers away" to sleep and his "will is bondsman to the dark"; but: "With morning wakes the will, and cries,/ 'Thou shalt not be the fool of loss.'" In dreams, however, the poet can also forget his loss; and he is thus led in the forty-third poem to equate sleep with death, "that still garden of the souls" situated outside time and space.

Sleep, then, may be courted as a form of mystical experience which releases the dreamer from the trammels of corporeal existence. Nevertheless, Tennyson had finally to admit that his dreams took the form of nightmares as often as not, and that he could find only sporadic relief through them. The life of the sleeping mind presented another version of the problem of appearance and reality which continually tormented him. In the famous fifty-fourth, -fifth, and -sixth poems of "In Memoriam" the spectacle of the struggle for existence leaves us in doubt whether it is Nature in conflict with God which "lends such evil dreams," or whether it is not man himself who is "a monster then, a dream,/ A discord."

All of Tennyson's thinking about the nature of dreams and their significance for the waking life is finally brought to bear on his immediate situation in the four extraordinary lyrics of In Memoriam which begin with the sixty-eighth. Sleep, again called "Death's twin-brother," restores Hallam to Tennyson; but their communion is imperfect because the Hallam of the dream is troubled. The poet awakens to realize that this trouble has had its origin in his own mind and that, therefore, the dream itself, as an instance of thought transference, possesses only such validity as can be attached to any act of the creative imagination.

A second dream, occupying the sixty-ninth poem, elaborates the idea that heartfelt grief isolates the sufferer from his fellows and subjects him to their contemptuous derision. Interestingly enough, this dream, although much more artificially wrought than the preceding one, compels the poet's belief in the truth of its testimony, apparently because its symbolism develops within an orthodox religious framework. The next lyric, almost surrealistic in its imagery, reverts to the earlier surmise that dreams are but a form of wish-fulfillment; but all uncertainty vanishes in the last stanza when the ugly welter of preceding visions is suddenly replaced by a mystic intimation of Hallam's spiritual presence:

Till all at once beyond the will
I hear a wizard music roll,
And thro' a lattice on the soul
Looks thy f air face and makes it still.

After this revelation the poet of the seventy-first lyric is no longer disposed to question the testimony of dreams. If sleep has such strong credit with the soul, then he will invoke its assistance to cancel time and to trace a magic circle within which he and his friend may continue to be together. Tennyson's eventual willingness after so much self-examination to rely on dreams as a source of spiritual certitude clarifies certain later affirmations in the poem, such as: "But in my spirit will I dwell,/ And dream my dream, and hold it true"; or:

Strange friend, past, present, and to be;
Loved deeplier, darklier understood;
Behold, I dream a dream of good,
And mingle all the world with thee.

It becomes apparent, then, that Tennyson located in the dream state one center of the life of the imagination, like others not always predictable in its operations, but ultimately rewarding as no exclusively objective awareness ever could be. Additional evidence in support of this contention is contributed by the long list of poems, from the very earliest to the latest of Tennyson's career, which in one way or another make use of dreams. During his formative period the traditional type of the dream-allegory strongly attracted the poet. "A Dream of Fair Women," "The Day-Dream," and "The Vision of Sin" are all ambitious experiments in this genre. Of these the last is the most successful and the most interesting for a variety of reasons. By representing the fantastic irrelevancies of the dreaming mind and by exploiting the vivid sense impressions which accompany this condition, the poet was able to say things which his audience would hardly have tolerated as undisguised statements of his own perceptions. One can hardly miss the erotic symbolism which plays through the first part of the poem; and the opening of the final section reveals a talent for the macabre which Tennyson too rarely displayed:

The voice grew faint; there came a further change;
Once more uprose the mystic mountain-range.
Below were men and horses pierced with worms,
And slowly quickening into lower forms;
By shards and scurf of salt, and scum of dross,
Old plash of rains, and refuse patch'd with moss.

By the same token the old rake's song in section four is a masterpiece of grotesque and mordant humor of a kind infrequently met in Victorian poetry and almost never in Tennyson's subsequent work:

You are bones, and what of that?
Every face, however full,
Padded round with flesh and fat,
Is but modell'd on a skull.
Death is king, and Vivat Rex!
Tread a measure on the stones,
Madam — if I know your sex
From the fashion of your bones.
No, I cannot praise the fire
In your eye — nor yet your lip;
All the more do I admire

Joints of cunning workmanship.
Lo! God's likeness — the ground-plan-
Neither modell'd, glazed, nor framed:
Buss me, thou rough sketch of man,
Far too naked to be shamed!

Although this kind of allegoric writing was later to fall into abeyance along with the other fanciful forms of the poet's early years, Tennyson's continuing reliance on the mechanism of dreams reveals the spectre of "otherness" which haunted his mind even when he most scrupulously masked its presence. The volume published in 1864 under the title of Enoch Arden and Other Poems is often cited as the work most illustrative of the author's final submission to Victorian literary conventions; and the three poems which stand first in this volume have come to seem prime examples of the weakness for complacent moralizing which so often spoiled Tennyson's attempts to treat domestic tragedy in a realistic way. It comes as something of a surprise, therefore, to find introduced into each of these poems an element of the supernatural, which is not only unrealistic, but is also in no way essential to the elucidation of the theme.

In "Enoch Arden" Annie's decision to marry Philip is motivated by her ironically misleading dream of Enoch sitting under a palm-tree, which she construes as meaning that her husband is dead and in heaven. In "Aylmers Field" Leolin dreams of Edith's death, and on the basis of this evidence commits suicide before confirmation can reach him. The significant thing to observe in both incidents is that the poet makes the motivation of two sufficiently commonplace characters depend on an intuitive faculty which is not really in the nature of either. The principal actors in "Sea Dreams" are equally unremarkable; and the sensational plot in which they are entrapped would hardly hold our interest were it not for the two dreams which suggest, quite in excess of the expressed moral content of the theme, that man's sentient existence is only a reflex of his unconscious being.

Tennyson had already shown in the second and third parts of "The Lover's Tale" unusual comprehension of the way in which dreams are shaped by stimuli provided by waking experi ence. In "Sea Dreams" the visions of the husband and wife are even more closely keyed to setting and situation. The crashing of a wave, the breaking of a glass, a child crying in the night assume momentous proportions in the depths of the sleeping mind. And despite the fact that the poet becomes overly explicit and so destroys the illusion in his anxiety lest the reader misinterpret the moral of the two dreams, the poem is noteworthy as a further example of its author's oblique approach to seemingly conventional material.

Dreams, however, were for Tennyson only one of several related manifestations of the mystery of man's inner being. In studies of minds unhinged by madness the poet found another way of sublimating his concern with the life of the imagination. For insanity has this in common with dream, that it releases the consciousness from active engagement in the affairs of the outer world and turns it inward on itself. Both dream and madness confuse truth and seeming; but whereas dream moves through seeming towards truth, madness reverses the process and becomes, in effect, an avenue of escape from the importunities of reality. Thus, dream usually appears in Tennyson's poetry as a condition in which the individual fulfills inherent needs of his nature; but madness is treated as a disease brought on by overexposure to harsh circumstance and expressing an inability to compensate. Through dreams outer and inner tensions are equalized; madness results from the failure to make any such adjustment.

The Tennysons were, of course, an extremely eccentric family; and the spectacle of erratic and often violent behavior which he had from childhood observed in his close relatives would in itself account for the poet's familiarity with mental aberration. Certainly his poetry shows an acquaintance with Symptoms of insanity which is as uncommon in its period as the somewhat similar interest in dream psychology. During the summer of 1840, while he was resident at Beech Hill, Tunbridge Wells, Tennyson formed a friendship with Matthew Allen, who was doctor-in-charge of a neighboring asylum. Allen had gained considerable reputation for his enlightened ways of treating mental patients (one of whom had been the poet, John Clare); and it seems likely that through this association Tennyson had a chance to study abnormal behavior at first hand.

As early as his unpublished poem, "The Outcast," Tennyson had used madness as a subject. And while there is no question of insanity in "Supposed Confessions of a Second-rate Sensitive Mind" or "The Two Voices," the suicidal depression of the speakers in both poems suggests a state of neurasthenia bordering on derangement. The same lack of intellectual equilibrium characterizes the central figures in "Mariana" and "Locksley Hall"; and in "Aylmees Field" actual imbecility is visited on the old baron as punishment for his inflexible pride. In these poems it may be observed that the madness, whether incipient or actual, is not directly the result of any congenital instability of mind so much as an outcome of the pressure of external events which have undermined the characters' powers of resistance.

More revelatory of Tennyson's true intent in exploring the theme of madness is Maud, which, despite its lukewarm reception, always remained the author's favorite among his poems? Here the protagonist's insanity is, significantly enough, a trait inherited from his father who had presumably killed himself in a fit of despondency. Throughout the first part of the poem Tennyson shows extreme skill in foreshadowing the d6nouement of the second part. In his variability between moods of dejection and exhilaration, in his animosity against the social order counter-balanced by attempts to bolster his self-esteem, in his fascination with concepts of violence, madness, and death, the gathering emotional strain on the hero's temperament is dramatically evoked. Then with the killing of Maud's brother in "the red-ribb'd hollow behind the wood," the shadow, which symbolizes guilt, appears and dogs the murderer overseas and through fits of uncontrolled despair until his mind gives way.

In the fifth section of Part Two, which is set in a madhouse, Tennyson shows his ability to deal with the nightmare visions of the disordered intellect. The hallucinations which parade before the speaker gather up and arrange in fantastic but meaningful patterns all the strands of his previous experience. And it is appropriately through the medium of his fevered imagination that the hero finally comprehends the nature of his transgression.

Selfknowledge comes as a result of intuitive perception of the meaning of the rose symbol and of the kind of passion which it exemplifies: "It is only flowers, they had no fruits,/ And I almost fear they are not roses, but blood." After this the third part of Maud, in which the hero vows himself to further purgation through a life of action in the Crimean War, seems hardly more than a sop to Victorian sentimentalism, though it is to be feared that its inclusion is one more indication of the poet's readiness to let his notion of the poet's public rôle usurp the place of artistic sensibility.

In "Lucretius" madness becomes the agency for dramatizing not only the life of the imagination, but also the tragic reprisals enacted on the rational mind. There is unmistakable irony in Tennyson's choice of Lucretius to formulate his theme; for the champion of philosophic materialism might be supposed the least likely of all persons to fall victim to fanciful delusions. Driven frantic by his wife's philtre, Lucretius experiences three dreams, each of which calls for close interpretation. The first is a monstrous version of his own system, showing an atomistic universe in a chantic state of flux. Here is symbolized the loss of control over the workings of the intellect. The second dream, which solicits the philosopher's senses through an orgiastic vision of Hetairai, "hired animalisms," represents the revenge of flesh on one who had always minimized its claims.

Lucretius then dreams of the naked loveliness of Helen of Troy, who stands for artistic beauty. The sword in this image is presumably the power of cold reason which threatens but is unable to subdue the aesthetic sense. In the lucidity of awakening Lucretius endeavors by rational methods to accommodate the meaning of these dreams within the limitations of the philosophy to which he has devoted his life. He fights a rear-guard action, retreating from one hard-won position to another and drawing ever closer to the despairing choice between confessed defeat and suicide.

To Aphrodite as instigator of sexual license he opposes the more abstract concept of the goddess in her guise of Venus Genetrix. But his accustomed view of the gods as elevated beings, enjoying the "sacred everlasting calm" to which he aspires, is shot through with doubts as to whether the laws of nature are after all compatible with a celestial order. And even granting the existence of the gods, does not their very remoteness from human concerns leave the individual alone responsible for his fate? In defense of suicide, Lucretius considers the vicissitudes which render life intolerable; and he concludes, recalling the sensual riot of his dreams, that the "worst disease of all" is

These prodigies of myriad nakednesses,
And twisted shapes of lust, unspeakable,
Abominable, strangers at my hearth
Not welcome, harpies miring every dish,
The phantom husks of something foully done,
And fleeting thro' the boundless universe,
And blasting the long quiet of my breast
With animal heat and dire insanity.

For reassurance Lucretius turns to Nature whom in her aspect as lawgiver he has always worshipped, only to realize that she condones the excesses to which he is now tempted. He beholds with fascinated loathing a classical vision of lust triumphant-the rape of an Oread by a satyr.

At first his sympathy goes out to the Oread as she flees her brutish pursuer, though the terms used to describe the nymph are significant of ulterior perceptions. There follow in quick succession moods of revulsion when the creature seems about to fling herself on him, and of relief when she is captured instead. At this point a sickening revelation of his interest in the scene is vouchsafed to Lucretius:

Hide, hide them, million-myrtled wilderness,
And cavern-shading laurels, hide! do I wish
What? — that the bush were leafless? or to whelm
All of them in one massacre?

In vain he tries to disprove the conjurings of his heated imagination by calling on philosophy to show that the satyr is outside the natural order of being: "Twy-natured is no nature." This latest vision, coming on top of the preceding dreams, has opened his eyes all too clearly to the double nature of man. Self-recognition destroys for Lucretius the hope of ever recovering "the sober majesties/ Of settled, sweet, Epicurean life"; for

now it seems some unseen monster lays
His vast and filthy hands upon my will,
Wrenching it backward into his, and spoils
My bliss in being ...

On the surface of this poem lies a moral teaching such as the age had come to expect from the author of In Memoriam: namely, that the unaided reason is not in itself strong or sure enough to discipline man's sensual nature.

In addition to its explicitly didactic purpose, however, Lucretius gives important bearings on Tennyson's aesthetic position at the most influential period in his career. The self-loathing which comes over the philosopher as a result of his madness, with its accompanying dreams and visions, destroys his confidence in his creative powers. Lucilia's potion has had a twofold effect:

For the wicked broth
Confused the chernic labor of the blood,
And tickling the brute brain within the man's
Made havoc among those tender cells, and check'd
His power to shape.
Hitherto it is for his writing that he has lived:
For save when shutting reasons up in rhythm,
Or Heliconian honey in living words,
To make a truth less harsh, I often grew
Tired of so much within our little life,
Or of so little in our little life-

The thought of leaving his poem uncompleted at first dissuades Lucretius from suicide: "and if I go "my" work is left/ Unfinish'd." And even when the decision to kill himself is finally taken, there remains the consolation that his masterpiece will survive and be of benefit as long as there are men to read it:

.. till that hour, My golden work in which I told a truth
That stays the rolling Ixionian wheel,
And numbs the Fury's ringlet-snake, and plucks
The mortal soul from out immortal hell,
Shall stand.

Since he holds this faith in the validity of his creative impulse, why does Lucretius take self-extinction as the best way out of his situation? The answer to this question leads back to the problem posed by Tennyson in "Supposed Confessions of a Second-rate Sensitive Mind" and "The Two Voices." Lucretius' madness is a metaphor for the mood of introspective, depression which throughout his life harried Tennyson's at tempts to fix his faith, but which he tried increasingly to sublimate in his poetry.

Furthermore, the daring dreams and visions which emerge from Lucretius' inner consciousness had, as we have seen, their counterpart in the poet's own imagination. It follows, then, that Lucretius' despairing recognition of the incommensurable elements in his nature reflects the dilemma which Tennyson himself faced in presenting a view of human experience which would legitimatize his assumed function as Victorian sage and at the same time be faithful to his intuitive perceptions. Insofar as the poem represents the vagrant imagination in conflict with a settled system of philosophic thought, it illustrates the author's double awareness and the tensions resulting there from.

In the seventy-first poem of In Memoriam a third plane of irrational consciousness is, by implication, brought into relation with dream and madness: "Sleep, kinsman thou to death and trance/ And madness." Trance, as used here, denotes a form of mystical experience equivalent to the traditional concept of the visionary power as a faculty of the poetic imagination. It is like dream in that it annihilates any logical ideas of time or-apace or the interrelations between cause and effect. It is normally, however, a waking condition of the mind, and in this way akin to mental derangement. Reference was made in the opening of this chapter to Tennyson's recurrent fits of abstraction when he passed into a trance-like state and lost all sense of individual identity. Indeed, he seems on occasion to have been able to induce such "day-dreams." On one occasion he wrote: "A kind of waking trance I have frequently had, quite up from boyhood, when I have been all alone. This has generally come upon me thro' repeating my own name two or three times to myself silently, till all at once, as it were, out of the intensity of the consciousness of individuality, the individuality itself seemed to dissolve and fade away into boundless being, and this is not a confused state, but the clearest of the clearest, the surest of the surest, the weirdest of the weirdest, utterly beyond words, where death was an almost laughable impossibility, the loss of personality (if so it were) seeming no extinction but the only true life."

In this connection it is perhaps significant that Tennyson discovered hypnotic powers in himself and successfully experimented with mesmerism.

As with sleeping dreams, therefore, Tennyson frequently introduces the vision or trance into his poetry for the purpose of suggesting an enlargement of experience beyond the more immediate implications of the matter in hand. But the same hesitancy to repose full confidence in extrasensory perceptions that we remarked in the poet's attitude towards dreams is also present in his treatment of visions. How could one be sure whether the revelation was a legitimate vision carrying supernatural authority, or whether it was not merely a self-imposed and superstitious delusion? For the fact that Tennyson's senses played phantasmagoric tricks on him there is biographical evidence.

His grandson tells how the poet would draw "the curious things which he said he often saw in the fire in the small hours of the morning-strange grim forms, half beast, half human." We are also told that in the highly nervous condition brought on by Charles Tennyson's death, the poet heard "perpetual ghostly voices."

In his poetry, however, such experiences, while described

with extreme clarity, usually go with the workings of diseased imaginations. The fearsome hallucinations of the soul in "The Palace of Art" and of "Saint Simeon Stylites" are motivated in this way.

On the other hand, the ultimate revelation that spirit is immortal comes to the poet of In Memoriam in a moment of trance-like exaltation quite obviously allied with true mystic vision. The ninety-fifth poem of the elegy describes how the poet was suddenly transfixed by a blinding apprehension of Hallam's presence, in comparison with which the testimony of the dream in the seventieth poem seems shadowy and inconclusive. The poet had lingered out-of-doors into the twilight. Left to himself, he was rereading his friend's letterswhen the illumination enveloped him:

So word by word, and line by line,
The dead man touch'd me from the past,
And all at once it seem'd at last
The living soul was flashd on mine,
And mine in this was wound, and whirl'd
About empyreal heights of thought,
And came on that which is, and caught
The deep pulsations of the world,
Æonian music measuring out
The steps of Time-the shocks of Chance —
The blows of Death.

And even though in the immediate aftermath the "trance/ Was cancell'd, stricken thro' with doubt," the more hopeful tone of the following lyrics leaves no doubt that for Tennyson this moment of insight was climactic and prepared the way for his subsequent attainment of religious faith. In passing, it is perhaps worthy of surmise whether, in greeting In Memoriam as an authoritative rebuttal to the modern spirit of scientific scepticism, the Victorian age ever seriously examined the nature of the evidence on which the laureate had erected his case.

Certainly Tennyson's argument derives from a kind of imaginative awareness which his contemporaries had shown themselves little disposed to condone in his earlier poetry, and which in its implications could not but run counter to the dominant materialism of the times.

Although the psychological complexity of the vision tended to limit its poetic uses, as compared, for instance, with the devices of dream and madness, Tennyson often employed it for the purpose of opening up unexpected and disquieting perspectives through conventional material. A prophetic trance enables the protagonist of "Locksley Hall" to look into the future; and it is as the result of a similar visitation that the poet of "The Golden Year" celebrates his faith in the Victorian ideal of progress.

More revealing in the present connection are the "weird seizures" under which the hero of The Princess suffers. They were not incorporated into the poem until the fourth edition, published in 1851; and since these additions are inappropriate either to the Prince's character or to the action and general tone of the poem, there has ever since been controversy about Tennyson's motives for including them.

The initial lines describing the symptoms of these attacks show once more the poet's obsession with the enigma of appearance and reality as a central problem of knowledge. The Prince is speaking:

There lived an ancient legend in our house.
Some sorcerer, whom a far-off grandsire burnt
Because he cast no shadow, had foretold,
Dying, that none of all our blood should know
The shadow from the substance, and that one
Should come to fight with shadows and to fall;
For so, my mother said, the story ran.
And, truly, waking dreams were, more or less,
An old and strange affection of the house.
Myself too had weird seizures, Heaven knows what!
On a sudden in the midst of men and day,
And while 1 walk'd and talk'd as heretofore,
I seem'd to move among a world of ghosts,
And feel myself the shadow of a dream.

Three times the Prince undergoes these dream-like trances, in which "all things were and were not," while

As in some mystic middle state I lay.
Seeing I saw not, hearing not I heard...

Finally the trial of the tourney restores him to normality and allows him to accomplish his manhood through selfless union with the Princess Ida, herself regenerate.

Equally arbitrary is the faculty of second sight ascribed to Enoch Arden on his desert island:

There often as he watch'd or seem'd to watch,
So still the golden lizard on him paused,
A phantom made of many phantoms moved
Before him haunting him, or he himself
Moved haunting people, things, and places, known
Far in a darker isle beyond the line...

This sixth sense, released through isolation, informs Enoch that Annie has accepted Philip. Thereby the story gains a certain element of pathos; but we feel, nevertheless, that Enoch has been made a vehicle for conveying the author's own preoccupation with the spirit world.

Dream, madness, and vision are all essentially internal conditions of being. The mind regards itself; it is, so to speak, bemused by self-consciousness, and inhibited from translating its insights into action. Lucretius' suicide is the ultimate negation of the active life; and to a lesser extent all the vision-haunted characters in Tennyson's poetry exhibit a centripetal movement in their psychological processes.

Their perceptions spin inward, isolating the core of consciousness from involvement in the outside world. Yet Tennyson was too much man of his time to put the life of contemplation above the life of doing; and in consequence we find in his poetry a release, having its origin, like dream, madness and vision, in the imagination, but, unlike the other three, more immediately productive of external consequences. When the poet undertakes to activate the mind's inner awareness, his characteristic method is the quest.

Again "The Two Voices" is the proving ground for a thematic device which was later to be elaborated. Recognizing man's native idealism, the voice of doubt derides the perennial search for intangible and unattainable truths. In reply the poet confesses ignorance of his goal, but finds reasons for optimism in the fact that there does after all exist in human nature an instinctual compulsion to fulfill itself through pursuing some sort of ideal. The language of the following passage is that of the spiritual pilgrim:

I cannot hide that some have striven,
Achieving calm, to whom was given
The joy that mixes man with Heaven;
Who, rowing hard against the stream,
Saw distant gates of Eden gleam,
And did not dream it was a dream;
But beard, by secret transport led,
Even in the charnels of the dead,
The murmur of the fountain-head-
Which did accomplish their desire,
Bore and forebore, and did not tire,
Like Stephen, an unquenched fire.

Tennyson was not to sound the full imaginative implications of the quest until late in his career; but his early poetry makes sufficient use of this motif to enable the reader to identify those aspects which principally commended it to the poet.

The summons to the quest usually takes the form of a visionary flash of illumination, experienced most ofte7n while the recipient is in a state of trance-like exhilaration, though it may be vouchsafed through dream or even madness.

Thus, the hero of "The Princess" is started on his search for Ida by a voice mingling with the wind in the wild woods and announcing: "Follow, follow, thou shalt win." But success in the quest is incidental to the faith which motivates it. The prince's wanderings in "The Day-Dream," Tennyson's version of the legend of the sleeping beauty, are thus described:

He comes, scarce knowing what he seeks;
He breaks the hedge; he enters there;
The color flies into his cheeks;
He trusts to light on something fair;
For all his life the charm did talk
About his path, and hover near

With words of promise in his walk,
And whisper'd voices at his car.

Finally, although the quest involves its devotees in a life of strenuous activity, frequently productive of good to mankind, its true purpose is individual self-realization; and to this extent it is anti-social. Sir Galahad in the poem of that name succors distress wherever he encounters it; but his pursuit of the Grail is a lonely and entirely personal trial which requires the sacrifice of all worldly ties and communal pleasures.

All these elements are exemplified in two poems explicitly concerned with the quest: "Ulysses," published in 1842 but written in the time of most intense grief over Hallam's death; and "The Voyage," which appeared in the "Enoch Arden" volume of 1864. For Ulysses the whole purpose of life is the search for experience beyond the limits of proven achievement:

Yet all experience is an arch wherethro'
Gleams that untravell'd world whose margin fades
For ever and for ever when I move.

The hero is an old man; but the gleam still beckons from beyond the horizon:

And this gray spirit yearning in desire
To follow knowledge like a sinking star,
Beyond the utmost bound of human thought.

This poem is often taken as expressing a point of view directly contradictory to that embodied in "The Lotos-Eaters." Actually the defeatism of "Tithonus" forms a more effective contrast; for Ulysses' final decision to give himself to a private vision is merely the counterpart in terms of action of the more passive self-obsession of the lotos-eaters. Furthermore, to read "Ulysses" as an intentional tribute to those solid public virtues most admired by the Victorians is wholly to misinterpret the author's central purpose. In setting out on further wanderings which have no clearly foreseen objective, the Greek hero is not restrained by any conventional scruples of duty either to his family or the people he rules.

The character of Telemachus, as somewhat contemptuously alluded to, approximates much more closely the

Victorian model of patriotic and domestic behavior. And the vaunted qualities of mind which will support Ulysses and his followers in their quest, the strength of "will/ To strive, to seek, to find, and not to yield," are here made to subserve a line of conduct which cannot be justified in any but the most individualistic terms.

"The Voyage" may be said to take up where "Ulysses" leaves off. The quest is its own "raison d'être" and the chosen band which mans the ship is blithely indifferent to social responsibilities. The one sceptic in the crew, unable to maintain throughout a lifetime the self-sufficiency of his shipmates, commits suicide.

If his death is a comment on the fate Tennyson conceived for Lucretius, then the perseverance of the others celebrates the dominance of mystic inward strength that supports the human spirit through the tribulations of earthly existence. And here it may be noted for future analysis that in his concept of the quest Tennyson was working towards a fusion of philosophy and aesthetics which would harmonize in a higher synthesis his underlying sense of alienation from Victorian society on the one hand and, on the other, his reluctance to give exclusive credit to the promptings of the artist's inner consciousness. For the dedicated seekers of "The Voyage" refuse to be stayed either by the sober household values of the North, or by the sensual exoticism of the East:

At times a carven craft would shoot
From havens hid in fairy bowers,
With naked limbs and flowers and fruit,
But we nor paused for fruit nor flowers.

The mysterious gleam which leads the ship on its endless quest has instilled in each member of the crew immaculate devotion to his individual vision:

For one fair Vision ever fled
Down the waste waters day and night,
And still we followd where she led,
In hope to gain upon her flight.
Her face was evermore unseen,
And fixt upon the far sea-line;

But each man murmurd, 'O my Queen,
I follow till I make thee mine.'

Considered separately, the devices of dream, madness, vision, and the quest might not perhaps seem to furnish conclusive evidence of the operation of private insights within poems ostensibly addressed to a Victorian audience. When these motifs are taken together, however, it will be found that in one or another combination they characterize a neglected aspect of Tennyson's genius which is all-important to an adequate comprehension of his poetry.

The truth of this statement may be tested by an examination of the Idylls of the King, the major creative effort of the poet's career, and one which occupied his thoughts for about fifty years from the first version of the "Morte d'Arthur," written as early as 1835, to the publication in 1885 of "Balin and Balan," the last of the Idylls. To the great majority of Victorian readers this work came to seem an heroic tribute to the values on which their society prided itself. Yet the modern reader may well be sensitive to overtones in the Idylls suggestive rather of the author's interior imaginative resources than of uncritical commitment to the manners and morals of the age.

To be sure, the Epilogue, addressed to Victoria, makes an overt appeal to the moralistic temper of the times. The Queen is asked to

accept this old imperfect tale,
New-old, and shadowing Sense at war with Soul,
Ideal manhood closed in real man,
Rather than that gray king whose name, a ghost,
Streams like a cloud, man-shaped, from mountain peak,
And cleaves to cairn and cromlech still ...

And, indeed, when read, as is too often the case, on its most accessible level of interest, the Idylls of the King has something of the quality of a relic of Victorian sanctimony, redolent of habits of mind which the twentieth century does not share. In the conventional view the focal figure in the poem is an idealized ruler, composite of the moral earnestness of Hallam and the exemplary hearthside virtues of the Prince

Consort. The adulterous passion of the Queen and Lancelot then becomes the principal agency for the downfall of Arthur's chivalric order, with each successive Idyll falling into place as a portrayal of the pernicious spread of the blight emanating from this pair.

Marital disharmony ("The Marriage of Geraint" and "Geraint and Enid"), fratricide ("Balin and Balan"), overthrow of reason ("Merlin and Vivien"), misprision of innocence ("Lancelot and Elaine"), betrayal of faith ("Pelleas and Ettarre") through the perversion of the ideals on which it was founded a social order decays until in the last Idylls we witness its ultimate dissolution into chaos.

The fact that the poem is so admirably shaped towards the exemplification of this theme certainly indicates that Tennyson wanted to invite just such a reading; and with this interpretation of the Idylls there is here no wish to quarrel. A modern audience, however, may be attracted to certain aspects of the poem's theme which are less conventional in their implications — may even be allowed to suspect that these aspects were the ones which most fully engaged Tennyson's own imagination.

There is no ignoring the sombre and doom-ridden atmosphere which from the very outset hovers over the Idylls of the King. (Idylls are here discussed in the order in which Tennyson finally arranged them. If, as seems certain, the overall pattern of the poem did not clarify itself in the poet's mind until after he had made a considerable amount of progress, then we may likewise assume that the sections latest in actual date of composition were written for the purpose of supplying lacunae in the narrative or strengthening certain aspects of the theme which had come to seem important.)

This is "Götterdämmerung." Of the ten poems entitled "The Round Table," only the first, "Gareth and Lynette," shows Arthur's knighthood in anything like its pristine health and vigor; and significantly, Gareth is very young, very nalif, and entirely new to the ways of the fellowship. With the two Idylls relating to Geraint and Enid the shadow of Guinevere's transgression begins to fall across the exploits of the knights, and it lengthens until all is dark. Much later, after she has fled from Camelot, the Queen dreams

An awful dream, for then she seem'd to stand
On some vast plain before a setting sun,
And from the sun there swiftly made at her
A ghastly something, and its shadow flew
Before it till it touch'd her, and she turn'd-
When lo! her own, that broadening from her feet,
And blackening, swallowd all the land, and in it
Far cities burnt ...

But the shadows that flit over Arthur's kingdom do not originate with the Queen's guilt; they were there from the first, lending an air of ambiguity to everything that happened. Tennyson shows great skill in establishing a tone of unreality. The very legitimacy of Arthur's title to the kinzship is shrouded in dubitty.

In "The Coming of Arthur" (text) Bellicent bases her testimony on the vision which Bleys and Merlin saw; and final confirmation comes to Leodogran in the form of a misty dream. Thereafter, the reader first beholds Camelot through the eyes of Gareth and his companions. It seems a kind of Palace of Art, and the poet deliberately leaves in question whether it is real or existent only in the enchanted realm of the imagination:

So, when their feet were planted on the plain
That broaden'd toward the base of Camelot,
Far off they saw the silver-misty morn
Rolling her smoke about the royal mount,
That rose between the forest and the field.
At times the summit of the high city flashd;
At times the spires and turrets half-way down
Prick'd thro' the mist; at times the great gate shone
Only, that open'd on the field below;
Anon, the whole fair city had disappeard.
Then those who went with Gareth were amazed,
One crying, 'Let us go no further, lord;
Here is a city of enchanters, built
By fairy kings.' The second echo'd him,
'Lord, we have heard from our wise man at home

To northward, that this king is not the King,
But only changeling out of Fairyland,
Who drave the heathen hence by sorcery
And Merlin's glamour.' Then the first again,
'Lord, there is no such city anywhere,
But all a vision.'

Throughout the following Idylls the atmosphere thickens until, as though, in Merlin's words, man's passage were veritably from the great deep to the great deep and all in between a dream, the concluding actions are almost lost in obscurity. There is, for example, the strange immateriality of Guinevere's parting sight of the King:

... so she did not see the face,
Which then was as an angel's, but she saw,
Wet with the mists and smitten by the lights,
The Dragon of the great Pendragonship
Blaze, making all the night a steam of fire.
And even then he turn'd; and more and more
The moony vapor rolling round the King,
Who seem'd the phantom of a giant in it,
Enwound him fold by fold, and made him gray
And grayer, till himself became as mist
Before her, moving ghostlike to his doom.

And finally, there is the description of Arthur's last battle fought in a haunted mist so dense as to obliterate all distinction between the real and unreal:

Nor ever yet had Arthur fought a fight
Like this last, dim, weird battle of the west.
A death-white mist slept over sand and sea,
Whereof the chill, to him who breathed it, drew
Down with his blood, till all his heart was cold
With formless fear; and even on Arthur fell
Confusion, since he saw not whom he fought.
For friend and foe were shadows in the mist,
And friend slew friend not knowing whom he slew;
And some had visions out of golden youth,
And some beheld the faces of old ghosts
Look in upon the battle; and in the mist

Was many a noble deed, many a base,
And chance and craft and strength in single fights,
And ever and anon with host to host
Shocks, and the splintering spear, the hard mail hewn,
Shield-breakings, and the clash of brands, the crash
Of battle-axes on shatterd helms, and shrieks
After the Christ, of those who falling down
Look'd up for heaven, and only saw the mist;
And shouts of heathen and the traitor knights,
Oaths, insult, filth, and monstrous blasphemies,
Sweat, writhings, anguish, laboring of the lungs
In that close mist, and cryings for the light,
Moans of the dying, and voices of the dead.

Thus insisted on, mist and shadow become symbols of the misgivings which assail the knights vowed to the fulfillment of Arthur's vision. Addressing the seer, Gareth expresses the bewilderment of his followers, and perhaps his own:

these, my men,-
Your city moved so weirdly in the mist-
Doubt if the King be king at all, or come
[46/47]
From Fairyland; and whether this be built
By magic, and by fairy kings and queens;
Or whether there be any city at all,
Or all a vision ...

To which Merlin replies:

And here is truth, but an it please thee not,
Take thou the truth as thou hast told it me....
For there is nothing in it as it seems
Saving the King; tho' some there be that hold
The King a shadow, and the city real.
Yet take thou heed of him, for, so thou pass
Beneath this archway, then wilt thou become
A thrall to his enchantments, for the King
Will bind thee by such vows as is a shame
A man should not be bound by, yet the which
No man can keep; but, so thou dread to swear,
Pass not beneath this gateway, but abide

Without, among the cattle of the field.
For an ye heard a music, like enow
They are building still, seeing the city is built
To music, therefore never built at all,
And therefore built for ever.

To Balin, self-distrustful because of his madness, the rigors of the King's service seems too severe:

Too high this mount of Camelot for me;
These high-set courtesies are not for me.
Shall I not rather prove the worse for these?

And the betrayed Pelleas raves: "we be all alike; only the King/ Hath made us fools and liars." Later Dagonet, the King's jester, jeers at Arthur in bitterness of spirit over the decline of the Round Table:

the king of fools!
Conceits himself as God that he can make
Figs out of thistles, silk from bristles, milk
From burning spurge, honey from hornet-combs,
And men from beasts — Long live the king of fools!

In the end, after the disintegration of all he has stood for, even Arthur gives way to self-doubt:

Hearest thou this great voice that shakes the world,
And wastes the narrow realm whereon we move,
And beats upon the faces of the dead,
My dead, as tho' they had not died for me?
O Bedivere, for on my heart hath fallen
Confusion, till I know not what I am,
Nor whence I am, nor whether I be king;
Behold, I seem but king among the dead.

In their confusing of the ideal and the actual, the principal actors in the Idylls of the King lead a sort of double life. An ulterior meaning shadows their actions. They exist not only in the outer world of postive achievement, but also in an interior world of conflicting motives. It is the interaction between the two realms of consciousness which gives the poem its strange quality of intensity. Every action has its imaginative counterpart through the instrumentality of dream, madness, vision, and the quest. A list of the characters whose dreams, too numerous to catalogue, interpret critical passages in the Idylls would include: Leodogran, Enid, Lancelot, Elaine, Pelleas, Tristram, Guinevere, and Arthur.

Inner stress induces madness in Balin and Pelleas, as well as Lancelot. In addition to the supernatural portents which attend the King's coming and passing, the vision of the Holy Grail, the phantom cup that comes and goes, is revealed with varying degrees of clarity to many of Arthur's knights. And the quest for the Grail is, of course, the very hallmark of fealty to the life of the imagination.

If a review of the Idylls be now undertaken with the foregoing observations in mind, there will be seen to emerge through the moral veneer which gave the poem its immediate appeal to the Victorian age a second and profounder theme. This theme, more consonant with Tennyson's habits of mind, reflects the under side of the author's twofold awareness, the side which faced away from society and towards his individual being as a creative artist.

For it was in the depths of his own consciousness that Tennyson had finally to confront and struggle with the problem of appearance and reality which remorselessly obsessed his imagination. It is only when regarded in the light of this conflict that the full meaning of the Idylls of the King becomes manifest.

The poet hints at his intent as early as the opening lines to "Geraint and Enid," where he departs from his usual practice in the Idylls and steps in front of the curtain:

O purblind race of miserable men,
How many among us at this very hour
Do forge a lifelong trouble for ourselves,
By taking true for false, or false for true;
Here, thro' the feeble twilight of this world
Groping, how many, until we pass and reach
That other where we see as we are seen!

The initiating situation in this Idyll is Geraint's unfounded suspicion of his wife's fidelity, which grows out of her intimacy with Guinevere. Geraint, jealous by nature, is unwilling to believe in his own good fortune. His distrust is played off against the cynicism of Earl Doorm, the first of many characters in the Idylls wholly possessed by sensuality. Doorm tempts Enid with food, drink, and finally with fine raiment. Her rejection of the latter brings into play the theme of shadow and substance on which Tennyson was to work so manv variations in the subsequent poems. For Enid's choice recafis not only the bedraggled condition in which Geraint first found her, but also the dream relating to her appearance at court, her actual presentation to Guinevere, and the Queen's gift of clothing.

A more tragic version of this conflict occurs in "Balin and Balan" which comes next after the Geraint and Enid story in the final ordering of the Idylls, although, significantly, it was the last of all to be written. The structure of this poem adroitly reinforces the irony of the central situation. Balin becomes Guinevere's knight as a means of averting further attacks of insanity; yet it is the disillusionment resultant on what Sir Garlon and Vivien tell him about the Queen's; clandestine life that plunges him back into his final fatal derangement. In granting Balin permission to carry the Queen's device on his shield, Arthur says:

Thou shalt put the crown to use.
The crown is but the shadow of the king,
And this a shadow's shadow, let him have it,
So this will help him of his violences!

Subsequently, Balin's frantic flight from the court takes place after he has overheard Lancelot and Guinevere talking together. To Lancelot's account of his symbolic dream of the lily, token of innocence, the Queen opposes her waking choice of the rose, flower of physical passion. But it is Vivien whose cynical estimate of the Round Table finally opens Balin's eyes to the maddening actuality of his situation. Vivien (along with Gawain) is the clear-sighted advocate of the life of sensation in the Idylls of the King; and, as such, she symbolizes the materialistic threat which Earl Doorm and his kind offer to Arthur's order.

This is the significance of her animistic hymn to the sun and its accompanying remark:

This fire of heaven,
The old sun-worship, boy, will rise again,
And beat the Cross to earth, and break the King
And all his Table.

The next Idyll, as its title, "Merlin and Vivien," indicates, carries on the pattern of bringing into opposition two characters, one representing the inner integrity of spiritual being, the other the corrupting powers of the world.

Vivien exerts the wiles of the flesh, not this time against the holy fanaticism of Arthur's knighthood, but against the authority of the intellect as vested in Merlin. The ensuing narrative presents interesting affinities with "Lucretius"; for both poems illustrate Tennyson's distrust of reason when it is not supported by some form of transcendental faith. Merlin knows that he cannot avert the fate which impends over Camelot. In deep despondency he has decided to withdraw from the court. The lines descriptive of his mental state Tennyson did not add until 1873, fourteen years after the first publication of "Merlin and Vivien" (at that time entitled simply "Vivien"), and furthermore, after the appearance of four Idylls concerned with later stages of the story:

Then fell on Merlin a great melancholy;
He walk'd with dreams and darkness, and he found
A doom that ever poised itself to fall,
An ever-moaning battle in the mist,
World-war of dying flesh against the life,
Death in all life and lying in all love,
The meanest having power upon the highest,
And the high purpose broken by the worm.

The symbol of Merlin's power is the spell bequeathed by a forgotten seer who had practised self-denial until

to him the wall
That sunders ghosts and shadow-casting men
Became a crystal, and he saw them thro' it,
And heard their voices talk behind the wall,
And learnt their elemental secrets, powers
And forces.

The victim of this spell loses all capacity to move and all

sense of time, and is condemned forever to behold only that person who has enchanted him. In the apathy born of the realization that the Round Table cannot be preserved by wisdom of the mind, Merlin yields to the fascination of the arch-realist Vivien with her mocking comment: "Man dreams of fame while woman wakes to love." So the power lodged in the spell passes into her hands; and Merlin's bondage becomes a token of the failure of Arthur's ideal in its intellectual aspect.

"Lancelot and Elaine" is, of course, a reworking of "The Lady of Shalott" (text) within a much wider context. Like the lady of the earlier poem, Elaine "lived in fantasy." The life of the imagination was her essential being;to shatter it would be to destroy her.

As with the Lady of Shalott also, the symbol of Elaine's inner existence is a work of art, the case that she has embroidered for Lancelot's shield. Which is the more real, the battle-scarred shield emblematic of Lancelot's exploits in the great world beyond Astolat, or its fragile covering? Here Tennyson's use of detail is especially subtle. Elaine is awakened each morning by the gleam of the shield. She fashions its covering "fearing rust or soilure." To a truthful depiction of "all the devices blazon'd on the shield" she

added, of her wit,
A border fantasy of branch and flower,
And yellow-throated nestling in the nest.

After Lancelot has returned to claim his shield, Elaine, like Mariana, lives on in her tower. Since her life depends on the delusion, she insists that it is her "glory to have loved/ One peerless, without stain."

The diamonds for which Lancelot is fighting operate symbolically against the main line of the story. Apparently so tangible and of such lasting beauty, they are no sooner found than lost; and possession of them is as unhappy as it is brief. Note the circumstances under which Arthur discovered the crown of the slain king:

And Arthur came, and laboring up the pass,
All in a misty moonshine, unawares
Had trodden that crown'd skeleton, and the skull

Brake from the nape, and from the skull the crown
Roll'd into light, and turning on its rims
Fled like a glittering rivulet to the tarn.
And down the shingly scaur he plunged, and caught,
And set it on his head, and in his heart
Heard murmurs, 'Lo, thou likewise shalt be king.'

In Elaine's dream, as her brother narrates it to Lancelot, there is no holding onto the precious stone:

...for, knight, the maiden dreamt
That some one put this diamond in her hand,
And that it was too slippery to be held,
And slipt and fell into some pool or stream...

A dream strangely premonitory of the fact. For Guinevere in her jealous fury is to cast Lancelot's trophy of nine years combat into the river at Camelot at precisely the moment when

slowly past the barge
Whereon the lily maid of Astolat
Lay smiling, like a star in blackest night.

Among the Idylls "The Holy Grail" not only marks the turning point in the history of the Round Table, but also calls forth the author's deepest speculations on the nature of appearance and reality. The beauty of the poetry does not permit us to question the vision in which the Grail appears to Percivale's saintly sister; but there is something suspect in the knights' eagerness to dedicate themselves to the quest. Lancelot's motive is suggestive of the sensation-seeking of declining order.

Hitherto, his sense of guilt has inflicted intermittent spells of madness; now, intoxicated by the hope of purging his conscience, he undertakes the search as an individual enterprise. Certainly in Arthur's view the ques is a form of self-deluding lunacy for all but the chosen few. It represents an over-indulgence of man's spiritual nature as harmful in its way as the sensuality for which Vivien stands. In sadness of heart he predicts that his knighthood will "follow wandering fires/ Lost in the quagmire!" Guinevere's reaction is equally perceptive: "This madness has come on us for our sins."

Tennyson selects five knights whose experiences

exemplify the ambiguity of the quest, though we are told that: "All men, to one so bound by such a vow,/ And women were as phantoms." Galahad and Gawain occupy the extreme positions. For the former the quest is the only reality and leads to beatification; for the latter it is a will-o'-the-wisp from which he soon turns back to earthly pleasures. Lancelot's way ends in frustration after exposing him to madness more humiliating than any he has yet known. Sir Bors' steadfast perseverance brings the desired vision, but his heart is never in the search.

For him the brotherhood of the Round Table takes precedence over self-fulfillment. On his return to Camelot he refuses to speak of his experience, but goes straight to Lancelot and grasps his hand. Sir Percivale is the narrator and his adventure is most illuminating of all. Setting forth alone, he finds himself "thirsting in a land of sand and thorns," where all the pleasant things of this world turn to dust at his approach. At last under Galahad's guidance he consummates the quest; but in after years the episode which lingers in his memory is curiously at variance with the ordeal as a whole. For he recalls how he found his first love and longed to remain with her until he

remember'd Arthur's warning word,
That most of us would follow wandering fires,
And the quest faded in my heart.

And even though he went on again in the wake of the vision, there is remarkably little solace in the recollection of temptation resisted:

... but one night my vow
Burnt me within, so that I rose and fled,
But waiPd and wept, and hated mine own self,
And even the holy quest, and all but her...

To which his marveling auditor, the monk Ambrosius, adds a chorus-like comment from the point of view of those who, like himself, "want the warmth of double life," and "are plagued with dreams of something sweet/ Beyond all sweetness in a life so rich."

It is Arthur, however, who out of his weariness and sadness places the final evaluation on the quest for the Grail.

Recognizing in it a portent of the fading of his ideal of the perfect society. He confesses that he too prone to visions such as dematerialize the phenomenal world. But such dreams, he says, do not belong to human life on earth, since they relate to a higher order of reality. Once man's work is done, however:

Let visions of the night or of the day
Come as they will; and many a time they come,
Until this earth he walks on seems not earth,
This light that strikes his eyeball is not light,
This air that smites his forehead is not air
But vision-yea, his very hand and foot
In moments when he feels he cannot die,
And knows himself no vision to himself,
Nor the high God a vision, nor that One
Who rose again.

Compare with these lines Tennyson's own statement, made in 1869:

Yes, it is true that there are moments when the flesh is nothing to me, when I feel and know the flesh to be the vision, God and the Spiritual the only real and true. Depend upon it, the Spiritual is the real: it belongs to one more than the hand and the foot. You may tell me that my hand and my foot are only imaginary symbols of my existence, I could believe you; but you never, never can convince me that the I is not an eternal Reality, and that the Spiritual is not the true and real part of me."

After the quest for the Grail, the scene darkens rapidly, while the Round Table enters on the final stages of decline. "Pelleas and Ettarre" is a bitter companion piece to "Lancelot and Elaine." By choosing a life of fantasy, and later death, Elaine retained her innocence; the actuality thrust on Pelleas destroys his innocence and reason together. For unlike Balin and Lancelot, Pelleas does not invite madness; it comes to him through circumstances over which he has no control. Lancelot's renunciation of Elaine is sorrowful, for his adultery ~Onjl makes him more honorable in all his other conduct.

Gawain already identified in "Lancelot and Elaine" and "The Holy-Grail" as the soulless materialist, is wholly cynical in his betrayal of Pelleas with Ettarre, who herself makes a mockery of chivalric love. Pelleas' disillusionment, then becomes symptomatic of the overthrow of an entire social order. In his Lear-like frenzy he imagines that human nature has debased itself below the level of animals.

Of all the narratives in the "Idylls of the King," "The Last Tournament," not published until 1871, is perhaps most skillfully contrived to bring out the theme of shadow and substance.

"The world/ Is flesh and shadow," says Dagonet; and the Tournament of the Dead Innocence mordantly embodies his meaning. As with the diamonds in "Lancelot and Elaine," the ruby carcanet has complex symbolic value. It is associated with "the maiden babe" who did not live after she was given into Guinevere's care. And it is won by Tristram for a last love-offering to Isolt of Lyonesse. Tristram's dream after his victory in the lists is filled with ironic implications:

He seem'd to pace the strand of Brittany
Between Isolt of Britain and his bride,
And showd them both the ruby-chain, and both
Began to struggle for it, till his queen
Graspt it so hard that all her hand was red.
Then cried the Breton, 'Look, her hand is red!
These be no rubies, this is frozen blood,
And melts within her hand-her hand is hot
With ill desires, but this I gave thee, look,
Is all as cool and white as any flower.'
Follow'd a rush of eagle's wings, and then
A whimpering of the spirit of the child,
Because the twain had spoil'd her carcanet.

Furthermore, the triangle of Mark, Isolt, and Tristram savagely parodies the situation obtaining among Arthur, Guinevere, and Lancelot, since Arthur could never have taken Mark's way, any more than Lancelot and Guinevere were capable of following the example of Tristram and Isolt in sacrificing all to love.

That Lancelot, in the King's absence, should preside over this last tourney is a further irony in view of the combatants' behavior. We hear the death-knell of the Round Table when Tristram, who alone has fought bravely, rejoices with Isolt in the triumph of lawless passion over the unnatural restrictions imposed by Arthur on his knights:

The vows!
O, ay-the wholesome madness of an hour-
They served their use, their time; for every knight
Believed himself a greater than himself,
And every follower eyed him as a God;
Till he, being lifted up beyond himself,
Did mightier deeds than elsewise he had done,
And so the realm was made. But then their vows
First mainly thro' that sullying of our Queen-
Began to gall the knighthood, asking whence
Had Arthur right to bind them to himself?
Dropt down from heaven? wash'd up from out the deep?
They fail'd to trace him thro' the flesh and blood
Of our old kings. Whence then? a doubtful lord
To bind them by inviolable vows,
Which flesh and blood perforce would violate;
For feel this arm of mine-the tide within
Red with free chase and heather-scented air,
Pulsing full man. Can Arthur make me pure
As any maiden child? lock up my tongue
From uttering freely what I freely hear?
Bind me to one? The wide world laughs at it.
And worldling of the world am I, and know
The ptarmigan that whitens ere his hour
Woos his own end; we are not angels here
Nor shall be. Vows-I am woodman of the woods,
And hear the garnet-headed yaffingale
Mock them-my soul, we love but while we may;
And therefore is my love so large for thee,
Seeing it is not bounded save by love.

And finally, as a counterpart to the Tournament of the Dead Innocence, there is Arthur's sally against the Red Knight when his newly-sworn followers behave in a manner indistinguishable from that of the enemy for brute ferocity and abandonment to evil passions. Throughout the greater part of the Idylls of the King Arthur is kept in the background, as if, in allowing his influence to be exerted indirectly, Tennyson had wished to explore alternative modes of behavior inspired by attraction to or repulsion from his example.

Now in "Guinevere" and "The Passing of Arthur" the King moves into the forefront of the action that we may judge the reality of his personal dream as a way of life. By modern standards Arthur's treatment of the Queen may seem unendurably self-righteous; but this must not be allowed to close the reader's eyes to the King's discovery that, however wronged, he is still a man in love.

Guinevere's betrayal has broken his heart and so tarnished his faith in the governing ideal of his life. No longer sustained by belief in the heavenly ratification of his mission, his mind is torn between vague and futile surmises. Either God is absent from the universe, or else mortal perceptions cannot fathom His purposes:

... for why is all around us here
As if some lesser god had made the world,
But had not force to shape it as he would,
Till the High God behold it from beyond,
And enter it, and make it beautiful?
Or else as if the world were wholly fair,
But that these eyes of men are dense and dim,
And have not power to see it as it is —
Perchance, because we see not to the close;
For I, being simple, thought to work His will,
And have but stricken with the sword in vain,
And, all whereon I leand in wife and friend
Is traitor to my peace, and all my realm
Reels back into the beast, and is no more.

The altogether human suffering inflicted by the Queen has condemned Arthur, like so many of his subjects, to walk the shadow line between seeming and reality:

Thro' this blind haze which, ever since I saw
One lying in the dust at Almesbury,
Hath folded in the passes of the world.

Gawain visits the King in dream; and his lament, "Hollow, hollow all delight," is a final comment on the life of the senses. But what is there to say for Arthur's vision after "that battle in the west/ Where all of high and holy dies away?" The ruined chancel with its broken cross, symbolizing the undoing of Christianity, to which Bedivere bears the dying Arthur would seem to negate the withdrawal of Guinevere, Lancelot, and Percivale to an existence of religious seclusion.

Surely the return of Excalibur to the Lady of the Lake signifies that the time for heroic action has passed. One may well sympathize with Bedivere's sense of desolation as he watches the outward voyage of the funeral barge. If Camelot is a nobler vision of the Palace of Art, then the "island-valley of Avilion" becomes at one further remove a symbol of total alienation. And for all Tennyson's pious tribute in the Epilogue to Victoria's "crown'd Republic's crowning commonsense," the final impression left by the poem is one of tragic incompatibility between the life of the imagination and the ways of the world.

Chapter 6

The Hidden World of Sight That Lives Behind This Darkness

The Idylls of the King is, for the purposes of the present argument, the culminating achievement of Tennyson's artistic career, since the poet here conceived a work of major proportions which spoke home to his age and at the same time gave full expression to his own deepest intuitions. In none of his later writings do we to any like extent sense the operation of this double awareness. In fact, after about 1870 a deliberate split is observable in Tennyson's aesthetic intent. He continues to write poems in conformity with the prevailing tastes which he had exploited so successfully from the 1842 volume on.

His invasion of the field of historical drama with Queen Mary in 1875 is perhaps the clearest evidence of his desire to reach as wide an audience as possible. On the other hand, in a return to and development of his earliest manner, he also produced a considerable number of poems anything but popular in nature, which are fully intelligible only if interpreted as projections of subjective states of mind. Whichever the category to which they belong, the poems published during the last two decades of Tennyson's life not only continue to employ the characteristic motifs of dream, madness, vision, and the quest, but do so in an even more highly selective way.

The pessimistic tone that darkens the concluding Idylls is strongly marked in the treatments of contemporary life which are the late counterpart of the English Idyls of the 1842 and "Enoch Arden" volumes. The poems in dialect are less humorous than their predecessors; and in such works as "The First Quarrel," "The Wreck," "Despair," and "Forlorn" the melodramatic situations, as the titles suggest, usually have a gloomy outcome. The vigorously challenging tone of "Locksley Hall" has given way to the somewhat shrill petulance of "Locksley Hall" "Sixty Years After." A comparison of the two poems indicates Tennyson's growing disquietude over the road Victorian England was travelling. The sentiments of the speaker in the latter have the querulous quality of a man driven almost frantic by the decay of those values which had seemed to guarantee social stability.

And, indeed, madness in Tennyson's later poetry is almost invariably a condition directly attributable to environmental pressures. Among other examples, "Rizpah" is the most forceful study of insanity as a form of individual release from the harsh workings of external circumstance. In the same way, as may be shown in such poems as "In the Children's Hospital," "Columbus," "Despair," and "Romney's Remorse," the value of dreams resides in the solace which they bring to wounded sensibilities.

Through sleep the sufferer escapes from actuality. Indeed, just as he tended increasingly to portray madness as an unproductive aberration, so the later Tennyson in those poems which celebrate the active life inclines to distrust the dream state as a form of self-indulgence. Saint Telemachus, tempted to the false asceticism of a Saint Simeon Stylites, hears a mystic voice, saying:

Thou deedless dreamer, lazying out a life
Of self-suppression, not of selfless love.

And Akbar feels that his dream of a universal church may by its very persuasiveness seduce him into complacency and so corrupt the will to act:

The shadow of a dream-an idle one
It may be. Still I raised my heart to heaven,
I pray'd against the dream. To pray, to do
To pray, to do according to the prayer,
Are, both, to worship Alla, but the prayers,
That have no successor in deed, are faint

And pale in Alla's eyes, fair mothers they
Dying in childbirth of dead sons.
I vowd Whate'er my dreams, I still would do the right
Thro' all the vast dominion which a sword,
That only conquers men to conquer peace,
Has won me.

On the other hand, a second body of poems proves that the ghostly promptings from the dark side of the human consciousness, which flicker through all Tennyson's work, visited the aging poet with greater and greater urgency. His need to believe in the existence of some controlling power outside the limitations of time and space had always been strong; towards the end of his life he was readier to accept the revelations of the inner mind, although its activities remained as much a mystery as ever to him.

Furthermore, the impulse to give expression while there was yet time to the complex intuitions of the imagination overruled that concern for the artist's communicative function which had led to the sublimation of the deeper meanings in so much of his previous writing. As a result, the later volumes contain such remarkable poems as The Ancient Sage and Vastness, in which the pretense of objectifying theme through didactic narrative is dropped, and the author lets his imagination have its way in highly personal and often cryptic utterance.

This poetry, as the voice of Tennyson's inner being, is shot through with visions of a transcendental kind. Nor is it surprising to find that the pilgrimage of the spirit towards ultimate truth presents itself, as often as not, under the aspect of a quest. The machinery of vision and the quest thus continues to motivate the themes of many of the later poems; and in the case of two of the most notable, "Merlin and the Gleam" and "The Voyage of Maeldune," it prescribes the form.

The first of these is a thinly disguised apologia for Tennyson's entire poetic career, viewed in terms of the generating impulses within each successive period. The "Voyage of Maeldune" is a broader allegoric representation of the life journey, rendered through symbols often perplexingly private. Analysis of these poems would only serve to explore ways of the imagination which have already been sufficiently travelled; but Tennyson's choice of the quest as a mode for embodying his profoundest spiritual convictions may suggest the inherently vitalistic habit of mind which is perhaps his strongest bond with the Victorian age. For in the quest, the active and contemplative life meet and are reconciled.

It is the finite objective of revenge which holds Maeldune and his companions together and makes them persevere in their long and arduous journey, even though the wisdom garnered along the way invalidates the goal when it is at last in sight. And as Tennyson himself tells us in "Merlin and the Gleam," the vision becomes all the more compelling after it has been challenged by sorrowful recognition of the disparity between shadow and substance, the actual and the ideal in this world:

Clouds and darkness
Closed upon Camelot;
Arthur had vanishd
I knew not whither,
The king who loved me,
And cannot die;
For out of the darkness
Silent and slowly
The Gleam, that had waned to a wintry glimmer
On icy fallow
And faded forest,
Drew to the valley
Named of the shadow,
And slowly brightening
Out of the glimmer,
And slowly moving again to melody
Yearningly tender,
Fell on the shadow,
No longer a shadow,
But clothed with the Gleam.

The argument which emerges from the foregoing

discussion should now be clear. Whether it be as an escape from actuality through dream or madness, or as an escape into higher truth through vision and the quest, the central emphasis in Tennyson's poetry develops from an inner rather than an outer awareness from the life of the imagination rather than from a sense of responsibility to society.

For the conflict between the appearance of the external world and the reality of the individual consciousness which we have found to be the real theme of the Idylls of the King runs through nearly all the more serious poems of Tennyson's later period. The aged protagonist of Locksley Hall Sixty Tears After says: "All the world is ghost to me, and as the phantom disappears"; and the narrator of The Sisters elaborates this sentiment as follows:

My God, I would not live
Save that I think this gross hard-seeming world
Is our misshaping vision of the Powers
Behind the world, that make our griefs our gains.

The fine poem, which Tennyson wrote on the birth of his son Hallam under the title of "De Profundis," originates in a like conviction that the world as we sense it shadows a higher realm of spiritual being. (The fact that the poet withheld until 1880 the publication of "De Profundis," although it was presumely written in 1852, might well be constructed as further evidence of his hesitancy in mid-career to reveal too openly the inner workings of his mind.)

The poet speaks of "that true world within the world we see,/ Whereof our world is but the bounding shore," and then continues, addressing his child:

O dear Spirit, half-lost
In thine own shadow and this fleshly sign
That thou art thou-who wailest being born
And banisYd into mystery, and the pain
Of this divisible-indivisible world
Among the numerable-innumerable
Sun, sun, and sun, thru' finite-infinite space
In finite-infinite Time-our mortal veil
And shatter'd phantom of that infinite One,

Who made thee unconceivably Thyself
Out of His whole World-self and all in all-

But because such intimations from the recesses of the unconscious are intermittent, the dialogue between faith and doubt that we first overheard in "The Two Voices" goes on. It receives crowning expression in "The Ancient Sage," the theme of which is "this double seeming of the single world." Here the voice of denial belongs to the young man who is, significantly, a lyric poet.

The sage advises his disciple to take up a life of human service as a means of making "the passing shadow serve thy will," and so extirpating from his thoughts the "black negation of the bier." As for himself, the sage, who, of course, speaks for Tennyson, has attained to full self-reliance, and as a result passed beyond the need for outside support. He admits that the truth as he knows it cannot be proved, but neither can the position of his skeptical pupil:

Thou canst not prove the Nameless, O my son,
Nor canst thou prove the world thou movest in,
Thou canst not prove that thou art body alone,
Nor canst thou prove that thou art spirit alone,
Nor canst thou prove that thou art both in one.
Thou canst not prove thou art immortal, no,
Nor yet that thou art mortal — nay, my son,
Thou canst not prove that I, who speak with thee,
Am not thyself in converse with thyself,
For nothing worthy proving can be proven,
Nor yet disproven.

But the sage, we find, has known mystic revelations of a kind which Tennyson himself experienced, and through them he has come to place unshakable trust in the imagination as the highest of human faculties:

If thou wouldst hear the Nameless, and wilt dive
Into the temple-cave of thine own self,
There, brooding by the central altar, thou
Mayst haply learn the Nameless hath a voice,
By which thou wilt abide, if thou be wise,
As if thou knewest, tho' thou canst not know;

For Knowledge is the swallow on the lake
That sees and stirs the surface-shadow there
But never yet hath dipt into the abysm,
The abysm of all abysms, beneath, within
The blue of sky and sea, the green of earth,
And in the million-millionth of a grain
Which cleft and cleft again for evermore,
And ever vanishing, never vanishes,
To me, my son, more mystic than myself,
Or even than the Nameless is to me.

Yet the imagination not only conceives, it also shapes; and so it is that for Tennyson inner awareness allied with the artistic act as well as with the apprehension of philosophic truth. The source of all true inspiration is within the intuitional consciousness of the individual. This sense of the immateriality of the outward show, of the strangeness and mystery that always lie just under the appearance of things, of the unknowableness of the human mind in its instinctual perceptions is the germinal impulse in virtually all of Tennyson's best poetry. Hence his uneasy conviction that the age with its obsessive materialism could not really supply him the materials with which to work; hence also his recognition of the subterfuges that were necessary in order to get Victorian society to listen to his message.

For these reasons Tennyson's genius was most at home when employed on traditional legends of proven narrative and moral interest, which could yet be made exemplificatory of deeper implications for the reader who cared to look below the surface. Two comparatively late poems of this kind best illustrate the author's final aesthetic position. One is "Demeter and Persephone." On first reading, this retelling of the familiar myth of the seasons seems hardly more than a rather tender rendering in elegiac terms of maternal devotion, consonant with the Victorian tendency to idealize domestic relationships.

Yet it will be noticed on closer analysis that it is only in the first access of grief, when she thinks of her daughter as irretrievably lost, that Demeter suspends her generative function. Persephone, appearing in dream, explains that her periodic withdrawal from the phenomenal world to the nether region of shadows does not really involve a loss, but is mysteriously necessitated by the process of creation:

The Bright one in the highest
Is brother of the Dark one in the lowest,
And Bright and Dark have sworn that I, the child
Of thee, the great Earth-Mother, thee, the Power
That lifts her buried life from gloom to bloom,
Should be for ever and for evermore
The Bride of Darkness.

When interpreted in this way, "Demeter and Persephone" becomes a symbolic representation of Tennyson's entire poetic career. Beneath his artistic productivity lay dark depths of consciousness on communion with which, rather than on any external stimulus, depended his will to create.

"Tiresias," which Tennyson kept by him for many years before he decided to publish it in 1885, yields insight of a different kind into the poet's dispute with Victorian society. The prophet of the "song-built" city begins by lamenting the decline of his powers:

These eyes, now dull, but then so keen to seek
The meanings ambusYd under all they saw,
The flight of birds, the flame of sacrifice,
What omens may foreshadow fate to man
And woman, and the secret of the Gods.

As with Tithonus, Tiresias' suffering is attributable to a vision of unearthly beauty. His punishment, however, entails loss of the faculty to compel belief through his art. The outraged goddess has decreed: "Henceforth be blind, for thou hast seen too much,/ And speak the truth that no man may believe." To his son Tiresias confesses that the vision still survives on the inner eye. The tragedy of his blindness is not that he cannot see what lies outside him, but that he is unable to share with the outer world the clarity of his interior perceptions:

Son, in the hidden world of sight that lives
Behind this darkness, I behold her still,
Beyond all work of those who carve the stone,

Beyond all dreams of Godlike womanhood,
Ineffable beauty, out of whom, at a glance,
And as it were, perforce, upon me flash'd
The power of prophesying — but to me
No power-so chain'd and coupled with the curse
Of blindness and their unbelief who heard
And heard not...

So "this power hath workd no good to aught that lives"; and the poet's impotent desire to influence the lives of his contemporaries has left him helpless victim to

The grief for ever born from griefs to be,
The boundless yearning of the prophet's heart —

Like Ulysses and like the Ancient Sage, Tiresias hands over the responsibility to act in society's behalf to less imaginative youth. In so doing he accepts his isolation with its burden of private intuitions. And the reasons which he gives epitomize the choice which the Victorian age sooner or later imposed on all its true artists, however earnestly they might seek grounds for compromise:

Virtue must shape itself in deed, and those
Whom weakness or necessity have cramp'd
Within themselves, immerging, each, his urn
In his own well, draws solace as he may.

Chapter 7

Irony and Comedy

In a famous passage, the narrator of Middlemarch expresses the central point of nineteenth-century irony:

We do not expect people to be deeply moved by what is not unusual. That element of tragedy which lies in the very fact of frequency, has not yet wrought itself into the coarse emotion of mankind; and perhaps our frames could hardly bear much of it. If we had a keen vision and feeling of all ordinary human life, it would be like hearing the grass grow and the squirrel's heart beat, and we should die of that roar which lies on the other side of silence."

When every life becomes tragic and the element of the special case is removed, human existence itself becomes ironic. Catastrophic disillusionment and destruction are not the lot of the godlike hero, invoking by his stature the terrible laws of retribution, but of every ordinary person going about the business of common life. There are, consequently, no heroes; there are no cosmic laws to be broken; there is no possibility of fixing our pity and fear on the suffering hero.

We are all victims, incapable of being "deeply moved" by what is common, uncaused, and without meaning. The tragic emotions are not released but focused and contained, and we are forced, in ironic art, to see ourselves as victims of the trivial, both trapped and released into the "illimitable inane" ("Lucretius," l. 40). We are all caught in the same incoherence, experiencing, as Melville's Ishmael says, the contradictory ironic states, floating isolation and total bondage ("And what are you, reader, but a Loose-Fish and a Fast-Fish, too?"). Increasingly in the nineteenth and twentieth centuries, we find a myth that stresses the two images of man as caught, wriggling on the deterministic pin, or loose, accidental, with only a vague hope "that nothing walks with aimless feet."

But this is not the only myth. There was, after all, the world of Mr. Pickwick, of Jane Austen, and much of Wordsworth: the world of liberated order, settled and humane values, sanctified and full life. The comic vision stood as an alternative to the ironic, dissolving the unrelieved tension of irony by reaffirming the dignity and power of the human will, the possibility of joy, and the continuity of all life. Comedy offered a means of surpassing the insistent "facts" of irony. Against the ironic insistence on the isolation of man, comedy posed the symbol of marriage; against the contrary insistence on bondage, it posed the symbol of the dance or the party: Christmas at Dingley Dell or Bob Cratchit's, the Mad Tea Party, cucumber sandwiches with Ernest Worthing.

The comic vision gradually becomes more difficult to sustain, perhaps, but it never dies entirely. The nineteenth century was much closer to Eden, and even its irony contains within it always the clear picture of what is lost. As Matthew Arnold says, the pain of isolation is not just increased, it is partly caused, by the memory or at least the legend of a union that once had been: "Who order'd, that their longing's fire / Should be, as soon as kindled, cool'd?" ("To Marguerite - Continued," ll. 19 – 20).

The comic thus stands against and enriches the ironic myth. Just so, irony begins to move to dominate all art, not necessarily because artists chose that myth, but because for serious writers of the last century or so, "irony is ... much less often a rhetorical or dramatic strategy which they may or may not decide to employ, and much more often a mode of thought silently imposed upon them by the general tendency of the times." But, by a striking further paradox, those artists most conscious of the advancing prevalence of the ironic view were precisely those who most aggressively resisted it. Those most sensitive to the present were also most deeply sensitive to the past: they saw that the comic life was lost but still remembered it most vividly. They continued to ask, with Hardy, "And why unblooms the best hope ever sown?" because they in part believed in — or at least remembered — the grand artistic, religious, and political hopes of the past.

The most crucial problem for these artists was contained in the perception that the present, the only thing really alive is void of meaning, while the past, which is dead, alone contains the meaning that can give life. The past is both immediate and beyond reach. The comic vision refused to yield completely to the ironic, and we find, in artist after artist, these forms existing side by side. One could argue, in relation to the past, from full and resonant comic grounds:

The Present is the vassal of the Past:
So that, in that I have lived, do I live,
And cannot die, and am, in having been —
A portion of the pleasant yesterday. ["The Lover's Tale," ll. 115-18]

Here our bondage to the past is made cause for an extension of personality throughout time, so that our being "a portion of the pleasant yesterday" helps define us in relation to time and insures that we "cannot die," implying not only that we have life in the past but that we will, by irrational but very compelling analogy, continue to live in the time that has defined us.

But "portion of the pleasant yesterday" recalls nothing so firmly as the grim lines from "The Lotos-Eaters": "All things are taken from us, and become / Portions and parcels of the dreadful past". It is not just that this "pleasant" past has become "dreadful"; time the protector has become time the ravager. This transformation locates for us the center of Tennyson's major poetry: the interplay and conflict of the comic and ironic modes. No other nineteenth-century writer is more responsive to the intense presence and distance of comic life, the memory that seems to make life possible in its promise of continuity and yet turns it into a mockery of genuine life, a literal death-in-life.

Tennyson's career can be seen as a and courageous resistance to the demands of ironic art, an art he had, moreover, mastered very early. If one sets aside his minor poems - the political and public verse, his English and domestic idyls, and his dialect and humorous poems – something like a semicircular pattern may be traced. The Poems by Two Brothers and the volumes of 1830, 1832, and 1842 all contain a few comic poems but show, in the main, a steady development toward more compact and rich ironic statement.

Beginning with The Princess however, and continuing through In Memoriam and Maud, Tennyson tries various and often unique comic strategies, only to return to irony in the late poems, and particularly in Idylls of the King, surely the major ironic work of art of the century. This development is neither simple nor pure - comic and ironic forms are used throughout his career – but the main outlines seem reasonably clear.

This suggested pattern differs markedly from that implied by what was once critical orthodoxy: the view that Tennyson and his poetry could best be apprehended by a series of contraries. Harold Nicolson made an admirably strategic division of the lyric, morbid, and mystic Tennyson from the public bard, and we have had, since, a good many developments and refinements of this view[4]. At present, critics frequently deny the dualism and assert one or another unity in its place. It is, however, surely just as dangerous to ignore the tension in Tennyson's poetry as to go on inventing new labels for it.

One can, of course, see how apt and expressive descriptions such as "life-weariness," "despair," "frustration," or "melancholia" [6] are in explaining the basis of Tennyson's art. Even more basic, it seems to me, is a larger formal battle carried out in his poetry between two alternate myths. One of these, irony, does express itself in the form of balanced, but unreconciled, opposites; the other, comedy, takes a firm, single direction. The first myth has often been approached indirectly by means of the dualistic view mentioned before; the second has largely been ignored.

TENNYSON'S IRONY

The narrative pattern of irony, what Northrop Frye calls

"the mythos of winter," frequently been characterized in discussions of "open" or "general" irony and distinguished there from the "specific" or "closed" irony that is more properly thought of as a technique. This general irony is noncorrective, presenting, like all irony, some conflict but insisting always that the conflict cannot be resolved. This is the irony of the impossible situation, an irony that includes us all as victims — characters, readers, even the ironist.

Art rooted in "unidealized existence" is likely, then, to formulate its structural principles and its narrative patterns in reference to general irony. There are no heroes and no heroic action; worse, there is no coherence to support any purposeful action whatever. Such heroism and such coherence are, however, often recalled in this irony in order that they may be parodied. In fact, parody seems to be the basic principle of this narrative irony. It feeds on the affirmations contained in the other traditional patterns: romance's idealizations, tragedy's cathartic sacrifice, comedy's liberation.

Practicing always a rhetoric of deception, this pattern forces us to anticipate resolutions that never come. Such rhetoric is deliberately unstable, seeking to disarm us, to include its audience with its victims. The characteristic themes are of disillusionment and meaningless defeat, the fall from freedom into bondage. While there is some specific irony in Tennyson — one thinks of "The Last Tournament" or the verse epistles — he is, clearly, not Donne. But he does utilize extensively the more general narrative pattern, especially in the depiction of dominant opposites which cannot be coordinated or made to cancel, but which demand equal and contradictory responses.

The tension between the religious, hopeful symbol on the one hand, and the tragic or melancholic symbol on the other, marks the center of Tennyson's poetry, the point being that his irony is not merely gloomy, almost never simply macabre. The contraries exist together, as brothers, an early poem says, stealing "symbols of each other" ("Song [Every day hath its night]").

The result is that no emotion can flow outward from us.

The comfort of comedy and the perverse comfort of decisive negativism are alike denied, and the reader is suspended between alternate emotional and intellectual responses to alternate, unreconciled themes.

Whatever Tennyson may have meant by his cryptic remark that "what the public do not understand is that the great tragedy is all balance throughout," " the "balance" he achieves and transmits is the ironic one presented in Moby-Dick, where the Pequod, tilting dangerously to one side under the weight of a whale's head lashed to it, hoists another on the opposite side, thus regaining her "even keel; though sorely strained, you may well believe." Ishmael goes on to point out the usefulness of this image as a symbol for the human mind, poised and paralyzed and unable to "float light and right." Irony, it may be said, causes so much horizontal strain that it makes any free forward movement impossible.

At its most obvious, Tennyson's ironic vision did insist directly and openly on the alternate truths: death is all, life is all – "All Things Will Die ..... Nothing Will Die," as the poems from 1830 put it. But we find the unresolved oppositions in much less dramatic and ostentatious form throughout his career. In the beautiful poem, "To the Marquis of Dufferin and Ava" (1889), for example, he deals with both the greatness of the Indian Empire (Lord Dufferin had been governor-general of India) and the sense that India was the treacherous fate that drew his son Lionel to his death. Toward the end of the poem, these views coalesce as Tennyson dwells on the terrible fact that his son died so far from him, with strange rites and in a strange sea:

Not there to bid my boy farewell,
When That within the coffin fell,
Fell-and flashed into the Red Sea,
Beneath a hard Arabian moon
And alien stars. [ll. 42-46]

The strong romantic associations packed into "Arabian moon" and "stars" are juxtaposed against the brutality of "hard" and "alien." But the romantic associations are not canceled by the adjectives, just as the speaker's belief in the

Indian enterprise or in the continuation of life through death are not shattered. The lines describing the death are, after all, contained in a tactful public utterance, which celebrates first the virtues of a good colonial ruler and ends in a vision of love in this life and the next. The poet-and the reader-perceives both visions with equal force: the private, despairing clarity of the image of a remote death, suggesting the alien universe and the absurd, causeless nature of life, along with the public, hopeful vision of reasonable and kindly political activity and a religion of love.

Neither wins. It is the great virtue of Tennyson's art that, as he matures, the diffuse and obtrusive "All Things Will Die" – "Nothing Will Die" dichotomies become compacted into phrases as suggestive and haunting as "hard Arabian moon."

Irony does not dominate all of Tennyson's poetry, but it does control the early poems (up to 1842) and many of the late ones, most prominently Idylls of the King. In the great middle period, the period of The Princess, In Memoriam, and Maud, Tennyson searched for means to transcend the ironic tension of vividly presented but unreconciled opposites. Transcendentalism helped, of course, and we find lively statements of it attributed to him: "Nothing worthy proving can be proven" ("The Ancient Sage," l. 66) or "Poetry is truer than fact," (Memoir, 2: 219) for instance.

But transcendentalism is likely only a small part of the major cause of Tennyson's liberation, which is the discovery of the possibilities of comedy. In fact, it could be argued that transcendentalism was convenient not primarily for its doctrine but for its ability to provide a happy surprise behind every false appearance, exactly paralleling the ending of comedy, where the disguises come off and reveal familiarity and promise. In any case, Tennyson spent the central part of his career writing comedy, imaging the very form he could also parody so completely. The movement from liberty to bondage was for a time reversed, as Tennyson sought to forge a unique and lasting comic vision.

Chapter 8

Tennyson's Comedy

Comedy" here is taken to mean the mythic pattern, not that which is funny. In this sense it duplicates in quality our sense of the term "irony"; that is, it is a narrative pattern, supported by an appropriate formal but unstated convention (or conventions). It clearly emphasizes liberation, freeing the ego from traps which are external and, especially, internal so that it may find, in its rejuvenation, a more or less exuberant social and personal life.

Comedy finds its source at the close of the basic myth, in the resurrection of the dead god and his restoration of fertility happiness to the community. It transforms an inhibiting condition, usually a social condition — symbolized by an unjust king, law, parent, personal vice or illusion — to a clarified and liberated one: from "law to liberty," as Frye says.

Comedy is especially satisfying because of its sense of completeness, its location at the very end of the myth, but also because of its magical way of solving problems that hinge on the contrary demands of the private self and of society. It takes as its hero a figure who confronts an unjust law boldly, and endures a period of neglect or even hostility in order finally to overcome injustice and gain recognition and reward from his society.

By means of a focus on the liberation and rewarding of the hero, comedy feeds the isolated egos of us all. At the same time, by attacking relentlessly all misanthropic and overtly egoistic tendencies and by regarding all extroverted and social traits as laudable, comedy supports community.

This union of the personal and the communal is effected

partly because we can easily identify both with the egoistic hero and with the society he redeems, but it is also true that comedy works very carefully to keep that heroic ego within certain bounds. One must, it suggests, be expansive in one's joy and, above all, charitable. Charity and forgiveness take the place of tragedy's iron justice and retribution and often stand in conflict with them.

Comedy emphasizes the miraculous and improbable; tragedy the necessary and inviolable. Thus, the hero is rewarded with gifts that will tend to social expression: marriage, which supports and prolongs the social order, and money, which is seen almost entirely in terms of its allowing the hero to give gifts, hold parties, and the like. In other words, if we are willing to define ourselves socially and accept [8/9] certain minor restrictions on our pride and our tendencies toward tyrannical or blind behavior, we can be rewarded with gifts that are both social and personal. After all, in comedy marriage implies a beautiful lady.

Comedy thus works against social definition seen broadly and impersonally (i.e. in terms of modern social science or the nineteenth century's political economy) and supports social definition seen narrowly and personally. Finally, comedy's position at the end of the myth means that, with the shadow of death and sacrifice behind it, it retains a very strong feeling about the preciousness of life itself and is always dedicated to it.

It is not often recognized that Tennyson's poetry contains a large element of this zest for experience, usually expressed indirectly but often coming to the surface in lines like, "One only joy I know, the joy of life" ("Life," l. 14). As Georg Roppen very perceptively argues, "Tennyson's obsessive preoccupation with death is the negative aspect of an insatiable life-zest which informs a considerable part of his poetry and seeks expression in various directions. His craving for immortality ... is not an aspiration to beatitude, but to continued, happy life."

But the comic sense that controls the major poems of the middle period is often realized in ways both puzzling and unique. The comedy is maintained only in the midst of difficulties so large that the form and even the values must be continually won and re-won. The conventional certainties of comedy are very difficult for Tennyson to accept, despite the fact that he had a strong artistic — and certainly personal — instinct to do so.

As a result, we have comedies which are not only highly specialized but which are haunted by their inverse: very sophisticated parodies of that comedy. The comic vision is never as purely expressed as is the ironic, and its tentative quality checks the resounding confidence that is usually necessary to bring off comedy's miraculous, nonlogical leaps. I am not suggesting that ordinary comedy can work only by establishing a mindless euphoria, but it seems clear that very little comedy is as dubious of its own affirmations as is Tennyson's.

This very distrust, however, can make the affirmations all the more striking. Easy as it is to make jokes about Queen Victoria's comparison of In Memoriam's comfort to that of the Bible, no one can doubt that the queen spoke sincerely and out of the depths of real need. It is no small thing to offer hope in the face of death; comedy has always tried to do just that.

But the tentativeness of Tennyson's great comedies helps to explain why he was never fully comfortable in that form. Despite the fact that In Memoriam, for instance, is a finer poem than "Rizpah," the latter is more unified and generically resonant.

Tennyson could growl on with "grim affection" about "Bones" — it is a fully finished and formed utterance — but he apparently disliked talking of In Memoriam — partly, I suppose, because he was so close to it, but also because it is so highly complex, almost generically mystifying, offering various directions for our emotions, only to pull them together at the end with a resolution that has not seemed fully satisfying to many.

In Memoriam is Tennyson's version of The Divine Comedy, but it lacks entirely the total confidence and the resultant easy coherence of Dante's poem. Tennyson, one feels, could have written ironic poems like "Rizpah" forever. It is a wonder and perhaps a clue to his greatness that he tried with such skill and against such odds to write a poem about a world that could be rescued for sense, loyalty, and love.

It is a great wonder principally because Tennyson seemed unable to delude himself, except in minor poems. Even Dickens could bluff-witness John Harmon and Bella Wilfer in Our Mutual Friend — if the genre so demanded. But Tennyson, in his major poems, is always turning over the comic coin, seeing if the affirmation can stand its own negation. This ironic tendency in his comedy is both remarkable and unsettling. Every comic generalization stands, but not on very steady legs.

First of all, while Tennyson could accept completely the necessity and even the beauty of a social or domestic life – "Come down, O maid," for instance, is one of the most complete lyric expressions of domestic comedy in our literature — he perceived at the same time that this vision could operate as a trap, killing the spirit of man and encasing him in deadly trivia.

There is a strong sense of this opposition in The Princess, "Ulysses" is a full statement of the problem, and Idylls of the King explores the pressures of the social life as subtly as Middlemarch and with very much the same view.

Second, Tennyson felt most uneasy about the principle on which comedy reverses tragedy: time's renewal. Time triumphs not only in The Winter's Tale but in every comedy, by having its linear march expose the false, restricting society, by its realization of a transcendent joy that lies outside time, or by its denial of time's dominion: they lived happily ever after.

Tennyson's ambiguous attitude toward the past has already been mentioned; it seems, however, that there was a larger ambiguity, involving change, which he could see both comically and ironically.

For instance, the comic expression asserts that change is comfortable, that it is for the better, and, most important, that it does not alter our real being: "We are all changed by still degrees, / All but the basis of the soul" ("'Love thou thy land, with love far-brought,' " ll. 43-44). The comic view of stasis and change takes as its symbols, respectively, eternity and regeneration. Turned about, however, these assurances become the two ironies that dominate much of Tennyson's poetry: comfortable change is transformed into meaningless flux; solid and unchanging being becomes an image of man trapped and unable to help himself.

Further, though comedy always has managed its defeat of time by a projection into future it has generally done so successfully only by convincing us of the powerful happiness realized in the present, "They lived happily ever after" has meaning only if they are happy now.

Tennyson seemed constitutionally unable, however, to imagine genuine and full comic happiness materializing for a long, long time; sometimes, one gathers, not until a few eons have passed.

It is a peculiar comic satisfaction that one can obtain from waiting for evolution to solve problems. Evolution is not nearly as rhetorically persuasive as, say, sex. Still, this is to oversimplify a more complex issue that involves what Spedding called Tennyson's "almost personal dislike of the present, whatever it may be." (Memoir, 1: 154). Existentialism is a modern term, but all effective comedy has contained more of it than Tennyson could muster.

Tennyson's tendency to complicate the comic mode is apparent even in very minor issues. His use of repetition, for instance, is, on the surface, highly appropriate to comedy, where the recurrence of events gives us a sense of the deep continuity of life and growth.

In Tennyson, however, the lulling reassurances contained in the repetitions of "Come down, O maid" can just as easily become the compulsive, desperately negative "Let us alone" of "The Lotos-Eaters" or "Tithonus," where the suggestions of life, ever awakening in similar patterns, are made hideous by burlesque.

Similarly, there is in Tennyson a distrust of the comic principle of prodigious abundance, of wild, almost uncontrolled generosity. He spoke of being appalled by "the lavish profusion ... in the natural world ... from the growths of the tropical forest to the capacity of man to multiply, the torrent of babies."

Still, though it is complicated and even tortured, comedy is central to Tennyson's vision, so remarkably strong that it could be maintained and finds long and continued expression despite ironic pressures from without and within. It is the interplay of these two forms that I wish to examine. Tennyson mediates between the two great myths that have become the dominant modes of modern artistic expression.

Chapter 9

The Minor Poems

There are, of course, other forms and other developments in Tennyson. It is a given that he wrote some extraordinarily interesting poems and some quite uninteresting ones, not that many would agree on which are which. It is not important to draw exact lines, though it is important to attempt an explanation of why poems like "The Spinster's Sweet-Arts" or "English Warsong" affect its as they do: with irritation or not at all.

Most of these minor poems are striking for their simplicity, their grim single-mindedness and relentless narrowing of emotion and focus. They stand in marked contrast to the complexity, suggestiveness, and expansiveness of the other poems. One way to think of them is as a relaxation from the great tensions of irony and the difficult sort of comedy Tennyson wrote. It may seem odd to speak of "tensions" being produced in this way, but we have seen for some time that Tennyson was caught between the worlds of Pride and Prejudice and Hyperion, between the practical, novelistic world and the visionary, mythical world.

The tension I am discussing, though not coincident with the other, ties over it and surely makes it understandable that simple poetic reductions might occasionally be inevitable. In any event, those poem which seem to me reductive fall into three groups: the political and public poems, the domestic idyls, and the humorous and dialect poems. Some of these poems are excellent in their way, but they do not, I think, constitute the major part of Tennyson's achievement, nor do they contribute a great deal to his present reputation.

When Tennyson's first child died at birth, the poet wrote to John Forster, describing the event with his strange and characteristic mixture of the naïve and the sophisticated, the immediate and the detached:

The nurse dressed up the little body in pure white. He was a grand massive manchild, noble brow and hands, which he had clenched in his determination to be born. Had he lived, the doctor said he would have been lusty and healthy, but somehow he got strangled. I kissed his poor pale hands and came away and they buried him last night in Twickenham churchyard. [Charles Tennyson, p. 262]

Notice how Tennyson uses the typical locutions associated with nineteenth-century sentimentality — "the little body," "pure white," "poor pale hands" — while suggesting the very opposite of sentimentality. The "core of toughness" always discernible in Tennyson's best poetry here controls and mutes the potential sentimentality by encasing it in accents of reserve and detachment. The bleak and naked quality of "but somehow he got strangled" or "they buried him last night in Twickenham churchyard," the staccato sentences, and the use of coordinations that simply string statements together, give the impression of artlessness, the refusal to rearrange, subordinate, and heighten — in fact, to interpret at all. The major impression is that of inexplicable awfulness temporarily mastered, of unbearable grief not overcome but suspended. The mixture of tones, in other words, provides a subtle and moving irony.

One way to look at the domestic idyls, the humorous poems, and the political poems is in terms of a dislocation of this ironic conjunction. The "core of toughness" is exaggerated into the uncontrolled energy and exhibitionistic release of the political poems; the tenderness and sentimentality become the humorous poems or the static and hazy idyls of the hearth. All represent a relaxation from the strain and difficulty of the ironic or comic modes one finds in the major poetry. One notices, for instance, that Tennyson seemed to find it necessary to write the domestic idyls only during periods when his major poems were ironic in form. The domestic idyls begin to appear in the 1830 volume, there are some dozen of them in the Poems of 1842, and he begins writing them again in about 1860, just one year after the publication of the first installment of Idylls of the King.

During the comic period, between The Princess and Maud, these poems virtually disappear. There is one exception: "The Brook" appeared in the Maud volume of 1853. Them were one or two, added to later editions of the 1842 poem too, but except for "The Brook," none was written in the "comic period," ie. between The Princess and Maud. There was apparently no need then for this therapeutic exercise, but they increase in direct proportion to the seriousness and dominance of his ironic vision.

Setting aside these minor poems, then, we are left with the poems that constitute Tennyson's claim to our attention, along with some revealing and interesting preliminary work. From The Devil and the Lady to Idylls of the King, the poet worked with irony and comedy, testing, reordering, and trying new combinations in an attempt to find an adequate form. In one of those irresponsible but penetrating remarks with which W. H. Auden filled the famous introduction to his edition of Tennyson's poems, he calls Tennyson "the great English poet of the Nursery."

There is not much truth in this, but there is some. Tennyson's poetry hardly seems to "deal with human emotions in their most primitive states," but it does express our most fundamental plights and hopes with an intensity and honesty that only a half-asleep Auden would ever call "stupid."

Chapter 10

Tennyson's Early Poems

Alfred Tennyson, the most representative, and by far the most popular, poet of Victorian England, born in 1809, was the fourth son of the rector of Somersby in Lincolnshire. His two elder brothers, Frederick and Charles, were also poets and must receive some mention later. They were all, not least the greatest of them, men of singular physical beauty and strength, dark and stalwart, and through most of them ran a vein of almost morbid hypersensitiveness and melancholy, to which, in Alfred, we may trace the rare delicacy and intensity of his sensuous and emotional renderings of nature and mood and dream, as well as the hysterical extravagances of some of the poems in which he touched on subjects, political and religious, that moved him deeply.

Educated at Louth grammar school (of which his only pleasant memory was the music of the Latin words *sonus desilientis aquae)* and by his father at home, Tennyson's genius struck its roots deep into that soil of family affection and love of country the alienation from which, in varying degree, of most of the earlier romantic poets—Wordsworth, Coleridge, Byron, Shelley—contributed to the independent, revolutionary tone of their poetry, and the slowness with which some of them gained the ear of English readers.

When Tennyson went up to Cambridge, Shelley's was still a name of doubtful omen. Tennyson was always to be—not entirely for the benefit of his poetry—in closer sympathy with the sentiments of the English middle-classes, domestic, distrustful of passion or, at least, of the frank expression and portrayal of passion, patriotic, utilitarian.

And the influence of these classes, politically and morally, was becoming dominant. Tennyson went to Cambridge a few months before Gladstone, the representative statesman of the coming era, went to Oxford.

The group of friends who gathered round Tennyson included Arthur Henry Hallam, Gladstone's most intimate friend at Eton. They were all of them young men of the high and strenuous seriousness which breathes from the letters of Sterling and Hallam—James Spedding, Richard Trench, Henry Alford, Edward Lushington. The life they led was a very different one from that which Byron describes in his letters of twenty years earlier. These have the hard, reckless ring of the age of Fox and his dissipated, aristocratic friends. The young band of "Apostles" who debated

On mind and art,
And labour, and the changing mart,
And all the framework of the land

were imbued with the serious, practical temper of the great merchant class which was to reshape England during the next fifty years. They were strangers alike to the revolutionary hopes that intoxicated the youthful Wordsworth, and the reactionary spirit of "blood and iron" against which Byron fought and over which Shelley lamented in strains of ineffable music:

Oh, cease! must hate and death return?
Cease! must men kill and die?

The era of conservative reform, of Canning and Peel, of attachment to English institutions combined with a philanthropic ardour for social betterment, had begun. The repeal of the Test act, Catholic emancipation, the first great Reform bill were all carried between the date at which Gladstone and Tennyson went up to college and a year after they had gone down.

Of this movement, Tennyson was to make conscientious efforts to approve himself the poet; but, as experience was to show, the conservative instincts of the would-be liberal poet were deeper and more indestructible than those of the young statesman who, in these years, was still "the rising hope of stern and unbending Tories." The same *via media* was the path followed by Tennyson and his friends in the region of theology and philosophy.

Disciples, some of them, of Coleridge, they were all more or less broad churchmen, Christian in sentiment but with little of Gladstone's reverence for dogma, and sensitive, as Gladstone never was, to movements of contemporary thought and science.

"Christianity is always rugging at my heart," Tennyson said, and his heart and mind were too often divided against one another to allow of his attaining to the heights of inspired and inspiring religious song. But in no mind of his day did the conflict of feeling and thought produce more sensitive reactions. In the widened and altered vision of the universe which natural science was slowly unfolding, Tennyson was to find, at moments, a fresh justification of the deepest hopes and instincts of his heart, at moments, their utter negation. To the conflict between his sensitive and conservative temperament and that Lucretian vision of the universe which physical science seemed more and more to unroll, we owe some of the most haunting notes of Tennyson's poetry.

But these notes were not sounded at once. Tennyson's first concern was with poetry alone, the object of his assiduous and patient quest being to discover and to master the style and measures in which he could best express the poetry with which his mind was charged to overflowing. *Poems, by Two Brothers* is negligible.

In these early verses, he threw off, as in a kind of mental measles, the infection of the more popular poets of the day—Byron and Moore and Scott. At Cambridge, Wordsworth and Coleridge and Shelley and Keats displaced their more popular rivals, and Tennyson's genius entered upon a period of experiment, of growing clearness and sureness of judgment, of increasing richness and felicity of diction and rhythm, the record of which has been preserved with unusual fulness in the successive *Poems, Chiefly Lyrical* (1830), *Poems* (1833) and *Poems. By Alfred Tennyson*, 2 vols.

The relation in which these stand to one another is not

unlike that of the different "states" of an etching, the successive "pulls" in which the artist studies the progress he has made towards the complex perfection of the final plate. Some poems were rejected altogether; others dropped only to reappear; a few suffered little or no alteration between the first edition and the last; yet others (and these are the most interesting and the most important) underwent an elaborate process of rearrangement of the component features, of rehandling that included every kind of erasing, deepening and enriching—processes of which the final outcome was the pomp and magnificence of the 1842 volumes, the beauty and glow presented in their final form by such studies as *The Lady of Shalott, The Miller's Daughter, Œnone, The Palace of Art* (considering the poem only on the side of its music and pictures), *A Dream of Fair Women* and *The Lotos Eaters.*

Tennyson's aim in all this elaboration is clear enough now, though it was not to such early critics as Christopher North and Lockhart—who were justifiably witty at the expense of the poet's lapses, if Lockhart was less justifiably blind to the final result to which the experiments tended. It was no deepening insight into his subjects and guided Tennyson's efforts, for they were to him subjects and no more. They were the common topics of his romantic predecessors, nature, English pastorals, ballad themes, medieval romance, classical legend, love and death.

But Tennyson was burdened with no message, no new interpretation of nature or the peasant, no fresh insight into the significance of things medieval or things Hellenic. Each and all were subjects that quickened his poetic imagination, and his concern was to attain to the perfect rendering in melody and picturesque suggestion of the mood which each begat in his brooding temperament. Much has been said of Tennyson's relation to Keats and Wordsworth; but a closer tie unites him to Coleridge, the poet. Like Coleridge, Tennyson is a poet not so much of passion and passionate thinking as of moods—moods subtle and luxurious and sombre, moods in which it is not always easy to discern the line that separates waking from dreaming.

And, like Coleridge, Tennyson, from the outset, was a metrist, bold in experiment and felicitous in achievement. Almost every poem in these volumes was a distinct, conscious experiment in the metrical expression of a single, definite mood. There were some failures, not from inadequate control of the poet's medium of verse (as Coleridge was inclined to think) but because, as Christopher North pointed out, Tennyson occasionally mistook for a poetic mood what was merely a fleeting fancy and recorded it in lines that were, at times, even silly.

Of the poems which survived the purgation to which Tennyson subjected his work, some are less happy than others, again not because the poet has failed to make the verse the echo of the mood, but because the mood itself was not one that was altogether congenial to his mind. In lighter and simpler strains, Tennyson is never quite spontaneous.

But, when the mood was one of the poet's very soul, luxurious or sombre or a complex blend of both, the metrical expression was, from the first, a triumphant success. *Claribel, Mariana,* "A spirit haunts the year's last hours," *Recollections of the Arabian Nights, The Dying Swan, The Lady of Shalott, the blank verse of Ònone, A Dream of Fair Women, The Palace of Art, The Vision of Sin, The Lotos Eaters*—all reveal (think what one may of the philosophy of some or of the faults of phrase and figure which marred the first transcripts) a poet with a command of new and surprising and delightful metrical effects as unmistakably as did the early poems of Milton, the masterpieces of Coleridge, Shelley's songs or Swinburne's *Poems and Ballads.*

The true character of the English verse foot which the romantic poets had rediscovered without all of them quite knowing what they had done, the possibilities of what Saintsbury calls "substitution," the fact that, in verse whose indicator is a recurring stress, the foot may be iambic, trochaic, spondaic or monosyllabic without altering the time-lengths of the rhythmical interval, Tennyson understood perfectly and he experimented on it with a conscious and felicitous art, combining with this subtle management of the foot a careful attention to the musical value of vowel and consonant combinations in which his precursors are Gray and Pope and Milton. And, for Tennyson, the guiding principle in every experiment, from *Claribel to The Vision of Sin,* is the dramatic appropriateness of verse to mood.

Many of the poems, as has been said, underwent drastic revision; but this revision seldom affected the metre, though the concluding stanza of *The Lotos Eaters* is a striking exception. It was the phrasing and imagery, the richly decorative and picturesque diction, that was revised before the eyes of the reader with wonderful results. The motive which dictated this labour was the same as that which controlled the varied cadences of the poet's verse, the desire to secure the full and exact expression for the single mood which dominates the poem throughout.

For each of Tennyson's shorter poems, at any rate—hence, perhaps, his preference of the idyll to the epic—is the expression of a single mood of feeling. It is seldom that one of his songs or odes or idylls carries the imagination of the reader from one mood of feeling to another, as does an ode by Keats or Wordsworth, while the stream of impassioned thought flows through the mind. In his longer poems, *In Memoriam* and *Idylls of the King,* as will be seen later, the plan of construction finally adopted is a concession to this quality of the poet's genius.

A brooding imagination, a fine ear and a vivid and curious eye, the eye of an artist who, also, was something of a naturalist—these are the distinctive qualities of Tennyson's poetic temperament. He divined, as Keats had before him (but Keat's eye was not, to a like extent, the dominant factor in his sensibility), that a picture presented with extraordinary precision of detail may, if every detail be relevant, contribute potently to the communication of a mood of feeling—the whole secret of pre-Raphaelitism. But he was also aware that mere description is no business of the poet who describes only to communicate feeling.

Accordingly, the alterations which Tennyson introduced into his work, in so far as they were not dictated by the ear, by the desire to secure a purer, more flute-like melody of vowel and consonant, had one of two purposes in view, either to present a picture with greater clearness of arrangement and vividness or wealth of detail, or, even more often, to diminish merely descriptive effects, to substitute one or two significant, suggestive details for a fully drawn picture, in every way to intensify the emotional, dramatic effect as by passing the stanza once more through the dyeing vat of the poet's own passionate mood.

Of passages in which the first aim predominates a classical example is the opening landscape in *Œnone,* but a shorter may be cited from *The Palace of Art:*

One seemed a foreground black with stones and slags,
Below sunsmitten icy spires
Rose striped with long white cloud the scornful crags
Deeptrenched with thunderfires,
compared with
And one a foreground black with stones and slags,
Beyond, a line of heights, and higher
All barr'd with long white cloud the scornful crags,
And highest, snow and fire

Of the other process, the subtle heightening of the emotional thrill, examples will be found in all the poems mentioned; but two short passages may be cited by way of illustration:

No time hath she to sport and play,
A charmed web she weaves alway,
A curse is on her if she stay
Her weaving either night or day,
To look down to Camelot,
compared with
There she weaves by night and day
A magic web with colours gay.
She has heard a whisper say,
To look down to Camelot,
or,
She moved her lips, she prayed alone,
She praying disarrayed and warm

From slumber, deep her wavy form
In the darklustrous mirror shone.
"Madonna," in a low, clear tone
Said Mariana, night and morn,
Low she mourned, "I am all alone,
Love-forgotten, and love-forlorn,"
compared with
Complaining, "Mother, give me grace
To help me of my weary load."
And on the liquid mirror glow'd
The clear perfection of her face.
"Is this the form," she made her moan,
"That won his praises night and morn?"
And "Ah," she said, "but I wake alone,
I sleep forgotten, I wake forlorn."

The heightened glow of the picture in the lines italicised is not more striking than the dramatic significance of "Is this the form," etc. But, perhaps, the supreme examples of the poet's power to enrich his verses by passing them once again through the mood in which the whole poem was conceived are the closing stanzas of *The Lady of Shalott* and of *The Lotos Eaters*.

The outcome of the severe course of training to which Tennyson submitted his art—a process that never quite came to an end, for later poems were, also, carefully revised after publication—was a style, the ground and texture of which is a pure, idiomatic English, mannered as, in a different way, the style of Milton is mannered, decorative as in a different way, the style of Milton is decorative, and a verse of wonderful variety, a felicitous adaptability to the mood of the poem, and a curiously elaborated melody of vowel and consonant. With the exception of Gray—for Pope's "correctness" is not entirely a poetical excellence—English poetry had produced nothing since Milton that is so obviously the result of a strenuous and unwearied pursuit of perfection of form.

Tennyson's range of topics is, also, fully represented in the 1842 volumes—studies of mood and character ranging from the first slight sketches of Adelines and Marianas to the complexities of Simeon Stylites, St. Agnes and Sir Galahad, and the nobility of Ulysses; studies of English rural life like *Dora,* among the least successful of Tennyson's poems, not because (as a critic has complained) they have too much of Wordsworth's "silly sooth," but because they lack the intense conviction which keeps Wordsworth from ever being "silly," though he may at times be absurd, and exalts his "sooth" into imaginative truth; medieval studies in which was now included *Morte d'Arthur,* starting point of the later *Idylls of the King;* classical legend represented by the early *Ònone* recast and *Ulysses,* for *Tithonus* though written was not yet published; and, lastly, poems in which Tennyson touches on the mysteries of life and death and immortality, themes round which his brooding imagination was to circle all his life with a sincerer passionate and pathetic interest than he felt for any other subject that engaged his art—seeking, finding, but never long sure that he really had found, like some lone, ghostly sea-bird wheeling round the luring, dazzling, baffling beams of a lighthouse on some stormy headland.

For all his questing, Tennyson was never to get much further than the vague hope of the closing section of *The Vision of Sin:*

At last I heard a voice upon the slope
Cry to the summit, "Is there any hope?"
To which an answer peal'd from that high land,
But in a tongue no man could understand;
And on the glimmering limit far withdrawn
God made Himself an awful rose of dawn.

The sombre note of the scene and the song which precede this close was to be heard more than once again in the verse of the poet who had already written *The Two Voices* and was yet to write *Vastness.* Of political pieces, the volumes included the very characteristic poems "You ask me, why," "Love thou thy land," "Of old sat Freedom" and the very popular, if now somewhat faded, trochaics of *Locksley Hall.*

THE PRINCESS

These latter poems, and such additions to his earlier work

as *Morte d'Arthur, Ulysses and Love and Duty,* were proof that not only had Tennyson completely mastered his decorative, musical style but that his poetry had gained in thought, in dramatic insight, in depth and poignancy of feeling; and the question for a lover of Tennyson's poetry in 1842 must have been, was this advance to be continuous, such an increasing dramatic understanding of the passionate heart of man as carried Shakespeare from *A Midsummer Night's Dream to Macbeth and Othello,* with all the change in style and verse which that process brought with it, or such an absorption in a great theme, the burden of a message, as produced *La Divina Commedia or Paradis Lost.*

For there were dangers besetting Tennyson's laborious cultivation of a new and rich poetic diction, dangers which betrayed themselves very evidently in the first considerable poem that followed the 1842 volumes, the longest poem Tennyson had yet attempted, and the first in which he set himself conscientiously (in the mood in which he had conceived *The Palace of Art)* to give to his poetry a didactic intention.

The Princess, first published in 1847 but revised and re-revised in 1851 and 1853, if it exhibits all the characteristic excellences of Tennyson's style, his mellifluous blank verse and polished, jewelled phrasing, reveals with equal clearness its limitations and faults. The blend of humour and sentiment and serious purpose is not altogether a success—"Alfred, whatever he may think," said FitzGerald, "cannot trifle. His smile is rather a grim one"—and of dramatic interest there is the merest suggestion in the grandlioquent princess, the silly prince and their slightly outlined companions.

Moreover, the style, with all its beauties, reveals, as some of the later *Idylls of the King* were to do, the radical want of simplicity, which is not really disguised by the purity, of Tennyson's style, a tendency to conceit and decoration which seeks to make poetry of a plain statement by periphrasis and irrelevant, even if beautiful, figure. Gladstone admired the skill with which Tennyson could make poetical the description of a game-pie:

Where quail and pigeon, lark and leveret lay
Like fossils of the rock, with golden yolks
Imbedded and injellied,

and describe mathematics as

The hard-grain'd Muses of the cube and square.

The Princess abounds in refinements of this kind, as when the prince

sat down and wrote,
In such a hand as when a field of corn
Bows all its ears before the roaring East,

or the remark that Cyril's wilder frolics are not the surest index to his character is thus adorned:

He has a solid base of temperament:
But as the waterlily starts and slides
Upon the level in little puffs of wind,
Tho'anchor'd to the bottom, such is he.

Even when the poem rises to a higher level of seriousness in the closing sections, the style is still elaborated and brocaded out of all proportion to the theme. Yet of such art the final perfection is found in an appearance of simplicity, and that, too, Tennyson achieved in the lyrics which were added to the third edition—the subtle "silly sooth" of "We fell out" and "Sweet and low," the pealing music of "The splendour falls," the sophisticated, coloured art of "Now sleeps the crimson petal," and, lastly, the melody, the vision and the passionate wail of "Tears, idle tears" the most moving and finely wrought lyric Tennyson ever wrote.

IN MEMORIAM

The quality which such art, with all its wonderful elaboration, lacks is that last secret of a great style which Dante indicates when he defines the *dolce still nuovo*—for what is true of love is true of any other adequate theme—

Ed io a lui:"Io mi son un che, quando
Amor mi spira, noto, ed a quel modo
Che ditta dentro, vo significando."

He had not yet written as when a great subject appears to take the pen and write itself. But, in 1850, Tennyson seemed to his readers to have found such an inspiring theme, when the poem on which he had been at work ever since the death in 1833 of his friend Arthur Henry Hallam was published under the simple title *In Memoriam,* for the theme, death and immortality, was that on which Tennyson ever felt most deeply, was most constantly haunted and agitated by conflicting hopes and fears.

In no poems had he written with more evident sincerity, more directness, a finer balance of thought and style, than in those poems which, like *Ulysses and The Vision of Sin,* were precursors of this longer poem on life and death and immortality, sorrow and sin and the justification of God's ways to men.

In Memoriam is not altogether free from the faults of Tennysonian diction, phrasing such as "eaves of weary eyes" or

And where the kneeling hamlet drains
The chalice of the grapes of God,

but, with few exceptions, the style is pure, direct and masculine, and to this not only the theme but the verse contributed, a verse which Ben Jonson and lord Herbert of Cherbury had used before him, but which Tennyson made his own by the new weight and melody which he gave to it. In Tennyson's hands the verse acquired something of the weight and something of the fittingness for a long meditative poem of the *terza rima* as used by Dante, the same perfection of internal movement combined with the same invitation to continue, an eddying yet forward movement.

The construction of the poem in separate sections, some of which are linked together in groups by continuity of theme, was that which gave freest scope to Tennyson's genius, allowing him to make of each section the expression of a single, intense mood. But the claim for *In Memoriam,* that it is not merely a collection of poems of varying degrees of beauty but a great poem, rests on the degree of success with which Tennyson has woven these together into a poem portraying the progress of the human spirit from sorrow to joy, not by the loss of love or the mere dulling of grief, but by the merging of the passion for the individual friend, removed but still living, into the larger love of God and of his fellow-men. 5 If the present generation does not estimate *In Memoriam* quite so highly as its first readers, it is because time, which has a way of making clear the interval between a poet's intention and his achievement, the expressed purpose of a *Paradise Lost* and its final effect, has shown that Tennyson failed to make this central experience, this great transition, imaginatively convincing and impressive.

It is not in the vague philosophy, with a dash of semi-mystical experience, in which is veiled the simple process by which the heart grows reconciled to loss and life renews her spell, nor in the finished and illuminated style in which all this is clothed—it is not here that the reader of to-day finds the true Tennyson, the poet with his own unique and splendid gifts, but in the sombre moods and the lovely landscapes of individual sections. "Old Yew, which graspest at the stones," "Dark house, by which once more I stand," "Calm is the morn without a sound," "To-night the winds begin to rise," "With trembling fingers did we weave"—sections such as these, or the passionate sequence beginning "Oh yet we trust that somehow good," and later, lovelier flights as "When on my bed the moonlight falls," "I cannot see the features right," "Witch-elms that counterchange the floor," "By night we linger'd on the lawn," "Unwatch'd, the garden bough shall sway," "Sad Hesper o'er the buried sun"—these are likely to be dear to lovers of English poetry by their expression of mood in picture and music, long after the philosophy of *In Memoriam* has been forgotten.

It is not the mystical experience of the ninety-fifth section which haunts the memory, but the beauty of the sunrise that follows when

the doubtful dusk reveal'd
The knolls once more where, couch'd at ease,
The white kine glimmer'd, and the trees
Laid their dark arms about the field:
And suck'd from out the distant gloom
A breeze began to tremble o'er

The large leaves of the sycamore,
And fluctuate all the still perfume,
And gathering freshlier overhead,
Rock'd the full-foliaged elms, and swung
The heavy-folded rose, and flung
The lilies to and fro, and said,
"The dawn, the dawn," and died away;
And East and West, without a breath,
Mixt their dim lights, like life and death,
To broaden into boundless day.

To the theme of the most agitated sections of the poem, those whose theme is not removal of the friend by death from the sight and touch of those that loved him, but the more terrible doubt as to a life after death, the poet was to recur again, to fight more than one "weird battle of the west," before he faced the final issue with courage and resignation and hope.

MAUD

In the year of *In Memoriam,* Tennyson succeeded Wordsworth in the post of poet laureate, and his first official poem was the fine *Ode on the Death of the Duke of Wellington* (1852), a bold metrical experiment, the *motif* for which is given by the funeral march and the pomp of the obsequies in St. Paul's. In the dramatic use of varying metres no poet was ever a more constant and generally felicitous experimenter than Tennyson, and in his next considerable poem *Maud,* issued in *Maud,* and *Other Poems* (1855), he employed the device of sections, not, as in *In Memoriam,* of like metrical structure, but varying in the boldest fashion from long six-foot to short three-foot lines, to tell in monodrama a story of tragic passion.

The hero and narrator is dramatically conceived, and Tennyson was very anxious not to be identified with the Hamlet of his story. But the political opinions which he put into his mouth were his own, in the main, and the morbid, hysterical temperament was his own, too, dramatically intensified and elaborated. The result was a poem which greatly disconcerted his admirers—alike those who would have had him content to remain the Theocritus of idylls like

The Gardener's Daughter and *The Brook* (which was published in the same volume as *Maud),* and those who were calling on him for a great poem, and were prepared to acclaim him—mainly on the strength of *Locksley Hall*—as the laureate of an age of "unexampled progress."

The latter were profoundly shocked at the poet's fierce exultation over war for a cause, his clear perception of the seamy side of commercial prosperity and his contempt for what he thought a mean conception of the blessing of peace. A great poem *Maud* is not. The heroine is too shadowy, the hero a Hamlet only in the hysterical instability of his temperament, with none of Hamlet's range of thought, or that ultimate strength of soul which held madness and suicide at arm's length; but "I have led her home," "Come into the garden, Maud," and "O that 'twere possible" are among the most perfect of Tennyson's dramatic love-lyrics.

ENOCH ARDEN AND DIALECT BALLADS

The same excess of sentiment, which, in a great poem, should have given place to thought and passion, and the same over-elaborate art, are apparent in the rustic idyll which gives its name to the volume published in 1864, *Enoch Arden, etc.*, a tragedy of village life founded on a story given to Tennyson by the sculptor Woolner, recalling, in many of its details, Crabbe's *The Parting Hour.* Fundamentally, there is more of Crabbe than of Wordsworth in Tennyson's tales of English country-life, for, though Tennyson is more sentimental than Crabbe and his treatment far more decorative, he does not idealise in the mystical manner of Wordsworth.

But, in style and verse, there could not well be a greater difference than that between the vividpictures, the tropical colouring, the sophisticate simplicity of *Enoch Arden* and the limited, conventional phraseology, the monotonous verse in which Crabbe tells his story with so much more of sheer dramatic truth. But it was in the direction of sheer dramatic truth, mastering and, to some extent simplifying the style, that Tennyson's genius was advancing most fruitfully, and the earnest of this is two poems which accompany *Enoch Arden,* the dialect ballads in six-foot anapaests, *The Grandmother and The Northern Farmer—Old Style,* the first of which owes its poignancy to the sorrow with which Tennyson gazed on his own first child born dead, while the latter is the earliest altogether felicitous expression of the vein of dramatic humour which ran through his naturally sombre temperament.

Tennyson could not trifle, but he had a gift of caustic satire to which he might have given freer play with advantage to his permanent, if not his immediate, popularity. The two farmer poems and *The Village Wife* are worth several such poems as *Dora and Enoch Arden.*

DRAMAS AND LATER POEMS AND BALLADS

"He bestowed infinite trouble on his dramas," his son says, and they bear every mark of a careful study of the sources, thoughtful delineation of character, finished expression and versification. What they want is dramatic life and force. The historical plays are the product of his patriotism and his dislike of catholicism; but the political interest is not, as in Shakespeare's plays, quickly superseded by the dramatic. The characters do not become alive and take the conduct of the play into their own hands, as Falstaff and the humorous characters in Shakespeare's English plays tend to do.

In *Queen Mary,* no single character arrests and dominates our interest, and the hero of *Harold,* as of many modern plays, is of the Hamlet type of character, without quite being a Hamlet, more interested in the conflict of his own impulses and inhibitions than the driving force of a play full of action and incident. The most single in interest and the most impressive is *Becket.* Thoughtful and accomplished as they are, none of Tennyson's dramas is the product of the imagination which begat the greatest and most characteristic of his poems.

It is in the poems beginning with the above mentioned dialect poems and continued in *Lucretius* (1868), *The Revenge: A Ballad of the Fleet* (1878), the starting *Ballads and Other Poems* of 1880 and the subsequent similar studies, published, some of them, separately and then collected in the successive volumes—*Tiresias, and Other Poems* (1885), *Locksley Hall Sixly*

Years After (1886), *Demeter and Other Poems* (1889), *The Death of Œnone, Akbar's Dream, and Other Poems* (1892)—that the later Tennyson appears in poems revealing the same careful structure and metrical cunning as the romantic studies that filled the two volumes of 1842.

But the romantic colour and magic are gone; gone, too, is the suggestion of an optimistic philosophy which has tempted some critics to apply the strange epithet "complacent" to the troubled, sensitive soul of Tennyson. What has taken the place of these is a more poignant dramatic note, a more troubled outlook upon life and the world around him, a severer but, in its severity, a no less felicitous style, rarely a less dramatic adjustment of rhythm to feeling.

Tennyson's sensitive imagination was ever responsive to the moral atmosphere around him. It was the high seriousness of Hallam and his Cambridge friends, their sympathy with moral and political progress, which had encouraged him to endeavour, even too strenuously, to charge his work with didactic intention, which had made him strive, often against his deepest instincts and prejudices, to sympathise with the claims of advancing democracy and which had instilled into his mind the one article of his vague and more emotional than dogmatic Christianity, the belief in the "far future," the ultimate triumph of love.

And now it seemed as though these high thoughts and hopes were illusions, and the morbid vein in which he had already written *The Two Voices* becomes dominant, strengthened by his consciousness of the times being "out of joint." Coleridgean Christianity had given place to modern science and the religion of Lucretius. Romance was yielding ground to a realism as sombre as Crabbe's, but more pathological and irreverent. Democracy had not brought all the blessings that were promised, and it seemed to Tennyson to be relaxing the national spirit, the patriotism and heroism which had made England great.

The feelings with which all these changes affected Tennyson are vividly reflected in all his later poems. The patriotic poems breathe a more fervent, a fiercer patriotism.

The Revenge, The Defence of Lucknow, The Charge of the Heavy Brigade are instinct with a patriotism which allows of scant sympathy with Indian rebels, "Russian hordes," or "the Inquisition dogs and the devildoms of Spain."

The ballads of peasant humours, as *The Spinster's Sweet-Arts* and *The Village Wife; or, The Entail,* and of peasant sorrows and tragedies, like *The Grandmother* and *Rizpah* are as realistic, sombre and humorous as some of the contemporary novels of country life—poems at the opposite pole from *The Gardener's Daughter* and *The Miller's Daughter.*

In stories of modern life, as already in the earlier *Aylmer's Field,* there is the note of hysterical feeling which betrays the jarring of the poet's nerves as he contemplated certain aspects of modern life in *Locksley Hall Sixty Years After, Despair, In the Children's Hospital.*

In the meditative poems in blank verse, classical idylls from *Lucretius to Tiresias,* idylls from history as *Sir John Oldcastle, Columbus, St. Telemachus* or more lyrical meditations like Vastness, his mind circles ever round one theme in various aspects, the pathos of man's destiny wandering between faiths which are rooted in fear and a widening knowledge that dispels the superstitious fears but leaves him no hope, the tragic grandeur of man's sensitive soul terribly environed, the cost and pain with which he has struggled forwards to

The worship which is Love, [to] see no more
The Stone, the Wheel, the dimly-glimmering lawns
Of that Elysium, all the hateful fires
Of torment, and the shadowy warrior glide
Along the silent field of Asphodel,

and the haunting fear that, after all, the purer faith may be a dream, melting in the cold light of physical science:

What is it all, if we all of us end but in being our own corpse-coffins at last, Swallow'd in Vastness, lost in Silence, drown'd in the deeps of a meaningless Past?

Tennyson was not able to expel, though he could subdue, the ghosts which haunted him. He never thought his way through any of the problems, political, moral or metaphysical, which the age presented, and, to the reader of to-day, it is not the thought of these poems which matters, but the reaction of this thought on their dramatic and poetic quality, the piercing note which it gave to poems that have lost the wonderful fragrance and colour—the rich bouquet if one might change the figure—of the 1842 poems, but in whose autumnal tints and severer outlines there is a charm more deeply felt than in the overwrought perfection, the deliberate intention of the middle period poems.

Chapter 11

Lord Alfred Tennyson, the Paramount Victorian Poet

Just as the title suggests, in analysing the poetry of Lord Alfred Tennyson, a 20th century reader gains almost direct access to the Victorian *Zeitgeist* which he can be said to typify. This is mainly due to Tennyson's sharing in the quality that most Victorian poetry has, that of being a form of fictionlised public letter-writing. This is striking for someone reading poetry after nearly one century of experimentally obscure lyricism in the *symboliste* key, or the surrealistic (dadaist) key, or, again, the factual classicism of the American imagism/ vorticism - in short, after the modernist revolution in letters in general and in poetry in particular.

Thus, Victorian poetry is *complicated and difficult in a very different way from the complications/difficutlies we have grown accustomed with in the 20th century*. (This does not mean that, as it will be seen immediately, Victorian fashions in poetry have been entirely shed or forgotten nowadays; on the contrary, they have added up to the conglomerate of conventions behind which the common mind of the 20th century has been hiding. And it is the purpose of today's lecture on Victorian poetry – and the others to follow - to make the readers aware of the Victorian heritage to the poetry and poets still cherished today in the space of the English language poetic craft).

The first thing worth noting is that the same didactic vein pervading Victorian literature in an age of realism in fiction paradoxically makes Victorian poetry be anything but realistic. This comes from its quality as public poetry in an age when the dominant ideology dictated a dogmatic turning to the past for discovering spectacular models of public action and public feeling materialised as "commendable, great literature". In plainer terms, therefore, Victorian poetry, just like the Victorian essay, is *obsessed by the great ideas of a fictionalised past,* it functions as a *popular encyclopedia* or commentary to myth or folklore and it is, consequently, a fashionable manneristic commentary to a variety of ideas. Consequently, the primary task of the 20th century student is to identify the idea(s) which a particular Victorain poem illustrates and to discover the precise manner in which it achieves this. (This is, of course, in direct opposition with the warning launched by the 20th century American formalist critics, W. Wimsatt or Cleanth Brooks against "the heresy of paraphrase", cf. Cleanth Brooks "The Well Wrought Urn", 1947)

This leads to the second general observation about Victorian poetry: if it is lyrical, a Victorian poem is so in an oblique, indirect way. In his 1932 text "New Bearings in English Poetry", F. R. Leavis refers to "the mischeviousness of the 19th century conventions of 'the poetical' " (*apud* Donald Thomas's excellent file of illuminating contemporary and later criticism in Victorian poetry represented by the lost book of the British Council Library in Bucharest, "The Post-Romantics" – which it unfortunately represents today *in absentia.*) Among these mischeviousnesses, Leavis enumerates:

- The dramatised poetic voice, which prompts to us here a jocose statement: poetry becomes ventriloquy (sic!), being voiced through a mask;
- Poetry amounts to allegory, voiced as fairytale or as medieval legend. More often than not, the reader of Victorian poetry has to grapple with streams of historically obscure consciousness projected outwardly or packed for the use of the Victorian public, with the Victorian public's own psychological or moral dominants. A pattern of double obliqueness or difficulty or, from the point of view of direct lyricism, *double difficulty,* underwrites any Victorian poem, whose sentiment hides behind two "veils": the

historically remote one, classicist or medievalista, in Tennyson's allegorical poetry and the, nowadays, remote veil of the intended Victorian lesson in spirituality. With Tennyson, the intended lesson in spirituality embraces the realm of art versus conventional life (in "The Lady of Shalott") or the opposition between the man of aspiration, in general, as compared to the man of convention (in "Ulysses") and grotesquely so, between the sentimental craving of man and his limited life doomed to defeat, old age dwindling and ultimately, decrepitude (as typified in "Tithonus"). Victorian lyricism in general is steeped in sadness and melancholy and seeks the weak consolations of oblivion, more often than not lethal oblivion. Orthodox Victorian poetry is, therefore, a kind of morbidly elegiac lyrical poetry, feeble, decadent and even – stuffy.

The resulting lack in lyrical vigour, was translated by literary history into a label for Victorian poetry as a whole: "Post-romantic poetry". When analysing this label from the point of view of Northrop Frye's "Anatomy of Criticism", the first essay, it is possible to detach a number of retained features that the Romantics had added to poetry, features that were not lost in Victorian verse.

- Regarding the poet, the Victorian poet, just like the Romantic, moves back in time and space, higher too and beyond the conventional experience, into a more imaginative order of experience. But whereas the Romantic remains lyrically elevated in/by that imaginative transport, the Victorian poet returns wiser and embittered, as a rule, to his present-day audience for whose sole benefit, it appears, he has soared into the provisional infinite; hence the shared elegiac tone associated to Victorian lyricism (cf. the ending of Robert Browning's poem "Two in the Campagna", that had masterfully uttered the cry: "Let us, O my dove,/Let us be unashamed of soul" only to check itself and conclude: "Only I discern-/

Infinite passion and the pain/ Of finite hearts that yearn") On a formal level, this points to the difference between the romantic love of (organic) metaphor and the Victorian alternative love of allegory, simile and dramatic representation in general. It is not by accident that the Victorian poets selected the form of the *dramatic monologue* as their favourite form of self-expression. (But the dramatic monologue will be analysed later, in connection with its greatest Victorian protagonist, Robert Browning.)

- Regarding the formal features shared by the Victorian with the Romantic poets, Frye mentions the tendency of the Romantics to develop encyclopaedic, grand, long poems in the form of epics, which is retained in Victorian poetry. The structures and motivations of these long epics can only be elucidated when relating the poetry to the poet's own design. The range of encyclopaedic epics includes:

Victorian replicas of mythological and religious or folk epics (respectively in Tennyson's Arthurian "Idylls of the King", 1859, Gerard Manley Hopkins's "The Wreck of the Deutschland", 1875 or Matthew Arnold's longer verse narratives "Empedocles on Etna", 1852 and "The Scholar Gipsy", 1853); allegorical epics (such as Tennyson's "The Palace of Art" or the feminist fable of "The Princess"); psychological epics of all hues: extensive and comprehensive spiritual autobiographies in a major elegiac key (e.g. Tennyson's peerless "In Memoriam" or Matthew Arnold's "Thyrsis"); dramatised alienist confessions (Tennyson's monodrama "Maud" or Robert Browning's long psychological and philosophical thriller "The Ring and the Book" 1868-9 high-mimetic novels in plain verse (Elizabeth Barett Browning's "Aurora Leigh", 1857)

But there are obviously missing features in the Victorian poems as compared to the Romantic ones: in addition to the above-mentioned *failure of the Victorian poets to radically turn away from the contemporary social or public thinking,* as the high Romantics had done, *the nature poetry of the Victorians lacks the nature – inspired sense of power,* and it is bland and outspoken or simply elegiac, where Romantic poetry had been mystical. As F. R. Leavis put it in the same text already quoted in Donald Thomas's book: "It was possible for the poets of the Romantic period to believe that the interests animating their poetry were the forces moving the world , or that might move it.

But Victorian poetry admits implicitly that the actual world is alien, recalcitrant and unpoetical, and that no protest is worth making except the protest of withdrawal").

Lastly, *the direct belief in the creative genius of the poet underpinning the fabric of any Romantic poem, be it great or small in size, is missing from each and every Victorian poem.* This belief is translatable as a kind of repressed manifestation of *a stunted when not downwardly ironic Victorian poet who is necessarily wearing a didactic, moralising mask.* Even the least sophisticated Victorian poet puts on an allegorical mask - pastoral, professorial, clinical – in the verse narratives. (These can no longer be called "ballads" because they are too learned to qualify for mere ballads; also they are by no means intended as lyrical, because they are learned allegories addressing well-informed gentlemen and ladies, as in Tennyson's "The Lady of Shalott" gathering for the purposes of poetic communion the typically elegant audience of "Knight and burgher, lord and dame") The more talented Victorian poet, however, has a correspondingly more difficult alternative: that of assuming the voice of a local *persona* who is heard speak in the dramatic monologue on a very partially visible scene.

The last consequence of all this is that, as in Matthew Arnold's poetry, *the lyricism of the Victorian poet is, as the French would put it, "déchiré", or as Northrop Frye would qualify it, a (self-) ironic lyricism dismayed by the spectre of the Greek sparagmos, the tearing to pieces of man to whom "heroism and effective action" are denied.* Now, Frye decidedly considers that *sparagmos* is "the archetypal theme of irony and satire" ("Anatomy...", p. 139).

This obviously leads one to the conclusion that as a whole and through its post-Romantic qualities, *Victorian poetry exists within the horizon of the ironic mode.* There is thus a major de-synchronisation that operates in the Victorian age: Victorian poetry, when lyrical, more decidedly manifests lay, modern man's universal and personal despair as (tragic) irony, whereas fiction still toys with romance and the self-important high mimetic forms of realism. (And this ultimately, and ironically speaking, "recommends" the Victorian age as a cultural age lacking in true, inherent stylistic and aesthetic greatness.

The Victorian age is great as a modern commentator only, as an impersonator or teacher of traditions and counter-traditions fabricated by other ages and other people. All the more so is the Victorian age essential for a Romanian modern student of letters, whom it can equip with the cultural background and critical spirit compulsory for a metropolitan intellectual.

In a way, the average Romanian student as a potential representative of a provincial, mass culture is in the position of Matthew Arnold's Philistine who is in need of major cultural instruction or, as John Henry Newman would put it, of Liberal Education in a University).

Chapter 12

Applying the General Features of Victorian Poetry to Tennyson's Poems

The first consequence of Tennyson's transposition of Victorian orthodox ideas in the neo-classicist key superimposed upon the key of late medievalism is the idyllic tone of a pastoral poetry which is elevating before being lyrical. Secondly, Tennyson's poems oscillate between a resulting epical grandeur (you can read here "grandiloquence") and a picturesque artificiality meant to move even the less refined middle-class average readers in the otherwise busy entrepreneurial circles, in their spare time.

Tennyson had a magus-like power of instilling dignity and picturesqueness in the domestic, everyday Victorian life as well as in many a public occasion, when people were eager to rejoice or mourn in public. For such occasions Tennyson had ready many a pastoral allegory or elegy, elevating the factual above itself, rendering it closer to the ideal. All this means that Tennyson's participative readiness fitted him, as a writer of occasional poetry for complying with the consumerist taste that was shared by this first age of mass communication which the Victorian age was. (It is quite clear that the Victorian consumerism was of an intellectual brand, not the raw, material consumerism advertised in today's media). As the contemporary Victorian literary critic Walter Bagehot put it in his review of Tennyson's "Idylls of the King"as excerpted by Donald Thomas in his book: there were "two audiences for

Tennyson's poetry: those with more youthful enthousiasm, the poet's admirers, and the wider public alienated from poetry". Actually, from the common status he had as the fourth child of eight sons born – in 1809 - to the Lincolnshire rector (in Romanian "vicar") of Somersby , Tennyson rose to the dignity of a national bard and the friend of the Royal Pair, being nominated "Poet Laureate", after Wordsworth, in 1850 and was chosen by Thomas Alva Edison to record his voice, among only three other famous 19th century voices (as Donald Thomas shows in his introduction to the Tennyson casebook in his "Post –Romantics").

From the point of view of the 20th century reader, there are two poets Tennyson, one readable, the other unreadable today, respectively, the lyrical poet and the occasional, public poet. This is mainly due to the fact that we are a different audience for poetry today than the public Tennyson enjoyed in the 19th century. We are neither enthousiastic in the youthful, naïve sense, nor alienated from poetry in the same way as the Victorian wider public. Rather, we form a middle (but not "middle-class"!) category of public who like to think of themselves as neither wide nor too enthousiastic readers of literature (this is the point of view of the average reader).

TENNYSON THE LYRICAL POET

Tennyson the lyrical poet fits almost perfectly the identikit portrait offered for the generic Victorian poet in this lecture's introduction, under 5.1 (this portrait might well remain an abstraction, were it not actually obtained by *ad hoc* extrapolation from Tennyson's particular case). Anyone can follow extensively in Tennyson's lyrical poetry what T. S. Eliot described in his essay on the Metaphysical poets as "the dissociation of sensibility", more and more refined language with feeling remaining more crude; or as Matthew Arnold complained, in the Preface to his First Edition of "Poems", morbid sufferance, sufferance in excess to accompany just rudimentary human action. Tennyson's poetry, which Walter Bagehot terms "ornate", exaggerates in all these ways the basic assumptions of lyricism. It is, just like Matthew Arnold's poetry, poetry suffused in" a universal note of sadness" (cf. the ending of the poem Dover Beach", by Arnold). This vein pervades Tennyson's poetry from his first volume, "Juvenilia", through the great elegiac sequence of "In Memoriam" which poetically attempted to come to terms with the death of a beloved friend and it echoed forth in the "Idylls of the King".

It has the power, praised by E. A. Poe in "The Poetic Principle", to offer "the elevating excitement of the soul", but it has two shortcomings: it is the only tonality of Tennyson's lyrical poems, always written in the elegiac, sick key and it is derived from a predictable plot describing human and universal decline.

This makes one read the same basic poem with few variations, irrespective of the title and the superficial accidents. It is worth comparing the feelings induced by the setting of the nature poem "Song", with the background of a poem about a dying swan in the same first volume, "Juvernilia", or with ... "other poems" in the later collections "The Lady of Shalott and Other Poems" and "English Idylls and Other Poems":

Heavily hangs the broad sunflower
Over its grave i'the earth so chilly:
Heavily hangs the hollyhock,
Heavily hangs the tiger-lily.

II

The air is damp, and hush'd and close,
As a sick man's room when he taketh repose
An hour before death;
My very heart faints and my whole soul grieves
At the moist rich smell of the rotting leaves,
And the breath
Of the fading edges of box beneath,
And the year's last rose.
Heavily hangs the broad sunflower
Over its grave i'the earth so chilly:
Heavily hangs the hollyhock,
Heavily hangs the tiger-lily. ("Song")
The wild swan's death-hymn took the soul
Of that waste place with joy

Hidden in sorrow : at first to the ear
The warble was low, and full and clear;
....
And the creeping mosses and clambering weeds,
And the willow-branches hoar and dank,
And the wavy swell of the soughing reeds,
And the wave-worn horns of the echoing bank,
And the silvery marsh – flowers that throng
The desolate creeks and pools among,
Were flooded over with eddying song. ("The Dying Swan")
or, at the beginning of "The Lotos-Eaters"
In the afternoon they came unto a land
In which it seemed always afternoon.
All round the coast the languid air did swoon,
Breathing like one that hath a weary dream.
Full-faced above the valley stood the moon;
And like a downward smoke, the slender stream
Along the cliff to fall and pause and fall did seem.
A land of streams! some, like a downward smoke,
Slow-dropping veils of thinnest lawn, did go;
And some thro' wavering lights and shadows broke,
Rolling a slumbrous sheet of foam below

From this atmosphere, Tennyson awakens into existence equally melancholy shadows of characters, incarnations of sad, slothful dreams themselves:

The charmed sunset linger'd low adown
In the red West: thro' mountain clefts the dale
Was seen far inland, and the yellow down
Border'd with palm, and many a winding vale
And meadow, set with slender gallingale;
A land where all things always seem'd the same!
And round about the keel with faces pale,
Dark faces pale against that rosy flame,
The mild-eyed melancholy Lotos-eaters came.
Branches they bore of that enchanted stem,
Laden with flower and fruit, wherof they gave
To each, but whoso did receive of them,
And taste, to him the gushing of the wave

Far far away did seem to mourn and rave
On alien shores; and if his fellow spake,
His voice was thin, as voices from the grave;
And deep-asleep he seem'd , yet all awake,
And music in his ears his beating heart did make.

with these lines extending into a whole fable of languidness, forgetfulness and doom enacted through the story of the public orgy represented by the opiate lotus eating. It is as if, from this suffused, oppressing memory, the great Romantic dreams and visions are projected as pale phantoms onto the Victorian canvass destined for public shows and not for visions.

Then at the opening of the other Greek fable of "Tithonus", the climactic outpour of similar imagery:

The woods decay, the woods decay and fall,
The vapours weep their burthen to the ground,
Man comes and tills the field and lies beneath.
And after many a summer dies the swan.

This overwhelming, nightmarish sentiment in the decadent romantic key will be further and systematically explored by Tennyson, and also to its ultimate transcendental implications, in the cumulative sequence of 131 philosophical lyrics forming "In Memoriam". These poems transmute the underlying phantom of death which haunted the Victorian universe of experience by directly confronting it. "In Memoriam" thus functions as a great exorcising poem on death and the human limitation regarded against the wider canvass of the world and time, for this age that feared its own shadow, in Jungian terms.

In poems such as III, XI and L, Victorian sentiments are expressed in the purest vein of lyricism, with a directness and clarity which amount the great action of coming to terms with experience rather than self-complacently toying with it. This last observation can be proved by comparing Tennyson's earlier sleep/languish poems, with the straightforward meditative discursiveness of poem IV in the sequence:

a There are various alternatively favourite histories in which Victorian artists manneristically find refuge. *The Pre-*

Raphaelite brotherhood painters and poets get transported to that period which marks *the threshold between the Middle Ages and the Renaissance*, which they identify from beyond its actual span as the period of the old Pre-Raphaelite school painters, Giotto, Angelico, Orcagna, John Bellini.

The poet Browning - who was also a man of subtle artistic tastes - and Walter Pater, the Oxford don and art theorist - who influenced all the later generations of Victorian artists and aesthetic theorists - opened the windows of their contemporary Victoriansm into *the Renaissance itself*. Matthew Arnold proclaimed a more general standard or ideal in *any "epoch of expansion"*, be it past or foreign, the period of Pericles' century in Athens, the Elizabethan period in England, the period of French academism which he saw to be successfully extended into the 19th century culture of France. Last but not least, the poet Gerard Manley Hopkins selected as his private model age that of the Oxford eccentric Duns Scotus's anti-Thomist scholasticism, which he revived through his militant devotional verse. In this way, Victorian escapism ends where it had started with Thomas Carlyle, namely in the Middle Ages of heroic ethics and enhanced vision.

To Sleep I give my powers away;
My will is bondsman to the dark;
I sit within a helmless bark,
And with my heart I muse and say:
O heart, how fares it with thee now,
That thou should'st fail from thy desire,
Who scarcely darest to inquire,
'What is it makes me beat so low?'
Something it is which thou hast lost,
Some pleasure from thine early years.
Break thou deep vase of chilling tears,
That grief hath shaken into frost!
Such clouds of nameless trouble cross
All night below the darken'd eyes:
With morning wakes the will, and cries,,
'Thou shalt not be the fool of loss.'
....

III

O Sorrow, cruel fellowship,
O Priestess in the vaults of Death,
O sweet and bitter in a breath,
What whispers from thy lying lip?
'The stars,' she whispers, 'blindly run;
A web is wov'n across the sky;
From out waste places comes a cry,
And murmurs from the dying sun:
'And all the phantom, Nature, stands-
With all the music in her tone,
A hollow echo of my own,-
A hollow form with empty hands."
And shall I take a thing so blind,
Embrace her as my natural good;
Or crush her, like a vice of blod,
Upon the threshold of the mind?

....

XI

Calm is the morn without a sound,
Calm as to suit a calmer grief,
And only thro' the faded leaf
The chestnut pattering to the ground:
Calm and deep peace on this high wold,
And on these dews that drench the furze,
And all the silvery gossamers
That twinkle into green and gold:
Calm and still light on yon great plain
That sweeps with all its autumn bowers,
And crowded farms and lessening towers,
To mingle with the bounding main:
Calm and deep peace in this wide air,
These leaves that redden to the fall;
And in my heart, if calm at all,
If any calm, a calm despair:
Calm on the seas, and silver sleep,
And waves that sway themselves in rest,
And dead calm in that noble breast

Which heaves but with the heaving deep.
....

L

Be near me when my light is low
When the blood creeps, and the nerves prick
And tingle; and the heart is sick
And all the wheels of Being slow.
Be near me when the sensuous frame
Is rack'd with pangs that conquer trust;
And Time, a maniac scattering dust,
And Life, a Fury slinging flame.
Be near me when my faith is dry,
And men the flies of latter spring,
That lay their eggs, and sting and sing,
And weave their petty cells and die.
Be near me when I fade away,
To point the term of human strife,
And on the low dark verge of life
The twilight of eternal day.

THE PUBLIC POET TENNYSON

Just like Dickens, Tennyson died rich and lionised by ordinary readers and officials alike, in 1892, and was buried in the Poet's Corner in Westminster Abbey. While still living he was also knighted as first Baron Tennyson of Aldworth and Farringford. All this was in recognition to his great merits as a public poet.

Today we may venture to read his official poetry for its documentary value if we want to study the ideas, environment, general mentality and lifestyle of the Victorian gentleman: the superior, gentlemanly ethics and refinement often voiced as a brand of chivalrous feminism as it happens in "The Princess", which very long poem bears the subtitle of "A Medley", as it allegorically sweeps through Victorian domestic and industrial life regarded in the light of Victorian culture as refinement and learning, Victorian colonial leisure, Victorian urbanity, Victorian fashion and sporting during a leisure day in the outing. As "The Prologue" explains, the setting is a

Victorian big house or mansion in the countryside which idylically recreates urban values, ambitions and intellectual debates from the elegant vista of Sir Walter Vivian's little palace which seems to concentrate in little the whole Victorian material and intellectual universe.

Facetiously and graciously then, this world will be counteracted by the poet's "fearful", actually farcical fairy-tale or fable of the all-feminine University-Convent of the Princess Ida, a man-eater who threatened the male I of the story-teller Prince with her whole army of chaste women or cultural amazons.

From The Prologue
Sir Walter Vivian all a summer's day
Gave his broad lawns until the set of sun
Up to the people: thither flocked at noon
His tenants, wife and child, and thither half
The neighbouring borough with their Institute
Of which he was the patron. I was there
From college, visiting the son, - the son
A Walter too,- with others of our set,
Five others: we were seven at Vivian-place.
And me that morning Walter show'd the house,
Greek, set with busts: from vases in the hall
Flowers of all heavens, and lovelier than their names,
Grew side by side; and on the pavement lay
Carved stones of the Abbey-ruin in the park,
Huge Ammonites, and the first bones of Time;
And on the tables every clime and age
Jumbled together; celts and calumets,
Claymore and snowshoe, toys in lava, fans
Of sandal, amber, ancient rosaries,
Laborious orient ivory shphere in sphere,
The cursed Malayan crease, and battle-clubs
From the isles of palm: and higher on the walls,
Betwixt the monstruous horns of elk and deer,
His own forefathers' arms and armour hung .
And 'this' he said 'was Hugh's at Agincourt;
And that was old Sir Ralph's at Ascalon:

A good knight he! We keep a chronicle
With all about him' – which he brought, and I
Dived in a hoard of tales that dealt with knights,
Half-legend, half-historic, counts and kings
Who laid about them at their wills and died.

While the visitors are given a tour of the park, in which the reader may visually participate like in a documentary movie on today's cable television, or like in a Zefirelli super-production set in the Victorian age, one feels overcome by the uninterrupted chain of gracious miracles and technological toys meant precisely for such a day of sporting, which playful miracles transform this park into a land of the 19th century fairies, or into an imagined International Exhibition of 1851 – only here imagined a few years in advance (as "The Princess" was first published in 1847):

....round the lake
A little clock-work steamer paddling plied
And shook the lilies: perch'd about the knolls
A dozen angry models jetted steam:
A petty railway ran ; a fire balloon
Rose gem-like up before the dusky groves
And dropt a fairy parachute and past:
And there thro' twenty posts of telegraph
They flash'd a saucy message to and fro
Between the mimic stations; so that sport
Went hand in hand with Science;

The same pairing of science with prowess, this time seriously rather than in jest, occurs in the strange poem "Locksley Hall", a confessive and didactic narrative and a thwarted love story yoking together feminism with progress:

"Here about the beach, I wander'd, nourishing a youth sublime

With the fairy tales of science, and the long results of Time

This poem contains some incredible injunctions, such as the following:

........................*forward, forward let us range*

Let the great world spin for ever down the ringing grooves of change (the heroic Homeric echo of "the ringing plains of

Troy" makes one vacillate between despair, disdain and mere laughter). But the poem continues with its heroic couplets in exactly the same incredibly encomiastic tone:

There methinks would be enjoyment more than in this march of mind

In the steamship, in the railway, in the thoughts that shake mankind

After all this praise of science and progress, we cannot wonder at the tone of Tennyson's topical "Ode Sung at the Opening of the International Exhibition"

Uplift a thousand voices full and sweet,
In this wide hall with earth's invention stored,
And praise the invisible universal Lord,
Who lets once more in peace the nations meet,
Where Science, Art, and Labour have outpour'd
Their myriad horns of plenty at our feet

Analytically speaking now, Tennyson as a public poet is obviously full of contradictions, because his occasional verse should be capable of flexibly moving from required lyricism to grandiloquence, as the case may be; sometimes, his public service as a Laureate required him to be sentimental; at other times, didactic. When sentimentally grandiloquent, Tennyson writes *idylls*.

As a kind of fixed allegorical poem, conventionally presenting a scene of rural, pastoral life, giving a sense of tranquil happiness ranging from serenity to euphoria (as J. A. Cuddon defines it in his "Dictionary of Literary Terms and Theory", Penguin, 1992) and again, conventionally transporting the reader to an idealized, remotely attainable past. When didactically grandiloquent, Tennyson writes *odes* (i.e., ceremonial, celebratory verse) dedicated to science and progress, to this or that member of the Royal Family, and even more particularly, to this or that historical victory on the battle fields of the Continent or at home, as at the opening of the International Exhibition in London in 1851. (the paeans of "Locksley Hall" are precisely that, and you can read Tennyson's explicit odes "To the Queen", "A Welcome to Alexandra", "A Welcome to Her Royal Highness Marie

Alexandrovna, Duchess of Edinburgh", "The Charge of the Light Brigade", "Ode on the Death of the Duke of Wellington" or "The Third of February, 1852") (All these occasional poems may be read as documents illustrating the age just like paintings in "The National Portrait Gallery" in London, and then their highflown language is atoned for, and they will immediately assume a humbler and more acceptable position among the Victorian Age exhibits).

This classification of Tennyson's official, "collaborationist" or occasional poetry into idylls and odes, brings us to one of Tennyson's most successful legitimating narratives in verse: his Arthurian "Idylls of the King" (1859- occasioned by the death of Prince Albert, the Royal Consort). Written in order to dignify in retrospect the life of the Royal Pair and to console the Queen for the loss of the Prince, they identified the dead Prince with King Arthur ("The Passing of Arthur" being especially topical, while it was also followed by the already quoted ode "To the Queen") and inaugurated a parallel soon to become the fashion, between the Victorian society as a whole and the legendary knightly court of King Arthur et comp.

In this way, the social and moral mythology of the inflated Victorian excellence and virtuous aspiration became a publically shared ideology. The epic thread of the twelve poems that make up the sequence has to do with the recognition of Arthur's excellence in war and in marriage, his fight for the moral restoration of the knights who have lost their power and purity by a life of sin.

There is an entire catalogue of allegorical virtues, vices and beneficial transformations high-mimetically connecting the Victorians with the Knights of the Round Table: thus, Sir Lancelot is the (sensual) good man who stands in need of being tamed; Queen Guinevere concentrates all the emotional hues of the human personality and points towards the need of controlling one's self through reason; the Sword Excalibur is the exemplary straightener and repository of the guiding Spirit in general. A pattern of mutual explicitation obtains therefore between the literal and the figurative levels of the allegory, which enriches both levels in their signifying power.

COMPARISON BETWEEN MATTHEW ARNOLD'S POETRY AND TENNYSON'S

The same lyrical themes and lyrical vein pervades Matthew Arnold's poetry, equally showing a preference for sea imagery. Like the Tennyson of "In Memoriam", Matthew Arnold the poet is profoundly meditative. His memorable poems "The Buried Life" and "Dover Beach" define the Victorian anguish as well as Tennyson's one hundred and thrity-one lyrics of "In Memoriam"; these poems indicate the same decentered, alienated position that man was felt to occupy in the universe during the 19th century.

In the poems mentioned, Arnold's poetry constructs even more pathetically profound allegorical images of the Victorian loss of vitality, reaching down to a rather more archetypal – and so, more romantic – level of symbolism and imagery. His poetry is less discursive and more metaphorical in its expressiveness.

But here the parallel with Tennyson has to cease, as the narrative and occasional poet Arnold employs predominantly neo-classicist topoi on which he comments in a late classicist manner tinged by romanticism rather than employ the romance, mediaeval topoi and manner. Thus, Arnold's poetry is less "popular" or "low-culture" in its mentality, much more intellectualised than Tennyson's, less suited for either mere youthful enthousiasts or the public alienated from poetry which Bagehot had indicated as the typical Tennysonian readership.

Also, unlike Tennyson, Matthew Arnold chose as his social profession of faith the intellectual one, when he decided to break up the habit of writing (romantic) poetry to become a professional and professorial teacher of poetry, cultural and literary criticism. (Thus he was dealt with as a representative of Victorian liberal intellectualism in these lectures and not as a poet whose ideology is also expressed by his prose of ideas)

But in the economy of the entire course of Victorian literature lectures, this hasty comparison between Tennyson's and Arnold's poetry may function as a good example of the "anatomical" difference between romance literature and the literature of Romanticism, which Frye justly discriminates in the first essay on historical literary criticism. Tennyson's facile allegorical nature poetry and celebratory poetry perfectly illustrates the literary mode of romance in the Victorian Age with the natural historical and ideological affinities it revealed as existing between Puritanism and Mediaevalism in their shared assumptions.

On the other hand, Arnold's post - romanticism can be demonstrated to move back in a typical manner for Victorianism, while intellectually "transcending" the idealistic mediaevalism of the Romantics and reaching towards *the universal ideas with the help of the classical intellectual topoi and manner*, which Arnold has already been shown to use in his meditations upon the opposition between man and nature, history and the cosmos, which represent his main theme not only in "Dover Beach" and "The Buried Life" but also in the curtly declarative sonnet "In Harmony with Nature". (to be read at the end of the lecture).

By an archetypal figure of speech, Arnold's poetry can be said to occupy the same middle position in the Victorian purgatory as the feminine Victorian novels or the later, more symbolic novels by Dickens, which converse on the same Romantic or at least romance topics and *topoi* but offer... "lower and lower mimetic solutions" to the spiritual problems raised beforehand. In Arnold's poetry, inspired by the classicist rationalism, romanticism is chastised and drawn into the precipice of its opposite pole, namely into the hellish precipice of satire and irony, as already stated in the introductory part of this lecture.

Chapter 13

Thomas Carlyle –A Fundamentalist Thinker

The lectures on the essay are meant to familiarize the student with the background ideas that shaped what is broadly called the cultural Victorian mentality (referred to as Victorianism in the introductory lectures). Also, the themes debated and shared by the Victorian thinkers can help the 20th century student of ideas connect the dominant themes of today, by comparison, to the ideas outlined in the Victorian essays studied.

On the other hand, the understanding of the composition (*inventio* of classical rhetoric, cf. A. J. Corbett, "Classical Rhetoric for the Modern Students"), the understanding of the structure and style characteristic for each essay as prose of ideas - completely different from what students currently analyse as "literature"-can represent a new, useful intellectual skill which a modern " young university scholar" had better acquire.

It will be as a result of acquiring this typological essay-writing competence that the reading and writing quality of this kind of Victorian press can best be assessed by a readership ready from now on also to appreciate more clearly and competently the journalistic prose written in the world and in Romania today, while also to better write the essay – assignments required during the Faculty years.

But the major purpose of the Victorian essay analysis is to revive and review what would otherwise probably remain a dead letter file of prose writings on issues of universal human interest, irrespective of the absolutist fashions of modernism and post-modernism self- sufficiently claiming that they know and understand absolutely everything better than the past generations did.

Thomas Carlyle (1795 – 1881) was in many ways the founding father of the Victorian literature of ideas. We can start by looking at his garrulousness, just as we did when we began the analysis of the novelists Dickens and Thackeray with their prolix communication in what was there termed the comic key. Carlyle's prose is incredible being in-formed by a whole *symphony of ideas* which he brings to bear upon his subject and by a *multiplicity of discourses* vying with each other on the same stage.

It is true that his texts seem meant to be physically uttered, enacted (with accompanying gestures and emotional outbursts) on a stage, by, in turn: an angry monologuist (just like the ones in Robert Browning's impassioned dramatic monologues); a military or political leader or strategist, or any other species of public orator, a preacher, a teacher, an actor even an itinerant saltimbanque, i.e., a juggler in ideas etc. This makes Carlyle's essays be hard reading for the unassisted student, who, especially if motivated by the rhythm and interests related to preparing for an examination, will grow impatient with Carlyle's verbal fireworks after the first page read.

If, however, Carlyle's prose is read disinterestedly (as Matthew Arnold would put it, meaning "with no ulterior purposes"), its incredible turns of phrase, its unexpected modulations – from oracularly held principles, through poetic argumentation, to anecdotes and real historical cases invoked as in a court room, only to descend back into the more widely and conventionally public benches usually occupied by press reporters participating in Parliament meetings, just as today, or in other important public events and milieus as TV cameramen and news editors do when they try to summarize the news and prepare a sample of lived history in a pertinent way: all these discursive stances are Carlyle's in turn and many more in addition.

And he appears not to prepare his reader for them in the least – either by more direct interventions from offstage or by observing a clearly presented plan, ever. This amounts to what N. Frye called, in the last paragraphs of his "Anatomy of Criticism" tantrum prose. The paradox is that, for all its rhetorical skill, Carlyle's prose is *informal prose, of the "table-talk" brand* (cf. J. A. Cuddon's Penguin "A Dictionary of Literary Terms and Literary Theory"); this prose seems rather meant to be heard in passing or *overheard,* in spite of the fact that Carlyle is more often than not literally thundering forth his discourses.

The explanation of all this is to be found in what we may term Carlyle's *fundamentalism* (or ideological passion and emotivity put in the service of strongly held – so strongly held that it becomes authoritarian - belief). As any other fundamentalism, Carlyle's own has a *positive belief* underlying it and a complementary... "legion" of *negations* accompanying it, negations of *criticised, tested, then noisily dismissed different beliefs and practices,* which obviously belong to what Carlyle, in the guise of a great military commander, believes to belong to the opposite, enemy's camp. On his battleground, Carlyle behaves as an avenging angel, first defending a set of traditional beliefs.

His campaign is the campaign for idealism in an age of materialism; sometimes Carlyle dresses up as a preacher and spells his nouns with capital letters as in the older versions of the Bible, or as in the romantic German philosophers's idiom – which he is actually copying also, in addition to the idiom of the English "Authorised Version" of the Bible. But Carlyle had made it clear that he spoke as a free-lance man of faith who feels he stands outside the fold of any particular church, outside the Calvinistic Presbyterian Kirk of Scotland into which he had been born and for whose service he studied to become a minister before he dropped out, when coming into contact with some lay German thinkers and writers such as Fichte and Goethe, directly and in translation or popularisation contemporary works. (He himself will translate Goethe's "Wilhelm Meister" into English.)

Critics gave the name of vitalism to Carlyle's positive creed, transcendentalism - or a popular version of metaphysics or spiritualism meant for the use of the contemporary middle-class audiences. Vitalism is another name for spiritualised humanism as the belief in man's soul and its aspirations over against man's other needs. For Carlyle, as is made clear in his most frequently read text "The Everlasting Yea", from "Sartor Resartus (1833-4), there is an infinity dwelling in man's chest, which should be let be and do its work, not obstructing it while catering for man's materialistic needs.

Carlyle rejects the utilitarian slogan of "the greatest *happiness* for the greatest numbers", authoritatively indicating that it is the individual, actual man who should alone form the object of the policy makers' concern, so as to lead this man's soul towards what Ralph Waldo Emerson would explicitely term in the contemporary 19th century America "the over-soul". The aim of living, Carlyle claims in "The Everlasting Yea" is to make man *blessed* rather than happy, in accordance with the sublime, spiritual standard, and not the worldly, communal one which may only , if ever, make man happy.

As the ending of "The Everlasting Yea" excerpted on pages 87 – 88 of PEV I clearly shows, man can answer the challenges of life by drastically reducing his claims and improving the spiritual powers inherent in his soul. What prevents man from achieving blessedness is precisely his search for happiness – which , Carlyle has only just demonstrated this in the "Everlasting No" and the "Centre of Indifference", will only lead to alienation. Carlyle's term for universal alienation is "the everlasting No": "The Everlasting No had said: "Behold, thou art fatherless, outcast, and the Universe is mine (the Devil's)". (The point is not that in the next sentence Carlyle rejects all this, but that the tonality and phrasing of these words perfectly resembles Gerard Manley Hopkins's terrible sonnet "No Worst, There is None" in "Fury had shrieked 'No ling-/ ering! Let me be fell: force I must be brief' ".

For all the spiritualised anguish underlying Carlyle's own plea against materialism, he has the playwright's instinct of dramatising and acting behind a multiplicity of masks and tonalities when taking action... against "the sea of troubles", as Hamlet soliloquised: so Carlyle stages an inexhaustible number of verbalised pageants, he allegorizes and metaphorically translates and slays with words his enemies in puzzling modulations and equations. in "The Everlasting Yea" (his handbook of metaphysical belief and vitalism) Carlyle employs at a climactic moment a mathematical syllogism for his demonstration which suddenly proves both the grace and the efficiency of the best in his talent and polymorphous personality: "So true it is, what I then said, that the Fraction of Life can be increased in value not so much by increasing your Numerator as by lessening your Denominator. Nay, unless my algebra deceive me, Unity itself divided by Zero will give Infinity" and, he continues, "Make thy claim of wages a zero, then; thou hast the world under thy feet.

Well did the Wisest of our time write: "It is only with Renunciation (Entsagen) that Life, properly speaking, can be said to begin" [He is quoting from Goethe who will also be invoked by Matthew Arnold, later as his inspirer] And, Carlyle declares, on the same page 88: "What Act of Legislature was there that thou shouldst be Happy? A little while ago thou hadst no right to be at all. What if thout wert born and predestined not to be Happy, but to be Unhappy! Art thou nothing other than a Vulture, then, that fliest through the Universe seeking after somewhat to eat : and shrieking dolefully because carrion enough is not given thee?

Close thy Byron; open thy Goethe." We can see the variety of Calyle's style in this short quotation – probably the most well-known words written by Carlyle – his experience as a teacher of mathematics prompts him in his ingenious demonstration of his point; next, he merges the social and political economy issues of his day with the universal, sermonic, theological perspective, in a sentence echoing Christ's temptation in the wilderness; in the following sentence he has the highflown courage of declaring, like a child in his wilful belief and innocence that – it is understood – Goethe was the wisest man of the time and he spells his adjective turned noun with a whimsical capital letter of respect; in the following part, he blends the judicial with the Biblical archaic language and judgment; then, like Silas Wegg and Mr. Boffin, in chapter 5, Book the First of "Our Mutual Friend", "he falls into poetry", with the image of the Vulture flying through the Universe – the Vulture and the carrion again having a Hopkinsian ring – only to culminate with an absolutely outspoken cry against Byronic romanticism and its morbid vanities, a cry to be taken up a few decades later, in 1853, more precisely, by Matthew Arnold, in his "Preface to the First Edition of Poems".

And with this we arrive at the more interesting paradox of Carlyle's creation: while opposing materialism, he was at the same time forging – as a founding father – the other part of the official doctrine of his age, namely the high moralism of the dominant puritanical spirituality, setting the tone of the cultural polemic for the few decades to come.

We can recognize not only in Matthew Arnold' cultural criticism but also in John Ruskin's aesthetic doctrine Carlyle's plea in "On Heroes, Hero-worship and the Heroic in History" for an order, a higher, heroic order of great men:men of letters, poets, priests, kings, whose mission it is to save mankind in historical times, just as had done in mythical times the divinities and prophets. What is more, in giving instances and names organised in a strict repertoire of qualities and a "scientifically understood" hierarchy, Carlyle inaugurates a whole paradigm of meritocracy which will be regarded as valid almost throughout the Victorian age, by classifiers and class-critics such as Matthew Arnold – in his "Culture and Anarchy", where the ... ill-behaved aristocracy who has resigned from its leading dignity is called a class of *barbarians* ; or by John Ruskin's canonical classification of painters, then of architecture, into first-order and second-order ones seems to observe a standard of rigid, absolute excellence inherited from Carlyle.

Carlyle's influence is no less important – via Ruskin – upon Oscar Wilde's or William Morris's utopian socialism, which seeks the legitimation of the individual as against the mass, average rights and aspirations advocated by the middle-class ideologues, followers of the Benthamite idealised political economy. Even today, in the American right-wing fundamentalism (you can read "traditionalism" instead) of the New Critics John Crowe Ransom or Allan Tate, we recognise the topical position of prestige that the man of letters occupies in the modern world. (The filiation is from Carlyle, via Matthew Arnold, through T. S. Eliot the critic, both American and European, and through Ezra Pound the international Arnoldian poet.

And in Britain, the contemporary trend of high culturalism inspired by F. R. Leavis and Q. D. Leavis, together with a whole now old generation of critical dames, such as Dame Helen Gardner or lords, leaders in criticism, knighted, as if according to the elitist population of an ideal Tennyson poem addressed to "knights and burghers, lords and dames")

With the high-mimetic and romance standard of heroism placing the spirituality of the cultural activist at the very top of the social pyramid, it is not to be wondered at Carlyle's downright opposition to:

- Democracy as the rule of the masses unaware of higher civilization standards and of greater historical necessity (cf. "Past and Present": "Labour" and "Democracy" (PEV I, pp. 171- 186)
- The age of mechanism as an age of damaging massification of the levelled human society (cf. "Signs of the Times", PEV I, pp 1 – 26, and especially, pages 4 and 12)
- The laissez-faire capitalistic State with its mercantyle cynicism, which Carlyle saw as a mere way in which the lawful political leaders, the elites had chosen to resign from their traditional position in the frame of the universally valid social contract (in French, the contrat social). (cf. "Chartism" – the excerpts in PEV I, pp. 103 –123). Here Carlyle's vision resembles Thackeray's frontal attack of middle-class society as "the vanity fair where all is bought and sold". Carlyle's allegory however, is more apocalyptical in

so far as he also opposes mercantilism in the guise of money worship or – in the next entry below

- Mammonism: the worship of money, the new religion of the Victorian middle-class capitalistic entrepreneurs (cf. "Past and Present", PEV p. 1621-7).

For all these "ills" Carlyle's discursive war or attrition of materialism offers positive counterparts or even solutions. Thus, he acts as what J. S. Mill indicated to be a desirable constructive thinker, in his essay on Coleridge, a thinker who does not only demolish like the negative thinkers, but after criticising puts something instead.

For "laisses-faire" Carlyle describes what "not-laissez faire " means; to the Mammon worshippers he offers for contemplation the ideal "Captains of Industry" linked to their labouring hands by a whole system of relationships amounting to respect, self-respect and, ultimately love, or agapé. (cf. "Past and Present", bk IV, ch. VI, PEV I, p. 186) (In John Ruskin's text "Unto This Last" a similar demonstration of exemplary social coexistence between full-fledged human beings is offered.

This demonstration will be followed in the spirit, when not in the letter, by the socialists, Wilde and Morris.) Carlyle chastises and scourges with his verbal, satirical, merciless verbal whip only in order to purge the actually existing institutions, social leaders and ideas of whatever is harmful from the spiritualised perspective.

His general cures for the Victorian sick patient include, on the other hand:

The doctrine of activism, which was borrowed from Goethe, clearly expressed in "Chartism", recommends man to perfect himself by means of work (a doctrine subsequently taken up by the socialists of all hues from the utopians with their respect for labour's dignifying power to the Fabian socialists such as George Bernard Shaw, to Marx himself and, in the 20th century, by the Lenininist communists who advocated work as the new ...opium for the masses (to obviously replace religion), while they, the communist politicians profited behind the stage and occupied Central and

Eastern Europe in the guise of liberators of the masses and the oppressed peoples creating Soviet concentration camps everywhere in their wake). (And it was precisely for reasons such as these that when the repressive communist propaganda in Romania used another naïve Christian believer, perhaps, the poet Ioan Alexandru, to preach in the press work and obedience and the ascetical doctrine of "less food, more spirituality" to the shamefully starving Romanian East – Europeans in the 1980s, it was precisely for this, then, that the intellectual community secretely resented and rejected this Christian preacher as a betrayer of the intellectual resistance through silence and as a mere collaborationist, which perhaps he was not.)

Now Carlyle did the same in the Victorian century, when he answered in written, in his essay, from above or within the upper strata of society to the oppressed masses pressuring for justice in the street in vain, during the Chartist movement.

In a way (but for nobler, idealistic reasons and without being anybody's but his own mouthpiece) Carlyle preached what the maddened ill-informed, manipulated masses yelled in the streets of Bucharest in response to the disciplined long demonstration of the Romanian thinking people of the Piata Universitatii civic forum: "Noi muncim, nu gindim". Carlyle preached, in "Labour" (p. 172, PEV I), the following:

"Blessed is he who has found his work; let him ask no other blessedness. He has work, a life-purpose; he has found it, and will follow it!" and after some compelling poetic allegory: "Labour is life: from the inmost heart of the Worker rises his god-given Force, the sacred celestial Life-essence breathed into him by Almighty God; from his inmost heart awakens him to all nobleness, - to all knowledge, "self-knowledge" and much else, so soon as Work fitly begins.

Knowledge? the knowledge that will hold good in working, cleave thou to that. Properly, thou hast no other knowledge but what thou hast got by working; the rest is yet all a hypothesis of knowledge; a thing to be argued in schools, a thing floating in the clouds, in endless logic-vortices, till we try it and fix it." Doubt, of whatever kind, can be ended by

Action alone." The general censorship of industrialised and urbanised modernization, being, for Carlyle, nothing but massification – inimical to man's nature and alienating, his thinking here includes a return from the present, a radical change of direction from the material to the spiritual values.

Carlyle chooses Medievalism as the cult of the discipline, morality and spiritualised order of the Middle Ages monastic culture. This will be his model fictionally typified by his 12th century excursion in "Past and Present" into the world of monastic civilization of St. Edmundsbury as revived in that little monastery thanks to the efforts of a good leader, Abbot Samson.

The virtues of the past indirectly exalted by Carlyle in Book II of "Past and Present" are simply translations of the virtues of Victorian puritanism, such as activism and high-minded modesty which Carlyle assumes, will naturally lead to inner-man's spiritual progress and to more dignified and peaceful social coexistence.

We have to do here with the undercurrent of utopian thinking accompanying medievalism, just as any other form of escapism, such as that wielded by Arnold's utopian modern age, a replica of classicist democratic culturalism, or the nostalgic return of the Pre-Raphaelites to the early Renaissance, which they would feign declare to still be part of the Middle Ages, but for investing it with the titanism in excess, as the cosmogonical theme in a lot of paintings and mystical Pre - Raphaelite poems indicate.

Similarly, the Gothic architecture of an ideal Venice or of specific Italian theologian painters whom Ruskin declares "modern" by an act of wishful thinking denotes pure cultural escapism. Not less so is the aestheticists exaggerate respect for this or that book, this or that avant-gardism recently posted from France or from Italy, the two great "races" who inherited the legacy of the Renaissance aestheticist belief in man. In general, as Browning's poetry or Pater's prose profusely demonstrate too, Italy and France vye with each other for precedence in matters of cultural refinement.

All this demonstrates how the Victorian cultural activists

and artists, all had a sense of guilt when they turned away from the vernacular contemporary or recently past Romantic practices in all the domains towards nations, periods and places more advanced on the paths of cultural progress , seeking for sources of elevating visionarism and for professions of faith everywhere and anywhere else than in their own home about which they only wrote masked complaints or romance fairytales, like Tennyson or direct elegies, like Matthew Arnold's stationed on Dover Beach or buried so deep in the frustrations of life.

Chapter 14

Characteristics Shared by the Three Feminine Novels

If the first lecture on the Victorian novels written by Dickens and Thackeray applied for unifying purposes Northrop Frye's combined algorithms of *the comic mode* (in the first essay of the "Anatomy") and of *the mythos of comedy* (as described in the third essay of the same book), in this lecture, as the long title indicates, what is attempted is an explanation of the way in which the low–mimetic *mode* lowers the high–mimetic and the romance modes by "weakening" the applicability of the *mythos* of summer (or romance) in the process of writing fiction intended as realistic. The novels "Jane Eyre", "Wuthering Heights" and "Middlemarch" shall serve as illustrations of this tenet.

On the other hand, it is necessary to anticipate on the main presuppositions of fictional realism as it will appear when analysing the novels by the three feminine authors as major fiction writers in the Victorian Age. Realism presupposes a respect for the dignity of living in reality which respectful attitude can be termed *organicism*. This is also associated with a *descriptive accuracy* that obviously transfers into the realm of fiction the empirical assumptions connected to the positivistic practices of science in the 19th century.

Thirdly, realism is currently associated with a lucid *criticism of stale, received ideas* which consequently *reveals* what is just faulty illusion, whatever is morally condemnable but people choose to hide from themselves and from others in ordinary, everyday social existence. Fourthly, and by applying

Matthew Arnold's systematic ideas, *realism amounts to "a criticism of life" – a deepened understanding of life since literature offers humanity an enhanced "interpretive power"*; in this respect, the task of realistic fiction is to lead readers towards conclusions that are the same as in real life.

Thus, when literary realism applies to the individual psychology and to the collective environment, it can be said to recreate, reveal in detail and in action what lies beneath the conventional, inert life that hasty or indifferent people share quite unreflectively: the inner conflicts and the hidden metamorphoses underlying individual or social existence. This further implies that in realistic fiction *the plots have the fluidity of life* and *the characters are endowed with psychological, social or natural authenticity*.

There are two important consequences of the first and the second part of this statement respectively, which are maybe less obvious than this otherwise common previous statement. The first consequence introduces *two brands of realism*, from this point of view. We can call spritual realism the realism *centred on introspection* and *the understanding/interpretation of human sensibility* when it is grounded in the mimetic intention of capturing the hardly controllable impulsivity or the unconscious in their own terms, as Freud or Jung would have it in the 20th century.

And we can call scientific realism that brand of realism which is grounded in either the *elevating ethics* of the consciously controlled and controllable beautiful souls, on the one hand and/or in *the liberal beliefs prompted by the ideal of harmonious, perfectible social living*, on the other hand. The second consequence of the statement about the fluidity and authenticity of realistic fiction is more rhetorical and theoretical. If the realistic plots manifest the fluidity of life, then they obviously work according to what Northrop Frye calls in his fourth essay of the "Anatomy" the rhythm of continuity, or prose.

This "rhythm" tends to lose its continuity when intense poetry or dramatism are applied to it, as it happens in so many Victorian low–mimetic romances, e.g., Charlotte Brontë's "Jane

Eyre". In the difference between the two "rhythms", of continuity, or prose and of association, or lyric, as Frye's rhetoric calls them, we can follow and, in our turn "anatomize" the way in which Victorian realistic fiction moves from social comedy (with the mythos of spring) to poetry (with the mythos of romance).

In the first lecture on the novel, we looked at this first, sociological hypostasis of Victorian fiction informed by comedy, and appearing, for this reason to be more amorphous because it imitates the social totality that is disorderly, more chaotic; consequently we described as "garrulous" and more digressive the narrative method inspiring Thackeray's panoramas and Dickens's symphonic observation of human nature in its social manifestation.

In this lecture we shall look at the effects the mythos of summer or`romance has over fiction, owing to its enhanced lyricism or poetic intensity that breaks the amorphous flow with punctual associations.

We can state that with the longer fictions published after the middle of the Victorian Age, i.e., for the novels "Jane Eyre", "Wuthering Heights"and "Middlemarch" that appeared respectively in 1847, 1848 and 1871–2, realism comes into its own and to terms with himself; or, it becomes by 20th century structuralist standards, structured. In the work of these women–novelists it is the functional design and the… narrative ambition that make the difference –especially as compared to the implied author Dickens's magnetism, which was mainly due to the power that his imagination and humour had of "simply" transfiguring the common world of his day.

The art of this lecture's protagonists resides more in the idea which they skilfully invite the reader to contemplate: *the confrontation of strength and weakness* which the encounter between (human) nature and society occasions. And this in itself is a task or theme compatible with the romance literature of sensibility or with the high–mimetic, demonstrative ideology; or, at any rate, this kind of literature is by no means compatible with comedy, which works with larger, coarser, more externally defined and impersonal blocks. The personalised pledge at the heart of the femine sensibility informs these authors' fiction with a functional, systemic construction. The plot and the characters, more often than not the setting or the dominant symbol, together with the narrative method chosen, perfectly motivate each other.

Thus, the functional or systemic form of these tightly–knit, acribious novels demonstrates the point which the feminine writers make, and this point has to do *with presenting experience as a whole,* revealing in its impact upon the sensibility, revealing in the amount of intellectual or symbolic lucidity, intensely compelling and expressive of, ultimately, one person's lifeworld, the feminine implied author's illuminated experience. Regarded from the inside, this narrative eloquence or talent amounts to ambition. Outwardly regarded, it is simply a realism of the sensibility, or spiritual realism, as it has been called earlier.

The feminine sensibility as ambition seems to focus the fictive lens on something that is not just, and often not really, low or common mimetism of existence but *a subjective transcription of experience whose result is a* kind of more intense meaning, a strong (because felt) radiation or beam of meaning, very different from casual significance (cf. Gottlob Frege's distinction between Sinn (sense) und Bedeutung (significance); also cf. the more recent twentieth century opposition between the paradigm of strong logic versus the paradigm of weak logic – which Horia Roman Patapievici applied at length in his description of modernity during the course of lectures he gave at the English Department of the University of Bucharest in the academic year 1998/9).

In Charlotte Brontë's "Jane Eyre", the confrontation between strength and weakness takes the positive form of an exemplary progress and metamorphosis involving basically the reciprocal transformation of interiority into strong, exemplary exteriority. Here, through the device of the intimate first–person narrative of interiority, an externally insignificant because ill–favoured person, an orphan girl, is followed, in stages, during her internal growth which amounts to ever stronger outbursts of interiority.

The narrative of mutual integration of the interior (Jane's soul, mind and spirit) with the exterior (Jane's social milieu) is effected by a corresponding progress in internal (spiritual) power and external (social) power. Jane's internal individual strength acting *as obstinacy* at first, *as sharper and sharper virtue*, later, is gradually and increasingly *validated* as *moral charisma* or *legitimate power* over the other inhabitants of the public space.

At the heart of the book "Jane Eyre" is an epiphany of purified power, obtained by the purification in the internal, spiritual order as a pre–condition for the subsequent purification in the external, social space. By fastidious, careful design, individual experience is presented first, then successfully transmitted as a form of initiation and growth. This is formally achieved by the implied author's building of provisional wholes to be demonstrably and didactically broken only in order to build superior, wider wholes, wholes capable of yielding ever "stronger" meanings.

Internal and external progress as illustrated by the plot is symbolically (i.e., poetically and so, discontinously, lyrically) presented as a staged journey whose *formative* stages correspond to some intiatic steps/stages. Thus, first at Gateshead and Lowood, Jane Eyre's soul is made and perfected as within a sanctuary, from whence she emerges strengthened in all her human faculties. In Gateshead, where she is kept, as it were, outside the house(hold), *at the gate*, she develops her imagination in loneliness and she is pushed to the limits of her identity in fear, terror of death and of herself.

(As a little girl of ten she is held culpable for every trace of her individuality by the fairy–tale like "step–aunt", she is daily tortured by her step–cousins, then she is exceptionally tormented in the gothic story dungeon of the savagely red Red Room. Fear and revolt mark or maim her, threaten to break her self in a kind of ritual death. Then in Lowood she is restored and brought back into the fold of shared humanity with/by Helen Burns who burns with godly lovingkindness and by Miss Temple, whose name itself points to the sacramental effects of Jane's stay at Lowod. Next, the newly acquired, serene, powerful and optimistic because spiritualised personality of the young governess at Thornfield Hall will be further subjected to the fire–test of temptation in the symbolically ambiguous paradise/hell of the wealthy mansion, whose significance appears to be "the field that seems peaceful only to work as an excruciating crown of thorns".

For Jane, Thornfield is, socially speaking, a potential "pleasure dome", to paraphrase Coleridge's phrase at the beginning of "Kubla Khan". Here she finds pleasure in complete fulfilment as a governness with power over the young (Adèle), the mature (Rochester) and the old (Mrs. Fairfax) alike. Here, therefore, her feminine identity has best prospects of being made whole in a social paradise. But the Puritanical obsession, the Biblical analogy, prompts the Victorian implied author with a detour.

The reader will have a chance of observing Jane re–enact with a difference the story of man's fall. Rochester will be cast for a moment as a mere tempter, having another, mad wife hidden in the attic even while proposing to Jane. When, therefore, after he has whispered the magic spell of his declared love in Jane's ear and asked her in marriage, and after she has accepted him, he is proved to be just like the serpent who can only make promises greater than he can keep; Jane realizes in time and gives thanks to the voices of her conscience awoken in the night–time that she has to leave unoccupied the position of legitimate power over the household as its mistress.

The reader will not be given time to doubt the heroine and wonder if she will exceed the mark, like Adam when prompted by Eve who set her eyes on and gave her ear to the serpent. (Here the gender roles are reversed, of course, with the male as the weaker of the pair!). No, Jane does not yield to the external temptation of deserved, but impossible external power. Instead, on realising what kind of mistress she could only become with Rochester already married to a former wife, Jane chooses to flee not fall.

She runs for her life through a self–imposed wilderness beyond the Eden that she does not lose by falling. The social wilderness she is courageous enough to confront will not crush her but reward her. Another set of founding, archetypal stories of the old world are echoed at this point in the story; and their purpose is to provide an external, social counterpart to the internal adventure in the heroine's powerful soul. First, like Moses and the chosen Jewish people, the trying exodus undertaken by Jane will be crowned by eventual triumph in Canaan, the land of milk and honey.

Here the Canaan is called Moor House. It will make for Jane the best household that she had ever lodged in, being both genteel and peaceful, and even more, providing a brotherly and sisterly family much more genuine than the Reed family of cousins Jane had had according to ordinary ties of blood or kinship at Gateshead. Secondly, Jane can be seen to flee from Thornfield Hall as if pursued by the Erinies, the furies of Greek tragedy. Only, these are not her own furies, but rather the shared furies of the rabid titans enchained together at Thornfield Hall: Bertha Mason and Edward Rochester.

Because Thornfield had actually been a household secretely ruled by disaster and fiery, secret rage in Jane Eyre's absence. (It would also be literally consumed by its fire after Jane's departure from – "the Thornfield …Hell"). By contrast to *fiery* Thornfield, Moor House will remain dominated by *ice* once the warm–hearted feminine figures of Mary and Diana Rivers leave it to become, just like Jane Eyre earlier, governesses in a big town of the south. The cause of this formerly harmonious household's freezing will be the apostolic parish priest St. John Rivers, Jane's new suitor.

Just like many a martyr in "The Lives of Saints", Jane will be subjected to the test of ice, after having been subjected to that of fire. In resisting St. John River's missionary appeals to her for becoming his companion in a brotherly marriage devoid of love, Jane Eyre's apotheosis is both internal and external : as a strong soul, Jane discriminates between what may be good in its own terms (a missionary's career) but not good for her own nature (becoming a man's wife without love); she does not mistake the externally good for the internally good, and this is her greater strength, as a round feminine character, than St. John's strength, a stock priestly character.

Ready to leave behind her external fulfilment as St. John Rivers' mate bound for Australia – just as she had been ready to leave behind internal self–fulfilment alongside with the external, social one as mistress at Thornfield, Jane Eyre's power will be momentarily impaired, it would seem, only to emerge even stronger in the end. The demonstrative structural amplification of Jane's circle of identity will be again effected by first breaking it radically. The rites of passage sequence of cyclical break–ups will end by the desirable climax of the renewed encounter with Edward Rochester crowned by marriage at Ferndean.

Here the dean, Rochester, venerable and shadowy as the fern among the flowers, will be met like a blind Lear or Oedipus elevated to the status of an external hero, having been in his turn purged by the fire and the *sparagmos* or ritual maiming, according to the best rules of romance. The mating of the royal pair of lovers and powerful beings will be effected now, at last, at the end of the journey which had been an ordinary trip through life for Rochester until he'd met Jane whom life had already singled out for becoming engaged in a quest–journey.

Jane, the inward rebel turned saint thanks to the external circumstances, several times over in the novel (as many times as there are stages to her journey after her going a–head once completely out of the gate at Gateshead) will thus apotheotically end up by appropriating – in marriage – the external, social, conventional realm, after her final marriage in strength with this realm's reclaimed fiend turned angel himself – as a result of his own shedding of weakness in favour of spiritual, moral, religious strength and rectitude.

In spiritualised terms, the vertical, intimately internal dimension reclaims, internalizes, appropriates the horizontal, social or public dimension. In this way, Victorian social reality and its values find themselves hallowed by Jane's progress, in Jane's name, by Jane's apotheotic marriage. This finally proves that the title of this novel was meant as more than an index for its centering merely on Jane's internal and external adventures in the Victorian social environment; it aimed further, in a sermonic gesture, at indicating the ritual transfiguraion of lived experience under the impact of spiritual belief.

By contrast, the other two feminine novels brush–up against romance in a less linear and less typical manner. Their forms of spiritual belief are of a very different brand. In *an agnostic, liberal commentary on religious or intellectual romance,* "Middlemarch" will simply *reverse and void* first the saintly legend of Saint Theresa's life of mystical aspiration on the vertical which is presented in "The Prelude"; it will effect this by emptying first Dorothea's intellectual and marital early aspirations; next it will *doom the spiritually ascending quest* of Tertius Lydgate's scientific romance by practically demonstrating that science and romance – in both senses – are mutually exclusive.

In this respect, "Middlemarch" demonstrates in best low–mimetic terms the attrition of heroism in real life, as it contemplates the reversal of power or strength into subjection and weakness, in an ironic exchange. It is an instance of critical realism in the two senses of the word "criticism". It criticises life by placing it against the background of the ideal, as Matthew Arnold advocated in his essays, and it shows in what way shared commonplaces are shallow. In the first sense, this novel draws its low mimetic power from the same standard feminine theme of the confrontation between good (power) and evil (weakness) usually encountered in the black and white colours of romance; also, it contemplates a panoramic hierarchy of social and psychological power in which the high–mimetic heroes as leaders of men are rather shown to be trapped in a web of deterministic relationships of their own make, which contradict their need for absolute power.

This is the crux of George Eliot's realistic matter. In this respect, "Middlemarch" uses the weakening of the vertical high–mimetic pyramidal structure in the service of the realistic criticism of social institutions and entire social milieus characteristic for Victorianism. But it is still the romance or high–mimetic presuppositions that offer to George Eliot the pretext for her tightly–knit structurality in "Middlemarch". Her acribious fictional structure which J. Hillis Miller symbolically projects in the form of the web is achieved by the choice of not one but two high–mimetic protagonists, endowed with potential heroic stature, Dorothea and Lydgate who are rendered maturer and disenchanted by low–mimetic plots.

They are caused by the implied author's choice of an adverse environment for her idealistic protagonists. They are placed in the provincial, narrow–minded environment of Middlemarch in which they will get involved too intimately, by marriage to stock low–mimetic social types (the intellectual and human fraud, Casaubon and the shallow but greedy puppet Rosamond Vincy, in every respect her brother's sister...) In this way, George Eliot starts where Charlotte Brontë ends: the progress is in "Middlemarch" from the blinding light of the illusions gloriously harboured inside the heroes' souls at the beginning, towards the subdued, middle light of experience or even the resigned penumbra at the end of the book; on the contrary, as shown above, in Charlotte Brontë's book the progress is from Jane Eyre's hardly contained ire at the beginning of the novel towards her radiating inner light that conquers an ever wider expanse in her exterior world from the middle of the book onwards.

For the best part of "Wuthering Heights", on the other hand, another opposition will reign, which reverses both Charlotte Brontë's triumphal marriage of true minds – at the same time a marriage of true social fringes with true social centres – and George Eliot's critical rejection of the same. This opposition reigning in "Wuthering Heights" is *the opposition between, on the one hand, the elemental* (as represented by Catherine Earnshaw and Heathcliff as a bachelor, by Hareton Earnshaw and Catherine Linton, as well as by the Heights itself) *and, on the other hand, the socially tamed nature* (as represented by the Linton clan at Thrushcross Grange, and by the Grange itself, by Nelly Dean and Joseph as inept servants at Wuthering Heights, and especially by the social and elemental outsider, Mr. Lockwood himself, through whose eyes we come into contact with the two opposed worlds).

We can further recognize a topical opposition of (the earlier) Victorianism: that between Carlylean vitalism with its emotional excesses and utilitarian Benthamism with its moderation; this renders the novel topical not only in view of its romantic intensity in an age of compromise but also as a landmark or stepping stone in "the living stream" of Victorianism, for once recognised as troubled, just as in William Butler Yeats's poem "Easter 1916".

Also, by comparison to Charlotte's serious parable of ascent into a socially virtuous Victorian heaven , "Wuthering Heights" is, archetypally speaking, a novel which explores *the fall of the elemental nature into the Victorian social purgatory*; this fall is comparable through its effects to a general fall of souls from paradise. The fall is in "Wuthering Heights" the cyclical fall from empathy: first, the fall from strict familial empathy of the Earnshaws, when the father, Old Mr. Earnshaw unwittinly brought along with him from the outside, remote space the alien/alienated/alienating orphan; next, the fall from empathy of the two elemental kindred souls Catherine and Heathcliff, dramatised at length in the novel; then the further fall of Heathcliff by "the mean gratification of his vengeance", his complete abdication from the dignity of human fellowship in the wake of his loss of identity after Catherine's betrayal and subsequent death.

All in all, a chain of falls: first the archetypal one, the fall of angels from heaven, next the socially induced estrangement from the vitality of childhood – in an ironically reversed interpretation of physical and social growth as degeneration; consequently, a last fall from every form of human dignity back into savageness: a case of genuine Freudian regression. No wonder then that the only anodyne to such a chain–reaction of falls remains death itself which ideally restores to quiet slumbers the set of the Victorian souls. And this slumber would be directly similar to the craving for lethal oblivion traceable in Tennyson's Greek parable or pastiche of "The Lotos Eaters" or in Swinburne's professions of faith in the

Proserpine poems – but for the novel "Wuthering Heights" swerving away into the backroads of ghostly romance, where the supernatural is allowed to let in the soothingly innocent air of reconciliation through the fantastic infinity.

Thus, it appears that the weakening of the romance conventions in the low–mimetic mode novels whose major aim is analytical, critical and classifying is effected by several signifying practices which mainly involve an increase in the myths' inclusiveness and applicability to the 19th century lifeworld. This is achieved by extending the scope of myths and archetypes while also diluting their punctuality : by overlapping various mythoi and archetypal imagery, as could be observed in the case of "Jane Eyre", i.e. by increasing the mythical density and strengthening the signifying power of one myth in the context of the neighbouring one, also by cutting, pasting and offsetting parts of myths and by combining archetypal imagery; by subjecting the vertical axis mundi to the test of the horizontal stream of conventional existence, as it happens in both "Middlemarch" and "Wuthering Hieghts" – in the case of the former novel by using experimentally intellectual techniques that separate elements from the romance (or high–mimetic) pattern and pit them against the critical patterns of received social observation, while in the latter novel, by simply distributing into radically opposing camps whole blocks of characters, temporal and generational social formations and repeating entire meaningful sets in cycles.

All these operations can be summed up as an instance when myths are used for social or psychological observation and commentary. But in this way, the ambitious commentary of romance interrupts with poetry and abstract artificiality the authentic flow or formal rhytm of continuity characteristic for realism. (In George Eliot's "Middlemarch", the very starting point which operates on the vertical represents an artificially exterior projection that "contradicts" the horizontal verisimilitude of the otherwise realistic enough narratological fabric of the web; also, the device of the two protagonists and main threads which the implied author of this long novel ultimately decided to weave together betrays the author's love of parallelism in opposition or viceversa; not to mention the set of conventional high–mimetic healthy, not always wealthy and wise, pairs of morally Victorian titans such as the Garth family in "Middlemarch" strictly opposed to pigmies that the equally Victorian Vincys represent in contrast to their "victors' " names (consider the Latin verb "vinco, vincere" and the ideal "amor vincit omnia").

THE STRUCTURALITY OF THE WOMEN NOVELISTS' NARRATIVE STRUCTURES

Retracing the narratological cohesion effects of the Victorian realistic romances already mentioned under 7.1, what ultimately interests us, however, is the exact manner in which these determined women–novelists managed to communicate so brilliantly their intensely felt ideas, when putting romance and the lyrically discontinous rhythm of association, as Frye puts it – or the symbolism of poetry, as anyone else could put it, for that matter – in the service of what we have called spiritual realism.

The ambitiously feminine novelists availed themselves of the purely symbolic power of repetition with variations, which is a principle of association, the principle of lyrical creation when not a downright theoretical *ars combinatoria per se.* We have demonstrated beforehand that the allegory of experience operates by cycles or stages in "Jane Eyre", building ever stronger and wider didactic or initiatic wholes. Similarly, we have shown how the plot of the novel "Middlemarch" springs forth from the system of parallelisms and dissonant clashes between aspiration and social determinism as represented by the web for every character caught in its nodal points.

Or, though not expressly stressed, in "Wuthering Heights" we have witnessed the implacable operation of chain reactions spanning over three generations whose histories are mutually and circularly determined by multiple associations. Narratologically speaking, the result is that the plot threads, the pairs of characters – more often than not placed in direct opposition –, the – usually symbolic – atmosphere and the narrative devices, such as the narrators' voices employed tend to absolutely or infinitely converge into or towards a structural or semantic centre in such romance–novels as "Jane Eyre", "Wuthering Heights" or the 'high–mimetic romance' "Middlemarch". (But Dickens's "Great Expectations" or "Bleak House" or "Our Mutual Friend" show a very similar tendency of being carefully staged novels, not to mention Thomas Hardy's novels cut into highly artistic dramatic chunks or phases).

The sensation, as recorded first by F. R. Leavis in his "The Great Tradition", is that such fictional universes become analysable in perfectly motivated plots as a function of the characters (and viceversa), better understood because supported by the general atmosphere of the book's setting and ultimately explicable owing to the narrative equation adopted. A tightly motivated, fully significant system of relations connects the stages of the plot with each other in deterministic patterns that are helped because they are further highlighted by the settings; the settings testify to the dangerous distance existing between the interior and the exterior of people in action ("Jane Eyre"), or to the troublesome freedom of untamed liberal spirits (in "Wuthering Heights" and at Wuthering Heights) also threatened by a similarly dangerous distance in space between freedom and civilisation as typified by the – physical and qualitative – milleage separating Wuthering Heights from Thrushcross Grange; the doubly unreliable point of view of the two dramatised narrators in "Wuthering Heights", Mr. Lockwood and Nelly Dean, is so chosen as to enhance the mystery of the narrative to which they remain practically exterior throughout the book.

In "Middlemarch" the social settings are ultimately rendered symbolical of the high likelihood of human ideals being suppressed amidst the stuffy provincial atmosphere of the actual life; this is achieved by means of the plot which indelibly places both Dorothea Brooke and Dr. Tertius Lydgate at cross purposes with their environment in which they get intimately involved due to the deterministic forces of their own psychological make–up. As personally flawed representatives of the most advanced Victorian ideas, the two protagonists work as avant–garde Victorians confronting mass Victorianism, they seem/are modelled on the suggested essay debates between the received Victorian conventions and their better versions, so that we, readers, can subsequently interpret intellectually rather than emotionally the appearance of Will Ladislaw as the lucky insinuation into the hopeless Victorian picture of the metropolitan air of Renaissance hedonism and classicist rationalism (translated as modern aestheticism or as liberal thinking in commonsensical matters of ideas and taste).

This makes us read "Middlemarch" for aesthetically contemplating the interaction between the intellectual or cognitive values which we have encountered in the essay too, with the purely human' values as Wayne Booth defined them in his "Rhetoric of Fiction", that connect the protagonists with their Victorian environment.

The narrative prowess of these feminine novels, the density of patterns amounting to "strong" wholes worth contemplating aesthetically recommends them for our theoretical, speculative purposes, i.e. for narratological or archetypal or Freudian and psychological analyses or sociologically Marxist or phenomenologically descriptive purposes typical for the 20th century horizon of expectations.

Chapter 15

The Action of Robert Browning's Verse

This lecture will open with a reading in the guise of a case study from one of Browning's early poems, "By the Fireside". To begin with, the readers' expectations are for a Victorian fire-side, perhaps a family scene or an idyll even. What we get instead is a reverie – but unlike the romance reveries that are set in nature, here, like in Vasile Alecsandri's "Pastel", nature is contemplated from beside the fire-place and at one further remote from nature than the fire-side, in the hearth of a home: from the cultural window that the "deep" study of Greek opens as an oblique vista of the mind.

Nature outside the fire-place in the house and the fire-place outside the book – of Greek prose, only prose –and the poetic "I" moving out – into imagination – there where every outside frame and vista ends. Indeed, to gain access to the spirit of Browning's poetry one has to open up a whole game of Chinese boxes, first the outermost box, then the next and the next all over again before you are "there".

At the beginning of this poem we meet not only Browning's genuine love of Greek, not at all like Tennyson's picturesque invocation of classical commonplaces to decorate his poetic studio like a painter (Browning was very much better educated than most of his contemporary Victorians, let alone Tennyson who had been to Cambridge, whereas Browning had read copiously, but on his own, in his father's library); but to return ... "by the fireside", we are also invited to slope with Browning "to Italy at last/And youth, by green degrees".

II	III
I shall be found by the fire, suppose,	Till the young ones whisper, finger on lip
O'er a great wise book as beseemeth age	'There he is at it, deep in Greek:
While the shutters flap as the crosswind blows	Now, then, or never, out we slip
And I turn the page, and I turn the page,	To cut from the hazels by the creek
Not verse now, only prose !	A mainmast for our ship!'

IV	V
I shall be at it indeed, my friends!	The outside frame, like your hazel-trees-
Greek puts already on either side	But the inside-archway narrows fast,
Such a branch-work forth as soon extends	And a rarer sort succeeds to these,
To a vista opening far and wide,	And we slope to Italy at last
And I pass out where it ends.	And youth, by green degrees.

Indeed, for Browning Italy signified all these and more, youth, the escape from the Victorian art of husbandry and tritely sublime industriousness. (Browning himself had sloped and, even, we could say, he eloped to the Italy he so loved, where he lived for half a life-time with his poet wife, Elizabeth Barett, until she died first, then he, 28 years later.) This is precisely what this poem does in its more external Chinese boxes, it takes us along "by green degrees" while it embarks upon a journey into the past on the wings of imagination.

The poem might even at this point still be regarded as a conventional reverie, were it not for the much more powerful entrance into the world of vision than in any of Tennyson's nostalgic allegories of experience and sentiment (in, say, "The Lotos Eaters" or even in Ulysses's dramatic monologue).

"The outside-frame, like your hazel-trees-
But the inside-archway narrows fast,
And a rarer sort succeeds to these.

i.e., to the hazel-trees and the outside-frames. (Compare this to the discursively intense statement, still just a statement in general, poor in dramatism, of Tennyson's "Ulysses": "Yet all experience is an arch wherethrough/ Gleams that untravelled world, whose margin fades/ For ever and for ever when I move")

The surprises continue: the journey is not a solitary reaper's or an exiled lonely soul's but a "journey *à deux*", so to say, by an inter-languages cooperative coinage, and the land of the journey is the land of love invoked with the discrete exclamation of subdued, just signalled emotion strengthened by the alliteration and assonance as "Oh, woman-country, wooed not wed" (And to think that Browning has been accused by his detractors of not having a musical ear!). In the following stanzas, the journey is crowned by standing "in the heart of things"(VIII) where it becomes possible for the two contemplators to be thrilled by the same thoughts:

XXVII

Think, when our one soul understands
The Great Word which makes all things new
When earth breaks up and Heaven expands
How will the change strike me and you
In the House not made with hands?

We are no longer there where F.R. Leavis generalised about Victorian poetry saying that "it was possible for the poets of the Romantic period to believe that the interests animating their poetry were the forces moving the world, or that might move it. But Victorian poetry admists implicitly that the actual world is alien, recalcitrant, unpoetical, and that no protest is worth making except the protest of withdrawal" (cf. the same earlier quotation in reference to Tennyson).

Indeed, after opening all the duly constructed boxes of one stage within a stage within a yet further stage, Browning's poetry points one over "the earth's break-up", where heaven expands to a kind of Wordsworthian mature, ripe age "an age so blest that, by its side/Youth seems the waste instead" (XXV). This is an age that *reveals* at one stroke, in the matter of a moment, before it asks anything, both the vision of eternity as a fact observable in time "For my heart had a touch of the woodland time" (XLI) and the mechanism of vision in a rational meditation upon it:

XXXIX

Oh, the little more, and how much it is!
And the little less, and what worlds away
How a sound shall quicken content to bliss,
Or a breath suspend the blood's best play,
And life be a proof of this!

A poem which ends in this key:

LI

I am named and known by that hour's feat;
There took my station and degree:
So grew my own small life complete
As nature obtained her best of me-
....

LIII

So, the earth has gained by one man more,
And the gain of earth must be Heaven's gain too,
And the whole is well worth thinking o'er
When the autumn comes....................
....

such a poem, then, is a poem in which individual belief matters much more than the public, plural, social Victorian self haunting literature in the second half of the 19th century. Also, this is one typical poem of Browning's poetry which deals with "huge" objects. So, the main difference between Tennyson's and Browning's poetry seemes to be a matter of very intimate choice: where Tennyson's talent selects external, circumstantial realities, objects or abstract ideas which he makes touchable, in the guys of toys for the immediate public imagination, Browning makes palpable huge trains of ideas, whole arguments about values, and ages and types of people.

Browning touches with his talent more universal, wider cultural contexts than Tennyson with his predictable, stock allegories; also, Browning does not choose the miniature story key but the confession of the intimate, hidden self; he does not work like in Tennyson's "The Princess" with models in little of the world, but with *expansions* of the individual to the universal. This is his key. And he does not remain just a

Laureate for an age to recognize its dear self in, but a poet as great as the romantics in his comprehensive range and approach to life.

As compared to the high Romantics, Browning is, however, not concerned with the higher order of the sublimer "other" of human life; but, in an equally titanic outburst of poetic energy, he is "interested in the dangerous edge of things", in "the grotesqueness of existence", side by side with its sublime outreach in moments of epiphany. (That like in "Porphyria's Lover", such moments of epiphany are in the grotesque key, as moments of vision entrusted to madmen, is not in the least meant to diminish the mechanism of vision itself, which is repeated again and again by Browning, no matter how despicable the occasions or agents for the visions may be)

Actually, Browning writes what Virginia Woolf wanted to find in the Victorian novel, when she commended George Eliot's literature intended for adults; only, Browning writes in verse and in poems that read like sketchy novels which wait for the reader to wake up and write further in his own mind; Browning's poems could be expanded any time and to the greatest lengths by the more ingenious readers – as the essay papers experimentally requested on "My Last Duchess" from the students of the current academic year proved. All the social, psychological, ideological connections imaginable are concentrated in Browning's concentrated scenes which embody what stanza XLIX of "By the Fire-Side" states:

XLIX

How the world is made for each of us!
How all we perceive and know in it
Tends to some moment's product thus,
When a soul declares itself – to wit,
By its fruit – the things it does!

In trying to understand extensively, on an incredible multiplicity of cases, in the judicial, clinical, anecdotal and sentimental key which his poems represent, this very statement about the world and every soul's declaration of itself by its fruit, Browning proves that he was interested, after all, in the life of the race, in its most ample variety, not in the life of the Victorian century and its particular themes and moods of self-assurance or anguish, as the case may be. This is what makes Robert Browning a greater poet, a poet for all ages, when compared to Tennyson, and a major poet.

What makes Browning's poetry major for all the fact that he was a poet without an audience for "a quarter of a century" after his 1840 volume "Pauline", as Martin Day shows in his "History of English Literature 1834 to the Present", was his ceaseless struggling with such sublime topics as infinity and the weight of the soul, this amphibian substance of man's life which is followed and ferreted through in all its accidents, no matter if grotesque or sublime under the game of appearances.

Like in Carlyle's "Sartor Resartus", Browning's grotesque characters begin the same main subject of the soul, albeit from the lowest level of the philosophy of appearances, i.e., of satire dressed up in the burlesque, carnivalesque garb of satire or "the philosophy of clothes". It can be stated that Browning starts from the margin in order to talk of the centre, by faithfully cataloguing each, and every, and all the *material movements* of this fabulous creature, the human soul...Browning makes the nice distinctions that render fully human even the last, most distorted, most grotesque human being.

Thus, in the publicly reproachable character of Fra Lippo Lippi, Browning embodies the strongest defensible hedonism by offering it the chance of getting directly connected to the ideal, "the best thing God invents":

Can't I take breath and try to add life's flash,
And then add soul and heighten them threefold?
Or say there's beauty with no soul at all –
(I never saw it – put the case the same-)
If you get simple beauty and nought else,
You get about the best thing God invents:
That's somewhat: and you'll find the soul you have missed,
Within yourself, when you return him thanks. (lines 213 – 219)

These are followed by a frontal declaration of faith in, and love of, life which is not equalled by any but the devotional poet's love of God and His nature, as can be seen in Hopkins's poetry.

And all this is complete with a protagonist for this declaration made on a stage and by means of the trick of rendering concrete and particular as a fictive character's voice one of Browning's own ideas:

And my whole soul revolves, the cup runs over,
The world and life's too big to pass for a dream,
And I do these wild things in sheer despite,
And play the fooleries you catch me at,
In pure rage! The old mill-horse, out at grass
After hard years, throws up his stiff heels so,
Although the milller does not preach to him
The only good of grass is to make chaff.
What would men have? Do they like grass or no –
May they or mayn't they? All I want's the thing
Settled for ever one way. As it is,
You tell too many lies and hurt yourself:
You don't like what you only like too much,
You do like what, if given you at your word,
You find abundantly detestable.
For me, I think I speak as I was taught;
I always see the garden and God there
A-making man's wife: and, my lesson learned,
The value and significance of flesh,
I can't unlearn ten minutes afterwards. (lines 250 – 269)

Once hedonism, "the value and significance of flesh" makes the man of sensibility grasp "the thing/ Settled for ever one way", "he can't unlearn [it] ten minutes afterwards". And through the methodical practice of intense living and thinking, this illuminated man who, archetypally speaking, has rediscovered the garden of Eden (and he is articulate about it being one among the professional Bible readers in a cloister), so he can "always see the garden and God there / A-making man's wife", this illuminated man, therefore, gains the right to teach a lesson back to the average man he is addressing as you who "tell too many lies and hurt yourself: / You don't like what you only like too much, / You do like what, if given you at your word, / You find abundantly detestable." This brings us to the important issue of the form and technique Browning employs in his versified plays of ideas in little. These plays are realistic and exemplary but from a distance, the distance that the stage and the plot introduce as *fiction*.

We shall now look at the devices or conventions which typically weave the gaudy fabric of Browning's allegories in the grotesque key. (Because, a play, especially a play in little, may also function as an allegory, only, it is unusual to refer to staged conflicts as allegorical. Also, the gaudiness of the fabric above-mentioned or the stridence of the speakers' voice in quite a number of poems by Browning are tokens of the grotesque.) (One more parenthetic addition is necessary here: If you wonder whether the poem just discussed was allegorical or not, you have to consider that it tells something very general too about two distinct tendencies that separate mankind into, on the one hand truth-seekers, usually artists, like Fra Lippo Lippi, like Fra Pandolf who painted the "Last Duchess" on the wall, or like Galuppi, Baldassaro! of "A Toccata of Gallupi's", also, more often than not truth tellers because enraged men, like the Duke in "My Last Duchess" or like "Childe Roland" or like the other soliloquist of "Soliloquy at the Spanish Cloister" and, on the other hand, blunderers in matters of truth, average men, who know not what they like and don't like and who stand to be chided in the same way as Fra Lippo Lippi is chiding "the silent interlocutor" who obviously represents a Victorian philistine, in Matthew Arnold's language.

And there is an ironic reversal, obviously, in the way the culprit Fra Lippo ends up teaching a more important lesson than the moral one to his interlocutor(s) who had clapped their torches to his face when they caught him, a monk, "at an alley's end / Where sportive ladies leave their doors ajar", at midnight).

BROWNING'S TECHNIQUE

At a first, descriptive level of analysis, *Browning chooses conventional situations "turned outside in", by an operation of reversal of expectations that turns the probable into the unlikely while the uncommon is provably shown to be the case in that particular circumstance.*

Thus, a deathbed scene with a bishop ordering his tomb at St. Praxed's Church in colloquy with his heirs proves his ultimately undefeatable love of life lived idiosyncratically and it gives the paradoxical sensation that death might not be parting with life but a more intense return to the core of being "human all too human" - in passion and blindness; Fra Lippo Lippi has just been shown to be ... turning the tables with his long arguments upon those who would silently accuse him of loving life more than ascesis, althoug a monk.

(It is obvious how much more dramatic and fit for the alert rhythm of drama Shakespeare's writing of Antony's funeral oration is as compared to Browning's dramatic monolgues which are *so very* long, and endowed with a dramatism of pure sentiments, not with the alert dramatism of genuine drama). Returning to the first characteristic... "trick" that Browning performs, another example is the Duke of Ferrara, an art collector, a connaisseur, who begins by praising to a visitor a beautiful portrait but proves to be a scandalously jealous villain, a murderer of the lowest order.

More often than not, it is friars, monks, bishops, childes (well-born youths, candidates for knighthood) or sublime lovers, in a word - elevated people who are expected to rise above the average rascal that Browning shows to be possessed actually by what would function as worldly furies when regarded from the conventional perspective of respectability and from the standpoint of the majority. But with Browning, the favourite device is to work with *richly ironic substitutions* of perspective and of roles made possible by novel combinations of lenses, mirrors, mirages, odd impersonations and masks which, Browning believes, alone can *give the unique value of the individual's mind and give it precedence over everything else.*

Figuratively speaking, Browning builds amazing word labyrinths and idiosyncratic pleasure domes threatening to baroquely turn at any time into scaffolding or scenes for demonstrating or exhibiting the power of *the one* (one mind, one soul, one imagination, will or passion) against *the many who, as Carlyle would indict them in "Signs of the Times", are organised into conventionally powerful flocks.*

All this amounts to the statement that Browning masterfully uses the technique of the dramatic monologue by which an essentially philosophical, general statement held as a personal idea by the poet is presented in action by a staged conflict between concrete people, "men and women" (cf the title of Browning's 1855 collection of poems). Although this dramatic presentation of a life situation is accompanied by gestures and a contextual frame clearly recoverable from the mentioned settings, from the inherently dissonant music of the text working itself as a background, as in genuine drama, this felt representation of life is not fully dramatic, because the general dynamics of a whole dramatic score is missing.

Instead, the dramatic monologue is just an updating in the 19th century of the classical figuration device of the prosopopoeia, whose major convention enables the poet to speak from behind the mask. Comparable to the intellectual literary species of the epistle, the prosopopoeia or dramatic monologue gives voice (in a kind of extended personification that gives voice to objects or animals) to people from past ages or other exotic spaces; also, in the Victorian age poetry, the voice is an introspective one, with Browning in particular speaking, as it were, directly from the viscerae and man's vital centre (conventionally speaking, the inmost soul) rather than, as the epistle does, from man's mere mind.

This enables the poet to voice profounder thoughts, more secret impulses than the ones normally observable during genuine conversations; the dramatic monologue therefore, is a kind of enhanced conversation, whose polyphonically confessive impact comes from presenting the communication between people, just like in fiction when the device of a dramatised narrator introduces a form of dramatic tension in every ordinary sequence of speech acts. And the difficulty of understanding Browning's dramatic monologues lies in the effort of understanding what the real circumstances of the ground situation are while the speaker only describes them subjectively. Linguistically speaking, the dramatic monologue apparently confronts the reader with straight utterances, which are actually richly connotative ones, and the reading task for the person who wants to find his or her way in this labyrinth or echo-chamber created by the richness of the interwoven connotations has only one chance: that of making a kind of propositional calculus by concentrating upon the situational presuppositions recoverable from the surface text.

But even the surface text poses problems to the lay reader of dramatic monologues. The surface text itself is conceived as a kind of stenogram of live conversation, with the poet-stenographer madly crowding the page with idiomatic, elliptical traces of speech acts as they can be caught/sampled in moments of broken psychological climax.

Browning's poetry in particular amounts to a kind of stream-of-dramatised-consciousness which is as spectacular as the stream of consciousness experiments of Joyce or Woolf or Faulkner, only, the Victorian dramatic monologues are perhaps even more difficult to decode as the phenomenon of speech is caught (like Hopkins's " dapple-dawn drawn morning minion" of "The Windhover") in overwrought verses using archaisms and set phrases meant to evoke not the objective ... "every-time" of the human psychological duration but the atmosphere of the Renaissance or the monastic Middle Ages situations which form the ground contexts of a Browning poem; or even the mythical atmosphere of the Greek legend, as in Tennyson's dramatic monologues "Ulysses" or "Tithonus"; and also the passage from what Matthew Arnold called Hellenism to Hebraism, as in Swinburne's poem "Hymn to Proserpine".

In the Victorian dramatic monologue another figure is superimposed on the already dramatic convention of the prosopopoeia : consciousness itself is only a mask for the unconscious and the stream, therefore, is a less technically mimetic stream- of- consciousness rather, as critics have already used the term when they wanted to characterise James' Joyce's "Finnegan's Wake": what we get is a disguised "...stream of unconsciousness".

The dramatic technique supplies in the Victorian dramatic monologue what the 20th century spectacularly experimental techniques will supply for catching the mystique of word and thought forming. From this point of view, the dramatic monologues written by Browning are *more sophisticated literary forms than the 20th century stream of consciousness novels* in so far as they, Browning's dramatic monologues, *capture the mystique of JUDGMENT forming,* which mystical experience is the privilege of the attentive members of the drama audience only.

If we can agree that the contemplation of judgment-forming is a more satisfactory form of literary contemplation, this will allow us to make a bold statement representing a pro domo suo' argument in favour of the ... superiority of certain sections of Victorian literature which almost nobody of the wider cultivated public still reads today, as compared to the fashionable literature for the educated elites of the 20th century. The bold statement goes as follows: it seems that *dramatism is a more profoundly writerly privilege than the programmatical privilege of so much modernist and high-modernist avantgarde writerly literature* (as Roland Barthes would describe it, cf. his "S/Z"), a privilege that the dramatic monologue enjoys over the ultimately *rawer prose* of the modernist experimenters, for example, whose surface prose is more sophisticated, but (especially in Virginia Woolf's prose), whose thoughts can be after all cruder, being mere recordings of human sensibility in action.

But, again, figuratively speaking, the ticket which the reader needs in order to "buy" his access to a Browningesque dramatic feast is represented by a reading competence superior to the mere technicalities of the writer-like competence which Roland Barthes designates by his terms "writerly literature". The reader of Browning's dramatic monologues, like the "wedding guest", at the beginning of Coleridge's "Rhyme of the Ancient Mariner", should let her-/ himself get contaminated first with Browning's relishing and cherishing of (Renaissance) art and of alienistic psychology. (cf. Ekbert Faas: "Retreat into the Mind: Victorian Poetry and the Rise of

Psychiatry", another book that got lost in the 1990s, this time not from the British Council but from the Teachers' Library of the English Department). With this proviso, any reader can freely begin to enjoy the stylistically (i.e., rhetorically) sophisticated and astute dramatic monologues.

After irony with the device of the prosopopoeia as its rhetorical form of expression, Browning's poetry challenges its audiences with the fictionalization of the ethical judgments which are set in older civilization contexts, in a sort of low-mimetic allegory or parable of man in general. We can wonder if what we find here again is a case of Victorian escapism, as that inaugurated by the late Romantic Carlyle's return to the ideal Middle Ages.

Were it not for the underlying intention of addressing psychological or cultural essentials in poetry, as demonstrated for the case of the poem "By the Fireside", we might answer in the affirmative. But, as it is, Browning's transpositions of cultural and philosophical debates that we also encounter in the essays or in George Eliot's "Middlemarch" make us rather see his poems as *thematizations of centrally Victorian ethical or existential issues, therefore exactly the opposite to any form of utopian or romance-mode escapism*. But this is also telling for the kind of acrobacies that realism or direct lyricism required from Victorian poets before they were allowed to address their audience bluntly.

Actually, Browning himself had to pay a big price for his choices in matter of subject and sophistication in verse: nobody read him in Victorian England for what Martin Day (loc. cit) called "a quarter of a century after 1840". The other outspoken Victorian poet who was not known - ever - by the wide Victorian public, Gerard Manley Hopkins chose silence too, from the beginning, together with sophistication in form and devotional sentiment as his poetic key.

Thus, the theme of Browning's dramatic poetry is confrontation - achieved through a game of eloquent masks, a confrontation between the individual and the tribe, and this amounts to two things: first, it works against the grain of the Victorian gregarious ideology, namely, it goes against the grain of the self-assured, utopian self-complacency of the Victorians who liked to imagine that ideological consensus also pointed to universal harmony; secondly, Browning's re-enactment of the conflict between, on the one hand, *conventional opinion* or *hypocrisy* (as, for example, the hypocrisy of the prior and his suite in Fra Lippo Lippi's Carmelite convent) and, on the other hand, *the impassioned loquacity of the "agonists" confronting the implied "chorus"* was meant for the benefit of Browning's contemporaries.

The dramatic monologues served as imaginative illustrations of some ideas understood and shared by the more advanced Victorian intellectuals. The underlying more enlightened opinion explains why the precise confrontation or opposition is not easy to define for Browning's poetry as a whole.

Because, for all the recurrence of artists, art collectors and connaisseurs, poets, lovers, monks, bishops and priors, they are sometimes cast as "positive"strong characters, mouthpieces for Browning's own vision on life, as in "A Toccata of Galuppi's", "Fra Lippo Lippi" or "Bishop Blougram's Apology" when the poem acts as a mere allegorical history, while at other times, the same gallery of characters is cast as absurd, grotesque representations of what Jung would have called "the archetype of the shadow", and what the purely realistic fiction writer would use as his vicious villains and even (potential) criminals (as it happens in the grotesque romance of "Porphyria's Lover", in the poems "My Last Duchess" or "A Soliloquy at the Spanish Cloiser").

Consequently, it becomes quite clear that Browning is not interested in making mere realistic inventories of characters, but he is rather intrested in the cases themselves as speaking of the way in which each human being, no matter what he or she is busy doing in the poem's plot, represents an instance of "the life of the race" (cf."By the Fireside"). This brings us to the last effect of the transpositions in times and places remote from the Victorian scene.

There is in Browning's poetic sensibility a need for detachment from the linear, conventional thinking which materialises as a *clinical interest* in the species "man". (This can also be called an anthropological, scientific interest that exceeds the conventional sharing of sentiment characteristic for lyrical or for public poetry, and that could be regarded as one of the secret springs of Browning's preference for the dramatic monologue in poetry.)

As a careful clinician or lab experimenter, Browning selects the most revealing, and complex cases and experiments which he also processes by an acribious use of judicial self-defence or apology; this makes the monologuists perfectly eloquent and, sometimes, to their horror, puts the readers in a corresponding perfectly empathetic relationship of sympathy with even the most inveterate criminals.

Thus, in a second reading moment, the lucid reader (as compared to the Victorian literalists who were dismayed by Browning's poems at first) checks his own immediate reactions and censures them.

Now, this effort of adaptation that the reader's sensibility has to perform like in stage drama in order to adjust to the world again by employing reason to check on momentary feeling, or in more directly rhetorical terms, this appeal to reason in a *secundo tempo* over against the *primo tempo* appeal to emotion finally casts Browning's dramatic monologues as fictionalised deliberative kinds of discourse in which the reader is him-/herself cast as a liberal reader, capable of making the apposite momentary distinctions or the right decisions in action because he or she is prompted by reason and not by sentimental whims or by stereotypes learned by heart that condition him like a Pavlovian dog.

It is very interesting to note here that the common root of the words "deliberative" and "liberal" is at this point shown to represent a real semantic affinity. The last effect of Browning's ideologically poetic transpositions is that they reveal the affinity existing between irony, dramatism and intellectual deliberation which seem to have been summoned for a ...summit poetic meeting in Browning's dramatic monologuesa.

Although the 133 individual sections of In Memoriam

present varying stages of doubt, faith, and consolation, they are all unified by the abba stanza form. Originally, Tennyson intended to call the poem "Fragments of an Elegy," and later often referred to his work as "The Way of the Soul." The actual title, however, was suggested by Emily Sellwood, Tennyson's future wife. In Memoriam has been argued by some critics to be deeply autobiographical, while others contend that it is foremost artistic and fictional; Tennyson himself claimed that the poem is actually the voice of all humanity, and not his own.

The style and form of the emotional verse preclude conclusive identification of more than a few characters. There may also be no definitive answer to the question of genre, as its interior struggle is both highly personal and universal. The poem expresses deeply personal emotions and questions of faith, often directly resulting from the loss of Hallam. Contradictions abound, however, and with each assertion of doubt in God, Tennyson complicates the emotion by offering verses, or even single images or words, of hope and renewal.

This culminates in section 95 when the poetic voice is reunited with the spirit of Hallam through a mystical experience. Finally, while closure is never truly found, the poem ends with a sense of consolation. Loss is accepted, faith is affirmed, and the presentation of a marriage leaves the reader with a measure of hope.

Most critics agree that In Memoriam can readily be divided into four sections marked by the three Christmas celebrations following Hallam's death. The mood progresses from despair, longing, doubt, and sorrow to hope, inner-peace, and faith. The poem considers death and the stages of bereavement as the narrator experiences intense grief, nostalgia, and disconsolation, as well as the contemplation of immortality with the desire for a future reunion with the dead. The eventual outcome of this renewed faith is tempered with knowledge of scientific advancement and is necessarily compatible with it. In Memoriam seeks to represent man's journey to understand suffering, love, and his own purpose.

Criticism of In Memoriam has been rich and varied. During Tennyson's lifetime, his poem enjoyed universal acclaim. The Victorian reader shared his own spiritual doubt with the narrative voice of the poem and found solace. After Tennyson's death, his poem and his reputation alike suffered critical backlash. Many twentieth-century readers found the dramatic melancholy and the questioning of faith to be dated and naïve.

The early twentieth-century vogue for dismissing Tennyson, and likewise In Memoriam, has largely passed, and critics since the 1960s have been greatly interested in the poem. Many scholars, including K.W. Gransden, consider In Memoriam to be an elegy. Gransden finds Tennyson's approach too tentative and exploratory as it seeks to adequately convey the poetic vision. Other critics have explored the influence of nineteenth-century scientific discovery on both Tennyson as a thinker and writer and on Victorian religious beliefs.

One critic, Robert Dilligan, turned to computer analysis to help unravel the syntax and prosody of In Memoriam. The vehemence with which Tennyson's poem longs for the lost Hallam has led some critics, including Christopher Craft, to examine the homoerotic underpinnings of the poem and to question whether the obvious passages of male love are simply written with a sensibility unique to its time or are indicative of a different level of comfort with homosexuality.

Likewise, analyses of the poem's linguistic structure, poetics, language, symbolism, and structure abound. In Memoriam remains an important work for critical examination as its themes of grief, doubt, loss, and longing are universal to humankind.

Chapter 16

The Charge of the Light Brigade

English poet, born at Somersby, Lincolnshire, on the 6th of August 1809. He was the fourth of the twelve children of the Rev. George Clayton Tennyson and his wife Elizabeth Fytche. The Tennysons were an old Lincoinshire family settled at Bayon's Manor. The poet's grandfather, George Tennyson, M.P., had disinherited the poet's father, who was settled hard by in the rectory of Somersby, in favor of the younger son, Charles Tennyson D'Eyncourt. The rich pastoral scenery of this part of Lincolnshire influenced the imagination of the boy, and is plainly reflected in all his early poetry, although it has now been stated with authority that the localities of his subject-poems, which had been ingeniously identified with real brooks and granges, were wholly imaginary.

At a very early age he began to write in prose and verse. At Christmas 1815 he was sent to the grammar school at Louth, his mother having kept up a connection with this typical Lincolnshire borough, of which her father, the Rev. Stephen Fytche, had been vicar.

Tennyson was at this school for five years, and then returned to Somersby to be trained by his father. In the rectory the boys had the run of an excellent library, and here the young poet based his wide knowledge of the English classics. The news of Lord Byron's death (19th April 1824) made a deep impression on him: it was a day, he said, when the whole world seemed to be darkened for me; he went out into the woods and carved "Byron is dead" upon a rock.

Tennyson was already writing copiously -- "an epic of 6000 lines" at twelve, a drama in blank verse at fourteen, and so on: these exercises have, very properly, not been printed, but the poet said of them at the close of his life, "It seems to me, I wrote them all in perfect metre."

The family was in the habit of spending the summer holidays at the coast of the county, commonly at Mablethorpe, and here Tennyson gained his impressions of the vastness of the sea. FitzGerald very justly attributed the landscape character of Tennyson's genius to the impress left on his imagination by "old Lincolnshire, where there were not only such good seas, but also such fine hill and dale among the wolds." In 1827 Frederick Tennyson, the eldest surviving brother, uniting with his younger brothers Charles and Alfred, published at Louth an anonymous collection of Poems by Two Brothers.

The two were Charles and Alfred (whose contributions predominated), and who shared the surprising profits, £20. On the 20th February 1828 Charles and Alfred matriculated at Trinity College, Cambridge, where Frederick was already a student. The poet subsequently told Edmund Gosse that his father would not let him leave Somersby until, on successive days, he had recited from memory the whole of the odes of Horace. The brothers took rooms at 12 Rose Crescent, and afterwards moved into Trumpington Street (now 157 Corpus Buildings).

They were shy, and made at first few friends; but they gradually gathered selected associates around them, and Alfred grew to be looked up to in Cambridge "as to a great poet and an elder brother" by a group which included Richard Chenevix Trench, Monckton Milnes (Lord Houghton), James Spedding, W. H. Thompson, Edward FitzGerald, W. H. Brookfield, and, above all, A. H. Hallam (1811-1833). Charles Tennyson afterwards took the additional name of Turner. He published four volumes of sonnets which have been highly praised. In June 1829 Alfred Tennyson won the Chancellors prize medal for his poem called "Timbuctoo."

With great imperfections, this study in Miltonic blank verse displays the genius of a poet, in spite of a curious obscurity both of thought and style. Here are already both richness and power, although their expression is not yet clarified by taste. But by this time Tennyson was writing lyrics of still higher promise, and, as Arthur Hallam early perceived, with an extraordinary earnestness in the worship of beauty. The results of this enthusiasm and this labor of the artist appeared in the volume of Poems, chiefly Lyrical, published in 1830.

This book would have been astonishing as the production of a youth of twenty-one, even if, since the death of Byron six years before, there had not been a singular dearth of good poetry in England. Here at least, in the slender volume of 1830, was a new writer revealed, and in "Mariana", "The Poet", "Love and Death", and "Oriana", a singer of wonderful though still unchastened melody. Through these, and through less perfect examples, was exhibited an amazing magnificence of fancy, at present insufficiently under control, and a voluptuous pomp of imagery, tending to an over-sweetness.

The veteran Samuel Taylor Coleridge, praising the genius in the book, blamed the metrical imperfection of it. For this criticism he has himself constantly been reproved, and Tennyson (whose impatience of anything like censure was phenomenal) continued to resent it to the end of his life. Yet Coleridge was perfectly just in his remark; and the metrical anarchy of the "Madelines" and "Adelines" of the 1830 volume showed that Tennyson, with all his delicacy of modulation, had not yet mastered the arts of verse.

In the summer of 1830 Tennyson and Hallam volunteered in the army of the Spanish insurgent Torrijos, and marched about a little in the Pyrenees, without meeting with an enemy. He came back to find his father ailing, and in February 1831 he left Cambridge for Somersby, where a few days later Dr. George Tennyson died. The new incumbent was willing that the Tennysons should continue to live in the rectory, which they did not leave until six years later.

Arthur Hallam was now betrothed to Emily Tennyson (afterwards Mrs. Jesse, 1811-1889), and stayed frequently at Somersby. This was a very happy time, and one of great physical development on Alfred's part. He took his share in all kinds of athletic exercises, and it was now that Brookfleld said, "It is not fair that you should be Hercules as well as Apollo." This high physical zest in life seems to have declined after 1831, when his eyes began to trouble him, and he became liable to depression. The poetical work of these three years, mainly spent at Somersby, was given to the world in the volume of Poems which (dated 1833) appeared at the end of 1832.

This was certainly one of the most astonishing revelations of finished genius ever produced by a young man of less than twenty-four. Here were to be read "The Lady of Shalott", "The Dream of Fair Women", "Oenone", "The Lotos-Eaters", "The Palace of Art", and "The Miller's Daughter", with a score of other lyrics, delicious and divine. The advance in craftsmanship and command over the materiel of verse shown since the volume of 1830 is absolutely astounding.

If Tennyson had died of the savage article which presently appeared in the Quarterly Review, literature would have sustained terrible losses, but his name would have lived forever among those of the great English poets. Indeed, it may be doubted whether, in several directions, he ever surpassed the glorious things to be found in this most exquisite and most precious book. It was well that its publication was completed before the blow fell upon Tennyson which took for a while all the light out of him. In August 1833 Arthur Hallam started with his father, the great historian, for Tirol.

They went no farther than Vienna, where Hallam, returning to the hotel on the 15th of September 1833, found his son lying dead on a sofa: a blood-vessel had broken in his brain. His body was brought back to England, and buried at Clevedon on the 3rd of January 1834. These events affected Tennyson extremely. He grew less than ever willing to come forward and face the world; his health became "variable and his spirits indifferent."

The earliest effect of Hallam's death upon his friend's art was the composition, in the summer of 1834, of The Two Voices; and to the same period belong the beginnings of the Idylls of the King and of In Memoriam, over both of which he meditated long. In 1835 he visited the Lakes, and saw much of Hartley Coleridge, but would not "obtrude on the great man at Rydal", although "Wordsworth was hospitably disposed." Careless alike of fame and of influence, Tennyson spent these years mainly at Somersby, in a uniform devotion of his whole soul to the art of poetry.

In 1837, to their great distress, the Tennysons were turned out of the Lincolnshire rectory where they had lived so long. They moved to High Beech, in Epping Forest, which was their home until 1840. The poet was already engaged, or "quasi-betrothed", to Emily Sellwood, but ten years more had to pass before they could afford to marry. At Torquay, in 1838, he wrote Audley Court on one of his rare excursions, for he had no money for touring, nor did he wish for change: he wrote at this time, "I require quiet, and myself to myself, more than any man when I write."

In 1840 the Tennysons moved to Tunbridge Wells, and a year later to Boxley, near Maidstone, to be close to Edmund Lushington, who had now married Cecilia Tennyson. Alfred was from this time more and more frequently a visitor in London.

In 1842 the two-volume edition of his Poems broke the ten years' silence which he had enforced himself to keep. Here, with many pieces already known to all lovers of modern verse, were found rich and copious additions to his work. These he had originally intended to publish alone, and an earlier privately printed Morte d'Arthur, Dora, and other Idylls, of 1842, is the despair of book-collectors.

Most of those studies of home-life in England, which formed so highly popular a section of Tennyson's work -- such as "The Gardener's Daughter", "Walking to the Mail", and "The Lord of Burleigh" -- were now first issued, and, in what we have grown to consider a much higher order, "Locksley Hall", "Ulysses", and "Sir Galahad."

To the older and more luxurious lyrics, as reprinted in 1842, Tennyson did not spare the curbing and pruning hand, and in some cases went too far in restraining the wanton spirit of beauty in its youthful impulse. It is from 1842 that the universal fame of Tennyson must be dated; from the time of the publication of the two volumes he ceased to be a curiosity, or the darling of an advanced clique, and took his place as the leading poet of his age in England. Among the friends whom he now made, or for the first time cultivated, were Thomas Carlyle, Rogers, Charles Dickens, and Elizabeth Barrett Browning.

Material difficulties now, however, for the first time intruded on his path. He became the victim of a certain "earnest-frothy" speculator, who induced him to sell his little Lincolnshire estate at Grasby, and to invest the proceeds, with all his other money, and part of that of his brothers and sisters, in a "Patent Decorative Carving Company": in a few months the whole scheme collapsed, and Tennyson was left penniless. He was attacked by so overwhelming a hypochondria that his life was despaired of, and he was placed for some time under the charge of a hydropathic physician at Cheltenham, where absolute rest and isolation gradually brought him around to health again.

The state of utter indigence to which Tennyson was reduced, greatly exercised his friends, and in September 1845, at the suggestion of Henry Hallam, Sir Robert Peel was induced to bestow on the poet a pension of £200 a year. Never was public money expended in a more patriotic fashion. Tennyson's health slowly became restored, and in 1846 he was hard at work on The Princess; in the autunn of this year he took a tour in Switzerland, and saw great mountains and such "stateliest bits of landskip" for the first time.

In 1847 nervous prostration again obliged him to undergo treatment at Prestbury: "They tell me not to read, not to think; but they might as well tell me not to live." Dr. Gully's water-cure was tried, with success. The Princess was now published, in a form afterwards considerably modified and added to. Carlyle and FitzGerald "gave up all hopes of him after The Princess", or pretended that they did.

It was true that the bent of his genius was slightly altered, in a direction which seemed less purely and austerely that of the highest art; but his concessions to public taste vastly added to the width of the circle he now addressed. The home of the Tennysons was now at Cheltenham: on his occasional visits to London he was in the habit of seeing William Makepeace Thackeray, Coventry Patmore, Robert Browning and William Charles Macready, as well as older friends, but he avoided "society."

In 1848, while making a tour in Cornwall, Tennyson met Robert Stephen Hawker of Morwenstow, with whom he seems -- but the evidence is uncertain -- to have talked about King Arthur, and to have resumed his intention of writing an epic on that theme. In his absent-minded way Tennyson was very apt to mislay objects; in earlier life he had lost the manuscript of Poems, chiefly Lyrical, and had been obliged to restore the whole from scraps and memory.

Now a worse thing befell him, for in February 1850, having collected into one "long ledger-like book" all the elegies on Arthur Hallam which he had been composing at intervals since 1833, he left this only manuscript in the cupboard of some lodgings in Mornington Place, Hampstead Road. By extraordinary good chance it had been overlooked by the landlady, and Coventry Patmore was able to recover it.

In this way In Memoriam was dragged back from the very verge of destruction, and could be published, in its original anonymous form, in May 1850. The public was at first greatly mystified by the nature and object of this poem, which was not merely a chronicle of Tennyson's emotions under bereavement, nor even a statement of his philosophical and religious beliefs, but, as he long afterwards explained, a sort of Divina Commedia, ending with happiness in the marriage of his youngest sister, Cecilia Lushington.

In fact, the great blemishes of In Memoriam, its redundancy and the dislocation of its parts, were largely due to the desultory manner of its composition. The poet wrote the sections as they occurred to him, and did not think of weaving them together into a single poem until it was too late to give them real coherency. The metre, which by a curious naïveté Tennyson long believed that he had invented, served by its happy peculiarity to bind the sections together, and even to give an illusion of connected movement to the thought. The sale of Tennyson's poems now made it safe for him to settle, and on the 13th of June 1850 he was married at Shiplake to Emily Sarah Sellwood. Of this union no more need be said than was recorded long afterwards by the poet himself, "The peace of God came into my life before the altar when I wedded her." Every species of good fortune was now to descend on the path of the man who had struggled against bad luck so long. William Wordsworth died, and on the 19th of November 1850 Queen Victoria appointed Tennyson poet laureate.

The salary connected with the post was very small, but it had a secondary value in greatly stimulating the sale of his books, which was his main source of income. The young couple took a house at Warninglid, in Sussex, which did not suit them, and then one in Montpelier Row, Twickenham, which did better. In April 1851 their first child was born dead. At this time Tennyson was brooding much upon the ancient world, and reading little but Milton, Homer and Virgil. This condition was elegantly defined by Carlyle as "sitting on a dungheap among innumerable dead dogs."

In the summer of 1851 was made the tour in Italy, of which The Daisy is the immortal record. Of 1852 the principal events were the birth of his eldest son Hallam, the second Lord Tennyson, in August, and in November the publication of the Ode on the Death of the Duke of Wellington.

In the winter of 1853 Tennyson entered into possession of a little house and farm called Farringford, near Freshwater, in the Isle of Wight, which he leased at first, and afterwards bought: this beautiful place, ringed around with ilexes and cedars, entered into his life and colored it with its delicate enchantment. In 1854 he published The Charge of the Light Brigade, and was busy composing Maud and its accompanying lyrics; and this volume was published in July 1855, just after he was made D.C.L. at Oxford: he was received on this occasion, which may be considered his first public appearance, with a "tremendous ovation."

The reception of Maud from the critics, however, was the worst trial to his equanimity which Tennyson had ever had to endure, nor had the future anything like it in store for him. He had risen in Maud far above his ordinary serenity of style, to ecstasies of passion and audacities of expression which were scarcely intelligible to his readers, and certainly not welcome.

It is odd that this irregular poem, with its copious and varied music, its splendid sweep of emotion, its unfailing richness of texture -- this poem in which Tennyson rises to heights of human sympathy and intuition which he reached nowhere else, should have been received with bitter hostility, have been styled "the dead level of prose run mad", and have been reproved more absurdly still for its "rampant and rabid bloodthirstiness of soul."

There came a reaction of taste and sense, but the delicate spirit of Tennyson had been wounded. For some years the world heard nothing from him; he was at Farringford, busying himself with the Arthurian traditions. He had now become an object of boundless personal curiosity, being already difficult to find, and the center of amusing legends. It was in 1857 that Bayard Taylor saw him, and carried away the impression of a man "tall and broad-shouldered as a son of Anak, with hair, beard and eyes of southern darkness."

This period of somewhat mysterious withdrawal from the world embraced a tour in Wales in 1857, a visit to Norway in 1858, and a journey through Portugal in 1859. In 1857 two Arthurian poems had been tentatively and privately printed, as Enid and Nimue, or the True and the False, to see how the idyllic form would be liked by the inner circle of Tennyson's friends. In the summer of 1859 the first series of Idylls of the King was at length given to the world, and achieved a popular success far beyond anything experienced before by any English poets, save perhaps Byron and Scott.

Within a month of publication, 10,000 copies had been sold. The idyls were four in number, "Enid", "Vivien" (no longer called "Nimue"), "Elaine" and "Guinevere." These were fragments of the epic of the fall of King Arthur and the Table Round which Tennyson was so long preparing, and which he can hardly be said to have ever completed, although nearly thirty years later he closed it. The public and the critics alike were entranced with the "sweetness" and the "purity" of the treatment. A few, like John Ruskin, were doubtful about "that increased quietness of style"; one or two already suspected that the "sweetness" was obtained at some sacrifice of force, and that the "purity" involved a concession to Victorian conventionality.

It was not perceived at the time that the four idyls were parts of a great historical or mystical poem, and they were welcomed as four polished studies of typical women: it must be confessed that in this light their even perfection of workmanship appeared to greater advantage than it eventually did in the general texture of the so-called "epic." In 1859 "Boadicea" was written, and "Riflemen, Form!" published in The Times. Urged by the Duke of Argyll, Tennyson now turned his attention to the theme of the Holy Grail, though he progressed with it but fitfully and slowly. In 1861 he travelled in Auvergne and the Pyrenees, with Clough, who was to die a few months later; to this year belong "Helen's Tower" and the "Dedication" of the Idylls to the prince consort, "These to his Memory."

The latter led to Tennyson's presentation in April 1862 to the queen, who "stood pale and statue-like before him, in a kind of stately innocence", which greatly moved his admiring homage. From this time forth the poet enjoyed the constant favor of the sovereign, though he could never be moulded into a conventional courtier. He now put the Arthurian legends aside for a time, and devoted himself to the composition, in 1862, of "Enoch Arden", which, however, did not appear until 1864, and then in a volume which also contained "Sea Dreams", "Aylmer's Field" and, above all, "The Northern Farmer", the first and finest of Tennyson's remarkable studies in dialect.

In April of this year Giuseppe Garibaldi visited Farringford; in February 1865 Tennyson's mother died at Hampstead in her eighty-fifth year; in the ensuing summer he travelled in Germany. The time slipped by with incidents but few and slight, Tennyson's popularity in Great Britain growing all the time to an extent unparalleled in the whole annals of English poetry. This universality of fame led to considerable practical discomfort; he was besieged by sightseers, and his nervous trepidation led him perhaps to exaggerate the intensity of the infliction.

In 1867 he determined to make for himself a haven of refuge against the invading Philistine, and bought some land on Blackdown, above Haslemere, then a secluded corner of England; here James Knowles began to build him a house, ultimately named Aldworth. This is the time of two of his rare, privately printed pamphlets, The Window; or, the Loves of the Wrens (1867), and The Victim (1868). The noble poem Lucretius, one of the greatest of Tennyson's versified monographs, appeared in May 1868, and in this year The Holy Grail was at last finished; it was published in 1869, together with three other idyls belonging to the Arthurian epic, and various miscellaneous lyrics, besides Lucretius.

The reception of this volume was cordial, but not so universally respectful as that which Tennyson had grown to expect from his adoring public. The fact was that the heightened reputation of Browning, and still more the sudden vogue of Algernon Charles Swinburne, Morris and Rossetti (period 1866-70), considerably disturbed the minds of Tennyson's most ardent readers, and exposed himself to a severer criticism than he had lately been accustomed to endure. He went on quite calmly, however, sure of his mission and of his music.

His next volume (1872), Gareth and Lynette and The Last Tournament, continued, and, as he then supposed, concluded The Idylls of the King, to the great satisfaction of the poet, who had found much difficulty in rounding off the last sections of the poem. Nor, as he was to find, was the poem yet completed, but for the time being he dismissed it from his mind. In 1873 he was offered a baronetcy by Gladstone, and again by Disraeli in 1874; in each case the honor was gracefully declined.

Believing that his work with the romantic Arthurian epics was concluded, Tennyson now turned his attention to a department of poetry which had long attracted him, but which he had never seriously attempted -- the drama. He put before him a scheme, which he cannot be said to have carried far, that of illustrating "the making of England" by a series of great historical tragedies. His Queen Mary, the first of these chronicle-plays was published in 1875, and played by Sir Henry Irving at the Lyceum in 1876. Although it was full of admirably dramatic writing, it was not theatrically well composed, and it failed on the stage.

Extremely pertinacious in this respect, the poet went on attempting to storm the theater, with assault upon assault, all practically failures until the seventh and last, which was unfortunately posthumous. To have really succeeded on the stage would have given Tennyson more gratification than anything else, but he was not permitted to live long enough to see this blossom also added to the heavy garland of his glory. Meanwhile Harold, a tragedy of doom, was published in 1876; but, though perhaps the finest of its author's dramas, it has never been acted.

During these years Tennyson's thoughts were largely occupied with the building of Aldworth. His few lyrics were spirited ballads of adventure, inspired by an exalted patriotism -- "The Revenge" (1878), "The Defence of Lucknow" (1879) -- but he reprinted and finally published his old suppressed poem, The Lover's Tale, and a little play of his, The Falcon, versified out of Boccaccio, was produced by the Kendals at their theater in the last days of 1879. Tennyson had reached the limits of the age 70, and it was tacitly taken for granted that he would now retire into dignified repose.

In point of fact, he now started on a new lease of poetical activity. In 1880 he published the earliest of six important collections of lyrics, this being entitled Ballads and other Poems, and containing the sombre and magnificent "Rizpah" In 1881 The Cup and in 1882 The Promise of May, two little plays, were produced without substantial success in London theaters: the second of these is perhaps the least successful of all the poet's longer writings, but its failure annoyed him unreasonably.

This determination to be a working playwright, pushed on in the face of critical hostility and popular indifference, is a very curious trait in the character of Tennyson. In September

1883 Tennyson and Gladstone set out on a voyage around the north of Scotland, to Orkney, and across the ocean to Norway and Denmark. At Copenhagen they were entertained by the king and queen, and after much fêting, returned to Gravesend: this adventure served to cheer the poet, who had been in low spirits since the death of his favorite brother Charles, and who now entered upon a phase of admirable vigor.

During the voyage Gladstone had determined to offer Tennyson a peerage. After some demur, the poet consented to accept it, but added, "For my own part, I shall regret my simple name all my life." On the 11th of March 1884 he took his seat in the House of Lords as Baron Tennyson of Aldworth and Farringford. He voted twice, but never spoke in the House. In the autumn of this year his tragedy of Becket was published, but the poet at last despaired of the stage, and disclaimed any hope of "meeting the exigencies of our modern theater."

Curiously enough, after his death Becket was the one of all his plays which enjoyed a great success on the boards. In 1885 was published another interesting miscellany, Tiresias and other Poems, with a posthumous dedication to Edward FitzGerald. In this volume, it should be noted, The Idylls of the King was completed at last by the publication of "Balin and Balan"; it contained also the superb address "To Virgil."

In April 1886 Tennyson suffered the loss of his second son, Lionel, who died in the Red Sea on his return from India. The untiring old poet was steadily writing on, and by 1886 he had another collection of lyrics ready, Locksley Hall Sixty Years After, etc.; his eyes troubled him, but his memory and his intellectual curiosity were as vivid as ever. Late in 1888 he had a dangerous attack of rheumatic gout, from which it seemed in December that he could scarcely hope to rally, but his magnificent constitution pulled him through.

He was past eighty when he published the collection of new verses entitled Demeter and other Poems (1889), which appeared almost simultaneously wilh the death of Browning, an event which left Tennyson a solitary figure indeed in poetic literature. In 1891 it was observed that he had wonderfully recovered the high spirits of youth, and even a remarkable portion of physical strength. His latest drama, The Foresters, now received his attention, and in March 1892 it was produced at New York, with Miss Ada Rehan as Maid Marian. During this year Tennyson was steadily engaged on poetical composition, finishing "Akbar's Dream", "Kapiolani" and other contents of the posthumous volume called The Death of Oenone (1892).

In the summer he took a voyage to the Channel Islands and Devonshire; and even this was not his latest excursion from home, for in July 1892 he went up for a visit to London. Soon after entering his eighty-fourth year, however, symptoms of weakness set in, and early in September his condition began to give alarm. He retained his intellectual lucidity and an absolute command of his faculties to the last, reading Shakespeare with obvious appreciation until within a few hours of his death.

With the splendor of the full moon falling upon him, his hand clasping his Shakespeare, and looking, as we are told, almost unearthly in the majestic beauty of his old age, Tennyson passed away at Aldworth on the night of the 6th of October 1892. Cymbeline, the play he had been reading on the last afternoon, was laid in his coffin, and on the 12th he was publicly buried with great solemnity in Westminster Abbey. Lady Tennyson survived until August 1896.

The physical appearance of Tennyson was very remarkable. Of his figure at the age of thirty-three Carlyle has left a superb portrait: "One of the finest-looking men in the world.

A great shock of rough, dusky, dark hair; bright, laughing, hazel eyes; massive aquiline face, most massive yet most delicate; of sallow brown complexion, almost Indian-looking, clothes cynically loose, free-and-easy, smokes infinite tobacco. His voice is musical, metallic, fit for loud laughter and piercing wail, and all that may lie between; speech and speculation free and plenteous; I do not meet in these late decades such company over a pipe."

He was unusually tall, and possessed in advanced years a strange and rather terrifying air of sombre majesty. But he was, in fact, of a great simplicity in temperament, affectionate, shy, still exquisitely sensitive in extreme old age to the influences of beauty, melancholy and sweetness.

Although exceedingly near-sighted, Tennyson was a very close observer of nature, and at the age of eighty his dark and glowing eyes, which were still strong, continued to permit him to enjoy the delicate features of country life around him, both at Aldworth and in the Isle of Wight. His Life, written with admirable piety and taste by his son, Hallam, second Lord Tennyson, was published in two volumes in 1897.

Chapter 17

Hang there like Fruit, My Soul, Till the Tree Die

Hallam reports his dying father as trying unsuccessfully to read this passage ("which he always called the tenderest lines in Shakespeare") before uttering the sentence "I have opened it,"and then speaking "his last words, a farewell blessing, to my mother and myself." Hallam's account is understandably edited and stylized, but it was clearly an impressive scene. Dr. Dabbs was more unrestrained in drawing out those elements of the poet's passing that lent themselves to a literary apotheosis. The Laureate dies with the majesty of his own King Arthur, and grips his Shakespeare as if it were his passport to the pantheon:

On the bed a figure of breathing marble, flooded and bathed in the light of a full moon streaming through the oriel window; his hand clasping the Shakespeare which he had asked for but recently, and which he kept by him to the end; the moonlight, the majestic figure as he lay there, "drawing thicker breath," irresistibly brought to our minds his own "Passing of Arthur." (Memoir, 2:428-429)

Dabbs's account is stagey and dated, but it is the private, rather than the public, aspect of the scene that is intriguing. Specifically, what did the play, and its final scene mean to Tennyson as he approached death? It is well known that the urgency of his reiterated request for the Cymbeline distressed his family who were alarmed by his response to reading some words from it on October 3, whereupon he mid the doctor that "now he was convinced of his approaching death" (Martin, p. 581).

Turning to the end of the play, we remember Imogen, restored to Posthumous after a period when they had been lost to each other, and when, her life threatened, she had had to brave exile from her sex and her family. Disguising herself as a male, she had entered a wilderness, and all but died, undergoing an episode of death-in-life, and a form of burial, before in the miraculous way of the later plays, she reveals herself and is restored to him.

In what follows, I take this scene as providing a kind of template, a symbolic narrative, that offers a model whereby we can think about what can be called the coexistence, entwinement, and alternation, in Tennyson's imagination, of male and female personae.

Broadly, I will hazard a hypothesis that Tennyson's works, like his life and career as a whole, aspired to ultimately masculine positionings of self, but that his work was always animated by an encrypted but constitutive dimension of (what is best called) feminine sensibility that yearned, like Imogen--against hope and experience, as it were--for self-revelation or expression.

My argument will be that this unfolding of femininity manifests itself in fundamental (if intermittent and often dissimilated) ways in Tennyson's poetry, largely in so far as an individual work projects an identity with, or as, its central female figure. Of course, as an obvious case like "Mariana" makes clear, this distinction is not a simple one, but it usefully allows me to explore two related but different kinds of case which I will use to frame my argument.

In the former, as I shall describe it, romance reveals a form of entranced symbiosis where difference between the masculine hero and a female other is suspended or transcended; and in the latter, the imagining of female identity is more directly enacted or voiced, entailing a conversion of gender. In this context, we can speculate that death represented itself for Tennyson as an opening as well as an ending, a crossing of the bar, where an alienating and constricting male disguise, compulsory for survival, can be miraculously discarded, as for Imogen, whose buried self is revealed at the end of the play.

So Anthony Hecht muses over "Now sleeps the Crimson Petal," and how Tennyson's scrupulousness over words could allow him to use the pronoun "she" in the sixth line for the male peacock, though he also notes within the poem "a deliberate and conscious shift from the masculine to the feminine posture of the mind."

In terms of this discussion, a close reading could grapple with the cryptic conjurations of perspective in the lyric, and the opalescent swathes of its language, to demonstrate indeed how its exotic diction (and its cancelling of everyday logic) serves to release a waking dream of female embodiment, one in which what is male may be held or may be lost:

"Now folds the lily all her sweetness up, And slips into the bosom of the lake; So fold thyself, my dearest, thou, and slip Into my bosom, and be lost in me." (The Princess, 7. 171-174)

One could multiply critical readings that have turned over the seemingly unfathomable riddles of gender in this poem (for instance by tying it more explicitly to Princess Ida than Hecht seems to do). However, what does appear unequivocal, if uncontentious and characteristic, about this lyric for my purposes is the subordination of the masculine self who is eclipsed by the poet's need to make the text a medium for an imagined female self-expression.

If Tennyson's work is indeed riven by the tension between the alternating claims of the public masculine and the private feminine voices within the poetry, it is nonetheless the aesthetic triumph of a poem like "Now Sleeps the Crimson Petal" that its enchantments can overcome the mere double-binds and contradictions of experience. Thus, the scenario and language of the poem conspire to accommodate the simultaneous necessity and impossibility of enacting this captive, exiled, subterranean, part of the self, this immured and proscribed female element.

Clearly, too, in arguing that these two aspects of the self, male and female, are separate but in constant circulation in Tennyson's work, my account intersects with, and recapitulates, many observations made about issues of gender and sexuality within it, from the earliest comments of celebrated contemporaries (such as Bulwer, Christopher North, J. W. Croker, Manley Hopkins, Charles Kingsley, and Alfred Austin), to more recent and influential discussions (by critics such as Kate Millett, Christopher Ricks, Alan Sinfield, Carol Christ, Christopher Craft, Marjorie Stone, Marion Shaw, Catherine Maxwell, James W. Hood, and James Eli Adams).

At the same time, these discussions appear to me to be often hampered by proceeding in terms of a series of competing and ultimately inadequate vocabularies. The either/ors--of homosexuality, bisexuality, and androgyny--that have held sway in Tennyson studies are inadequate to the complexity and dynamics of a case that is better subsumed (so my argument tends) under the rubric of what we are learning to call the transgendered.

Closer to this emphasis would be Richard Cronin's remark, of the early Tennyson, that he wrote "quite uninhibitedly as a woman," though one needs to acknowledge here that Cronin rather collapses the insight by interpreting this as a career move, and so a cultural matter. For Cronin, "writing as a woman" ultimately was a strategic mode by which Tennyson responded, adapted, to the predominantly femininized values of poetry in the 1830s.

In what follows, I shall argue that it remained a central component in Tennyson's literary imagination, and evident in many major texts, even as it took often circuitous routes, and was increasingly subject, as Cronin also hints, to self-censorship and disguise.

My aim is twofold: to account in plausible ways for a key dynamic that underlies the distinctive aesthetic values and modes of individuation, even temporality, operative in Tennyson's work, and to offer a heuristic contention that removes many of the creases, dead-ends, and shortcomings that bedevil critical discussions of gender and sexuality within it.

I

Much, then, in Tennyson criticism needs to be acknowledged, but also reinflected, in so far as it anticipates, or just stops short, of the case being made here. Alan Sinfield, one of Tennyson's subtlest and most probing critics, cites the notorious reviews of In Memoriam--the declaration that "these touching lines evidently come from the full heart of the widow of a military man," and the Times reviewer (in this case mindful of Tennyson's authorship), who commented on the verses.

Books by Kathryn Ledbetter and Kirstie Blair form the most notable contributions to Tennyson studies in 2006. In Tennyson and Victorian Periodicals: Commodities in Context (Ashgate, 2007 [released December 2006]), Kathryn Ledbetter examines sixty-two poems authorized by Tennyson to appear in thirty-two periodicals. Ledbetter not only takes up material ignored in earlier publishing histories by Edgar Shannon (Tennyson and the Reviewers, 1952) and June Steffenson Hagen (Tennyson and His Publishers, 1979) but also revises some well-established reference points in Tennyson studies.

As her chapter on Tennyson's contributions to literary annuals demonstrates, his "Ten-Years' Silence" was not so silent after all. Instead Tennyson followed the practice common to William Makepeace Thackeray, Charles Dickens, and others of speaking slightingly of annuals in letters or conversation while seeking berths as contributors. If several of Tennyson's contributions ("O that 'twere possible," "Come not, when I am dead," "St. Agnes' Eve") resulted from his network of well-connected friends such as Arthur Henry Hallam, whose work on Tennyson's behalf Ledbetter compares to that of a literary agent, Ledbetter also persuasively argues that his appearance in widely read annuals brought Tennyson useful notice from reviewers at the outset of his career and helped him hone a feminine aesthetic that characterizes much of his early verse.

Ledbetter makes extensive use of Tennyson's letters and publishing records to track his engagement with serial publications over his entire career. Tennyson's collected correspondence has been available since 1990, but the clear evidence of Tennyson's immersion in periodicals has remained largely invisible until Ledbetter originated the idea to look for it.

Tennyson's vaunted hatred of all publicity and high conception of art give way in Ledbetter's study to a far more nuanced view of a poet who was quite savvy about strategically adopting periodical publication and who read widely in contemporary newspapers and magazines. In the chapter on Tennyson's political poetry, for example, Ledbetter retraces the news reports on which Tennyson drew to show how deliberately he wove contemporary references into poems.

Above all, she demonstrates his knowingness about his celebrity and the stature of his poetry, which was already "branded" (to use Gerhard Joseph's term in "Commodifying Tennyson: The Historical Transformation of 'Brand Loyalty,'" VP 34, no. 2 [1996]) in periodicals at mid-century.

Emily Tennyson, incidentally, comes off less well: she insisted that Tennyson stay aloof from periodicals--a directive he honored in the breach--to avoid the taint of commercialism while reasoning that he could obtain higher profits through book contracts.

Tennyson could be virtually assured of placing his poems in periodicals whenever he cared to, since his poems augmented sales and a periodical's prestige.

Chapter 18

Performing "The Solitary Reaper" and "Tears, Idle Tears"

In the years since Susan Sontag's "Against Interpretation" (1964) and Roland Barthes's Le Plaisir du texte (1973), there have been numerous attempts to distinguish between interpretative/hermeneutic models of literary criticism and other models. In some cases, the alternative model has been performative. Helen Vendler, for example, drew on Barthes's work in arguing that interpretative and aesthetic models were "radically incompatible."

Practitioners of the former look "for meaning, import, philosophy, social truth; [they] remind us of the links between literature and its social and philosophical milieu." It is from this model, "with its persistent allegorizing tendency, that the vulgar notion of there being a `hidden meaning' in literature has arisen."

Aesthetic critics, on the other hand, remind one "of the links between literature and the other expressive arts--music, painting, and sculpture." They offer explication rather than interpretation; their "analysis is, so to speak, admiration methodized." They are interpreters not in the exegetical sense, but rather "as a pianist or a conductor is an interpreter, holding up the work in a new and coherent manifestation." Their analysis is "terminable rather than interminable, as every performance of a musical work implies final choices of emphasis and color."

Since critics of both sorts "are always with us, though

under different names," Vendler's distinction has a general usefulness. But her account is too simplified to be helpful in more than a rudimentary way. For one thing, the analogy between a literary and a musical artwork is not well grounded.

Vendler could, for example, have made use of Barbara Herrnstein Smith's reflections on Nelson Goodman's Languages of Art, which led her to formulate a distinction between literary works that are "representations of inscribed discourse" and thus "constituted by their own texts," and those (for example, lyric poems) which, "as representations of spoken discourse, bear [a] special relation to their own texts... that is, the relation between a performable work and its score."

Moreover, the medium of literature is words, not simply sounds, and while Vendler's two models might be logically distinct, it is hard to think of them as empirically distinct. Any aesthetic rendering of a literary artwork will involve choices and emphases closely similar to, even if not coterminous with, interpretative operations.

And if aesthetic pleasure can arise from appreciation of the manner in which "the cognitive content, moral import or political message" of literary work is "embodied in or communicated by the work's specific elements and organization," such appreciation will presuppose at least some degree of interpretative inquiry.

A more nuanced distinction between interpretative models of criticism and other models has been attempted by Paisley Livingston, who contrasts two "broad kinds of question": (a) "What does a particular text mean?"; and (b) "What are the consequences of an utterance in the context of the interaction in which it occurs?"

The former is "an indeterminate question, whereas the latter is determinate relative to the specifications of context, agents, and so forth." Since the specific determinants that Livingston has in mind are "concrete interactional systems requir[ing] a reliable knowledge of the social history in question," it might seem that, from Vendler's point of view, his two questions simply discriminate between interpretative emphases.

But when the literary artwork in question is a lyric poem, it could be argued that the primary interactive context is interpersonal, between speaker and listener, and that the "utterance" is the latter's performance of the work.

This suggestion, however, need not involve the disregard of the "social history in question" or of other contextual factors. One way of showing this would be to pursue the analogy between the performance of a lyric poem and that of a musical work. Stephen Davies, for example, has described the "thicker characterization" of the ontology of the latter (the characterization that allows one to say that the work is created rather than discovered) "as necessarily including a performance-means and as necessarily being indexed to a person, time and place." And he has insisted that an authentic performance of a musical work (as opposed to "improvising or fantasising on that work") must respect these properties.

In reflecting on these matters, it is useful to consider particular poems. When one does so, the "criterion of... validity" of a critical model "becomes the profitability of what it proves capable of doing." I propose to consider two of the best-known nineteenth-century lyric poems in English-Wordsworth's "The Solitary Reaper" and Tennyson's "Tears, idle tears."

The subject of the former is its speaker's reception of a song that is sung in a language he does not understand. The latter was first published in Tennyson's narrative poem The Princess, where it is presented as a song sung by a young woman to the accompaniment of a harp. My discussions, which include a consideration of the genesis of each poem, will suggest that while interpretative analysis (as of any artwork composed of words) is always possible, an aesthetic rendering may more satisfactorily account for and integrate the essential features of a poem, including those pointed up by that analysis.

I shall also suggest that the difference between a hermeneutic critical model and an aesthetic one is analogous to the difference between reading a lyric poem with the eyes only and listening to it or performing it.

1

The Solitary Reaper
Behold her, single in the field,
Yon solitary Highland Lass!
Reaping and singing by herself;
Stop here, or gently pass!
Alone she cuts and binds the grain,
And sings a melancholy strain;
O listen! for the Vale profound
Is overflowing with the sound.
No Nightingale did ever chaunt
More welcome notes to weary bands
Of travellers in some shady haunt,
Among Arabian sands:
A voice so thrilling ne'er was heard
In spring-time from the Cuckoo-bird,
Breaking the silence of the seas
Among the farthest Hebrides.

Will no one tell me what she sings?--Perhaps the plaintive numbers flow

For old, unhappy, far-off things,
And battles long ago:
Or is it some more humble lay,
Familiar matter of to-day?
Some natural sorrow, loss, or pain,
That has been, and may be again?
Whate'er the theme, the Maiden sang
As if her song could have no ending;
I saw her singing at her work,
And o'er the sickle bending:--I
listened, motionless and still;
And, as I mounted up the hill,
The music in my heart I bore,
Long after it was heard no more.

On 7 November 1805, Dorothy Wordsworth wrote to a correspondent from Patterdale in the Lake District, enclosing a transcription of a poem that her brother William had written two days before. She explained that "The Solitary Reaper" had been "suggested by a very beautiful passage in a Journal of a Tour among the Highlands, by Thomas Wilkinson."

On the poem's first publication two years later, Wordsworth gave the same explanation in a note, adding that its last line was taken verbatim from Wilkinson. The source passage reads as follows: "Passed by a Female who was reaping alone, she sung in Erse [Highland Gaelic] as she bended over her sickle, the sweetest human voice I ever heard. Her strains were tenderly melancholy, and felt delicious long after they were heard no more."

William and Dorothy had toured the Highlands of Scotland two years previously, and Stephen Gill is no doubt correct in saying that if Wordsworth had not himself "seen isolated figures set against the immensity of the Highland landscape the poem would not have been written."

But Gill does not speculate on why this particular passage had such an impact on the poet. In the poem's opening stanza, the reaper's isolation is repeatedly emphasized ("solitary," "single," "by herself," "alone"), an auditor is directly addressed, and his/her attention insistently drawn to this figure ("Behold her," "Stop here," "Listen").

At first sight, this might suggest that the particular attraction of the Wilkinson passage was owing to Wordsworth's longstanding interest in pathetic subjects and their focalization. But there is a crucial difference between "The Solitary Reaper" and such poems as "The Ruined Cottage" and "The Thorn," which also center on solitary females in particularized natural settings and have narrators who directly address an auditor.

These poems are calculated mixtures of lyrical and narrative elements; but there is little of the latter element in "The Solitary Reaper." And since the speaker does not know the language in which the maiden is singing, he cannot apprehend the "theme" of her song, cannot determine what story, if any, it tells.

I suggest that Wordsworth's attraction to the Wilkinson passage may have been owing not to the pathetic subject per se, but rather to a related and equally longstanding preoccupation with the "effect... always produced in pathetic and impassioned poetry": i.e., the way in which "the music of harmonious metrical language" tempers "the painful feeling always found intermingled with powerful descriptions of the deeper passions" and "imperceptibly contribute[s]" to "a complex feeling of delight" in the listener/reader.

In any event, both the provenance of "The Solitary Reaper" and its opening imperatives call attention to a distinctive feature of the poem. It contains two overlapping relationships: that between the reaper's song and the poem's speaker; and that between the speaker's utterance and the poem's addressee.

Despite the difficulties posed by the reaper's use of an unknown language, there are several important indications of the song's character. Let us begin by considering the last two lines of the opening stanza, in the sound of which Dorothy Wordsworth found "something inexpressively soothing to me": "O listen for the vale profound/ Is overflowing with the sound."

Profound: deep, inclusive, solemn. The syntactical reference is to the Highland valley; but the word can refer to both objective and subjective states, and to the ear "profound" modifies its rhyming word, "sound," as much as it does "vale." What is profound, then, is the setting as filled with the melancholy singing of the maiden. Overflowing: outgoing, copious, fluid, reverberating, ramifying, expanding, resonant. This quality is intimated verbally by the poem's repetitions: "solitary"/"single"/"by herself"/"alone"; "old"/ "far-off"/"long ago;"/"Sorrow"/"loss"/"pain"; "motionless"/"still."

And it is enacted by the expanding, rippling outward effect of what Geoffrey Hartman called the poem's "fluidifying doublings": reaping and singing; cutting and binding; stopping or passing; things and battles; perhaps... or; has been... may be again.

In addition, as Hartman also pointed out, the overflowing quality of the song is intimated by the dynamics of the stanza form: the fourth line of each stanza is a foot shorter than the other lines; this slight contraction leads to a sense of expansion or flowing outward in the following rhyming tetrameter lines.

This feature of the stanza form is particularly noticeable in the second and third stanzas, the former of which uses two striking images to suggest the qualitative impact of the reaper's singing. There is a pedagogic old chestnut concerning this stanza. I quote from Brooks and Warren's Understanding Poetry:

If we omit the second stanza, we are given an account of the situation and of the effect of the girl's song upon the traveler. What, then, would be lost--if anything--had the poet decided to cancel the second stanza?

Consider as carefully as you can the meaning of the girlbird comparison. In what specific ways does the song of the girl resemble the song of the birds? Is the poet simply suggesting that the girl's song is beautiful? Or is he defining a special quality and significance for the traveler who overhears it?

Clearly, the speaker is attempting to express the complex effect the song is having on him. The song is a "melancholy strain" sung by an isolated figure doing back-breaking agricultural labor in a stark, inhospitable natural setting, which is understandably likened to a desert or to northern seas in winter. And yet (a paradox) the plaintive song in a foreign tongue refreshes and renews; it is like the song of a nightingale or a cuckoo; by metonymy, it is like an oasis to desert travellers; or like the arrival of spring in northern islands.

The opposites further suggest the elemental inclusiveness of the song: an oasis offers coolness in the midst of heat; the harbinger of spring brings the promise of warmth in the midst of cold. The particulars, like the reaping, are emblems of the basic necessities of human life: grain (food) to satisfy hunger; water to satisfy thirst and to cool; spring to bring warmth and allow for germination.

Another feature of the stanza is its geographical range: the song overflows the Highland vale and moves outward to the tip of northern Europe at one end and to the Orient (the Middle East) at the other. Of course, this doesn't happen literally; it happens figuratively. What is being figured or suggested? One answer would be the universality of the melancholy strain--of what in "Tintern Abbey" is called "the still, sad music of humanity."

A better answer--better because the effect of the song on a particular listener in a particular place is re-emphasized--is that extensiveness in space is a poetic transformation of intensiveness in feeling. In this implicit metaphor, distance is the vehicle, subjective profundity or intensity is the tenor.

In the third stanza the song continues to expand--this time temporally rather than spatially. The movement is from "long ago" to "to-day," from the catastrophic national sorrows of the always defeated Highland Scots to the ordinary ("natural") sorrows of an individual person's life. Three questions are asked in the stanza; none is answered because what they want to know is inessential.

The questions are a pretext for the foregrounding of loss and suffering as the abiding conditions of human existence. This realization seems encapsulated in the strong rhyme of the stanza's closing couplet: "pain"/ "again." Syntactically, loss and suffering have been in the past and may be again in the future; but the resonating rhyme intimates not possibility but inevitability.

The poem distracts one's attention with what turn out to be unanswerable questions about the song's content, while at the same time suggesting that this content is as unimportant as it is local, particular, and transient. But while the song cannot be understood, it can be deeply affecting. The urgent questions are themselves an indication of this in that the speaker would have no desire to know the song's content had he not been moved by its formal effects.

Whatever its particular subject, then, the "plaintive" quality of the song seems expressive of the universality of "passions and thoughts and feelings [that] are the general passions and thoughts and feelings of men" and that are connected with "the operations of the elements, and the appearances of the visible universe... with cold and heat, with loss of friends and kindred."

This explication can be buttressed by examining the three substantive changes that Wordsworth later made in the text of the poem that Dorothy transcribed in November 1805: in line 10, "More welcome notes to weary bands" replaced "So sweetly to reposing bands"; in line 13, "A voice so thrilling ne'er was heard" replaced "No sweeter voice was ever heard"; and in line 29 "I listened, motionless and still" was substituted for "I listened till I had my fill." In the first two revisions, the incipiently sentimental sweetness taken over from the source passage is removed.

Wilkinson's epithets "sweetest," "tenderly melancholy," and "delicious" all carry the suggestion that the reaper's song is "a tale of pleasing woe," to use the phrase Keats applied to Byron's "sweetly sad" melody. But something rather stronger is suggested by "thrilling" and by "welcome notes" to "weary" travellers. And "till I had my fill" suggests dessert rather than deserts, quantity rather than quality, and satiety rather than the receptive intensity of "motionless and still."

Another felicity of this last revision is that it removes any indication of why or when the speaker stopped listening to the song and continued on his way. There is "literal precision" in the line "As if her song could have no ending": the song is "one of those Gaelic... chants that go on and on like the droning of a bagpipe."

But there is a figurative level as well: the suggestion of a continuation of the expanding spell of the song, the music of human suffering and endurance continuing into the future--into other vales and other times. At the same time, in the dying fall in the ing rhymes ("ending"/"bending") there is the impression that the singing is growing indistinct; and in the repetition of "sang"/"song"/"singing" there is a sense that the song is becoming detached from its temporal setting and becoming part of psychic time for the listener.

This level of suggestiveness is intensified in the poem's closing lines, in which "the music" (itself a more general and inclusive term than song) is said to continue to resonate internally long after it has ceased to be audible. This process of internalization had been adumbrated in the middle stanzas of the poem. As Earl Wasserman noted, while the last stanza returns to the scene described in the first, there is "an essential difference" between the two. In the intervening stanzas the maiden's song "is stretched out in space... and in time," losing its specificity and becoming "quasi-spiritual." This is the precondition for passage into the "inner consciousness" of the Wordsworthian speaker: "the object is perceived vividly, usually with great specificity; the husk is then dissolved; and when the phenomenon has at last become `spiritualized' it passes into the core of the subjective intelligence."

As Wordsworth was to explain in the 1815 Preface: the imagination, "either by conferring additional properties upon an object, or abstracting from it some of those which it actually possesses [enables it to] re-act upon the mind which hath performed the process, like a new existence."

There is another important difference between the first and last stanzas of "The Solitary Reaper." At the poem's beginning, there was the illusion of immediacy; the scene was presented as if happening before the speaker's eyes and those of a companion; but the poem ends in the past tense and it becomes clear that the scene described is a remembered one that the speaker had witnessed in the past.

One now realizes that the earlier verbal gestures ("Behold her"/"Stop here") were addressed not to an auditor within the poem but to the reader, who has been arrested by the speaker just as the speaker had been earlier arrested by the singer.

In "The Solitary Reaper," then, there is an overlay of two aesthetic experiences: the effect of the young woman's song on the speaker; and the effect of the speaker's utterance (the poem entitled "The Solitary Reaper") on the reader. The implications of this large-scale example of repetition or doubling must now be considered.

Are the effects similar or different? Does a process of internalization similar to that adumbrated in the poem take place during the reader's engagement with the work? Is the reader refreshed and renewed by the poem as the speaker is by the song? Does the poem similarly stay with the reader "long after" his/her engagement with it is concluded?

In answering these questions in the late twentieth-century North-American critical context, a deconstructive reading along the following lines is likely to result. The song-speaker/poem-reader distinction is without a difference. We know from Dorothy's letter and William's note that there was no "real" experience of hearing a solitary young woman singing in a Highland valley. Even if there had been, there could be no question of the reader accessing this experience; all one would have is an after-the-fact verbal representation of an event, which would inevitably differ from the event itself.

It is the speaker's words and feelings that are overflowing. Thus, the whole poem is a mise-en-abime of itself, an affective effusion about the effect of an effusion. We are trapped in the self-referentiality of the text, and must say what Hillis Miller said of Wordsworth's "A slumber did my spirit seal": "the reader is caught in an unstillable oscillation unsatisfying to the mind and incapable of being grounded in anything outside the activity of the poem itself."

The poem's conclusion is thus an inevitable let-down; the reader cannot have (experience) what the speaker has. He has the music; the reader has only the words. The burden of the song is absence not presence, loss not plenitude, and this is effectively communicated. The reader shares a sense of loss; but he/she does not share in the uplift of the music. At the very least, we must say of "The Solitary Reaper" what Tilottama Rajan says of Wordsworth's "The Two April Mornings":

At issue in this temporal duplication is the imitative nature of poetry, as a claim to recapture "the spiritual presences of absent things" and to "arouse the sensual from their sleep / Of Death" (Excursion iv,1234; "Prospectus," ll. 60-61)... it is not so easy to see whether poetic reproduction is an "imitation" which masters the very essenceof the object of desire, or a "copy" which merely represents it and therefore reveals "an emptiness... an unreality" [Coleridge, "On Poesy or Art"] within the fabrications of language.

As an interpretative analysis, this reading has much to recommend it (as my citations of two distinguished critics are intended to suggest). But from another point of view, this account of "The Solitary Reaper" may be regarded as an inauthentic rendering that does not respect the poem's aesthetic properties--as the cerebral exercise of a critic who engages poems only with his/her eyes--who reads a poem but does not listen to it or perform it.

An aesthetic rendition is particularly appropriate in the case of "The Solitary Reaper." Part of the power the maiden's song had for the speaker lay in his inability to comprehend it (since it was in a tongue he didn't know), and there is a comparable situation with reference to Wordsworth's poem and the person who listens to it.

The formal, stylistic and figural properties of the poem create an "indefinite, imprecise suggestiveness" which, like the maiden's song, eludes comprehension. The poem shows that one can receive a song aesthetically even when it cannot be received semantically and suggests that this mode of reception may be a locus of both the universality and the comfort of art.

When "The Solitary Reaper" is received aesthetically (when it is performed rather than read with the eyes only), it can be found to express the same properties that it exemplifies. To speak for myself, each time I return to the poem and engage myself with it, I am caught up in its rhythms, rhymes, repetitions, doublings, gestures, metaphors, and images; and the magnetically tenacious image of a solitary young woman reaping and singing sorrowfully in an inhospitable natural expanse is evoked.

The poem is grounded in the abiding pain and sorrow of human existence, but at its conclusion I find that I have been refreshed and warmed by its inexpressively soothing sounds. I hear in the poem something that cannot be read in it: the sorrow, loss and pain that have been may be a gain when they are tempered by the music of harmonious metrical language.

2

In his essay, "Why Distant Objects Please," William Hazlitt identified a distinctive feature of the nineteenth-century sensibility:

How any object, that unexpectedly brings back to us old

scenes and associations, startles the mind! What a yearning it creates within us.... It is not the little, glimmering, almost annihilated speck in the distance, that rivets our attention... it is the interval that separates us from it, and of which it is the trembling boundary, that excites all this coil and mighty pudder in the breast. Into that great gap in our being "come thronging soft desires" and infinite regrets. It is the contrast, the change recollection with its giant strength...

One of the vehicles for articulating this feeling was a short lyric poem in which something explicit or implied, often a natural setting or an aspect of it, evokes in the speaker an intense feeling of the presence-absence of the past and a piercing sense of its unrecoverability. The poem is the expression of this intense emotion. It ends not with the assertion or suggestion of compensation but with the completion of the emotional discharge.

These poems tend to be short and to center on a specific moment. The longer and more generalized they become, the more the emotion tends to be dissipated by reflection or adulterated by self-pity. In redefining the sonnet as "a small poem, in which some lonely feeling is developed," Coleridge assessed the advantages of brevity from the point of view of the audience. A limited number of lines was essential "in order that the reader's mind having expected the close at the place in which he finds it, may rest satisfied; and that so the poem may acquire, as it were, a Totality,--in plainer phrase, may become a Whole."

The many nineteenth- (and twentieth-) century examples of this kind of lyric include some excellent poems;(31) but the preeminent example, the paradigmatic lyric, is Tennyson's "Tears, idle tears":

Then she, "Let some one sing to us: lightlier move
The minutes fledged with music": and a maid
Of those beside her, smote her harp, and sang.
"Tears, idle tears, I know not what they mean,
Tears from the depth of some divine despair
Rise in the heart, and gather to the eyes,
In looking on the happy Autumn-fields,

And thinking of the days that are no more.
Fresh as the first beam glittering on a sail,
That brings our friends up from the underworld,
Sad as the last that reddens over one
That sinks with all we love below the verge;
So sad, so fresh, the days that are no more.
Ah, sad and strange as in dark summer dawns
The earliest pipe of half-awakened birds
To dying ears, when unto dying eyes
The casement slowly grows a glimmering square;
So sad, so strange, the days that are no more.
Dear as remembered kisses after death,
And sweet as those by hopeless fancy feigned
On lips that are for others; deep as love,
Deep as first love, and wild with all regret;
O Death in Life, the days that are no more."
She ended with such passion that the tear,
She sang of, shook and fell, an erring pearl
Lost in her bosom.

"Tears, idle tears" was written in the mid 1830s and first published in 1847. In later years, Tennyson made several comments on the poem. He told one friend "that it was not real woe, as some people might suppose; 'it was rather the yearning that young people occasionally experience for that which seems to have passed away from them forever.'"

On another occasion, he observed that the poem expressed a longing "in a way like St Paul's 'groanings which cannot be uttered.' It was written at Tintern when the woods were all yellowing with autumn seen through the ruined windows. It is what I have always felt even from a boy, and what as a boy I called the 'passion of the past.'" This last phrase was glossed in a third comment: "The passion of the past, the abiding in the transient, was expressed in 'Tears, idle Tears.'"

The germ of the poem is found in a short lyric entitled "No More," written in 1826 when Tennyson was seventeen.

Oh sad No More! Oh sweet No More!
Oh strange No More!
By a mossed brookbank on a stone

I smelt a wildweed-flower alone;
There was a ringing in my ears,
And both my eyes gushed out with tears.
Surely all pleasant things had gone before,
Lowburied fathomdeep beneath with thee, no more!(36)

As Christopher Ricks has noted, this poem contains much of the vocabulary of "Tears": sad, sweet, strange, no more, eyes, tears, fathomdeep/depth. But the words are brutally compacted; the poem is convulsive gush during which the reader is rhetorically drenched. Moreover, there is no sense of the abiding in the transient. The choice of smell as the sensory trigger of the emotion is telling.

Of itself, smell has no memory. Unlike other sensory experiences, olfactory ones cannot be recalled: "memory can restore to life everything except smells, although nothing revives the past so completely as a smell that was once associated with it."

That is to say, smell cannot detect the co-presence of the abiding and the transient; it is rather a case of all or nothing. In reworking the verbal materials of "No More," Tennyson was obviously concerned to avoid declamatory intensity. One decision was to make "Tears" longer than its prototype. But why wouldn't the fourteen pentameter lines of a sonnet (identified by Coleridge as the obvious medium for this subject matter) have done the trick?

Because the sonnet form could not easily have accommodated either the lack of rhyme or the refrain, the two most crucial compositional choices that Tennyson made. Eric Griffiths has analyzed the subtle effects achieved by the employment of blank verse:

Cadence and refrain combine to give a sense of formal stability which we have in the past found with rhyming stanzas, and which leads us now to imagine rhymes where there are rhymes no more. The sound of "Tears, idle tears" is the sound of prosodic days that are no more . . . each line at once preserves its own integrity and is shaded and absorbed into the whole. A similar double being, at once its own and not its own, affects the individual stanzas and their relations one to the other. The refrain also contributes to this double being. It tends to make each stanza into a discrete entity deploying its own images and figures to convey the speaker's complex apprehension of what is common to them all and reiterated in each bottom line: "the days that are no more." It also tends to make the poem non-progressive: there is a sense of temporal suspension--not duration, but deepening intensity.

Moreover, in the refrain phrase itself there is a similar suggestion. If the line is recited with a slight pause after are rather than after days one has a small-scale example of the abiding ("the days that are") and the transient ("no more") in suspended balance.

The principal effect of both these formal devices is to give a musical quality to the poem. Edgar Allan Poe identified the "intrinsic and essential character" of "true musical expression" as "indefiniteness" and described Tennyson's genius as leading him to strive for "a suggestive indefiniteness of meaning, with a view to bringing about a definiteness of vague and therefore of spiritual effect."

There is no better example than "Tears, idle tears," which Poe quoted in toto in "The Philosophy of Composition." The refrain and the rhymelessness contribute to indefiniteness of meaning; the shape of the poem contributes to definiteness of effect.

"Every short poem," Tennyson once remarked, "should have a definite shape, like the curve, sometimes a single, sometimes a double one, assumed by a severed tress or the rind of an apple when flung on the floor." In many lyric poems there is a movement of thought, the configuration of which is the shape of the poem.

There is no such movement in "Tears," but rather a back-and-forth, slowly oscillating motion that expresses a condition of being. The dominant figures and locutions are oxymoronic: "divine despair"; "sad and fresh"; "sad and strange"; "dark . . . dawns"; "Death in Life." The conjunction of opposing states has a similar effect: rising tears/happy fall of the year; looking/thinking; rising sun/sinking sun; the light of nature dawning while the light of sense is being extinguished; real kisses/

feigned kisses. And other details similarly suggest a suspension between two states: half-awakened birds; a man hovering between life and death; "idle tears." On the literal level, the tears gather to the eyes but do not fall; they idle there. The phrase may be equally taken as a transferred epithet suggesting the suspended state of the speaker's consciousness.

A simultaneous centripetal, downward-and-inward movement gives the poem a double shape. There is a gradual deepening and intensifying of emotion as the contrasting images and conditions become more and more intervolved. This can be traced by noting the changes in the dominant or focusing sense in each stanza and the way in which the objects of perception become increasingly closer to their subjects. Sight is dominant in the second stanza, and the objects of visual perception are at a distance.

As the Victorian critic R. H. Hutton explained: the mingled freshness and sadness in contemplating the days that are no more are likened to "a mixture of the feelings with which we see the light upon an approaching sail that brings us friends from the other hemisphere, and the light upon a retreating sail which takes them away thither; for does not the memory of those days both bring and take away? does it not restore us the vivid joy of the past only to make us feel that it is vanished?"

The third stanza, in which both sight and sound figure, presents a partially analogous situation. The contrast between dawning sun and closing eyes is similar to the dawning/waning contrast of the previous stanza; but we are now indoors, in a confined space. And the waning is that of dying eyes in which the objects of visual perception blur into "a glimmering square" (as if tears have gathered in them).

The glimmer recalls the glitter of the previous stanza; but while the latter is hard and constant, the former suggests a simultaneous brightening and fading. There is thus no need for a contrasting image, as reddening was needed to complement glittering.

The final stanza is the culmination of both the oscillating and the centripetal movement. The dominant sense is touch, in which (in contrast to sight and sound) there is an interaction between perceiver and perceived. And when memories of real kisses and of feigned kisses become equally affecting, the distinction between objective and subjective, palpable and impalpable, has disappeared.

The adjectives "deep" and "wild" refer as much to the consciousness of the speaker as to the memories; the stanza's penultimate line is the only line in the poem that "ends with a sharp closed syllable--regret--a poetic stop to this hitherto fluent emotion"; and there is a further note of finality in "Death in Life," which picks up from the second stanza the subterranean suggestiveness of "underworld."

How desolating are the implications of "Death in Life," the strongest figure in the poem? Does "Tears, idle tears" end with its speaker in a "wild" frenzy and in utter despair like the speaker of "No More"? How this question is answered will depend on the kind of critical model that is used. Since the 1940s, when Cleanth Brooks included a chapter on the poem in The Well-Wrought Urn, "Tears, idle tears" has been the subject of a good deal of excellent commentary.

The most recent example is a deconstructive analysis by J. Hillis Miller, which may be regarded as the exemplary late twentieth-century interpretative reading of Tennyson's poem. For this reason, it is my principal point of reference in addressing these questions and arguing that an aesthetic model can provide a more comprehensive and satisfying answer than an interpretative model can.

Like Miller, most recent commentators regard the poem's first line as setting out an interpretative task for both speaker and commentator: the discovery, or the production, of the meaning of the tears. Gerhard Joseph, for example, writes that the poem's structure "arises from a speaker's repeated need to explain . . . what the seemingly inexplicable tears of the opening line 'mean'"; and another commentator speaks of "the poet's active search for the meaning of the past, his attempt to fill in the absent meaning emblematized by the image of the tears." These are erroneous assumptions.

The speaker initially says he does not understand the

meaning of the tears, that is, why he is feeling the way he does. But in what follows he does not try to understand the cause (the meaning) of the tears; he is rather concerned to find images and figures to express and communicate his emotional state. By the end of the poem he has accomplished that task. At the same time, he has also clarified the question of why he feels the way he does (the meaning of the tears).

This clarification resides in the metonymic or synecdochal aspects of the figures he employs in expressing himself. That is to say, clarification of the meaning of the tears comes not through thinking or interpreting, but as a result of the creative activity of mind involved in the poem's composition. The comprehension of his emotional state is the artwork itself. It is not something that can be extracted from it by hermeneutical operations.

In order to understand the speaker's tears, the reader has to comprehend the poem aesthetically. This can only be done by performing the poem and determining what Jerrold Levinson calls the "utterance meaning." For Miller, the tears "signify the non-being of what they represent. They are like a word repeated so often that it loses its meaning and becomes pure meaningless sound"; they are both "cognitively empty" and "performatively void."

They are not symbols in Coleridge's sense: they are "an allegorical sign [which] does not participate synecdochically, as part for a whole, in what it signifies." We are given "an allegorical time of perpetual loss and absence." Miller's reliance on Paul de Man's interpretative procedures has clearly desensitized him to the musical suggestiveness of Tennyson's poem and to its double being. From an aesthetic point of view, the poem is different from, and less desolating than, his decoding of the tears suggests.

Take, for example, "divine despair," the striking figure of speech in the poem's second line. "If it means anything," Miller insists, it "must mean despair of some god." But divine has both a subjective and objective reference: it can refer to the intensity and the ravishing quality of the emotion as well as to its object. Of course, it can hardly be denied that the felt absence of a compensatory providential design in human experience may be heard in the phrase.

There is too much circumstantial evidence in the poem, too many images of death and bereavement, to allow one to think the speaker's idle tears are unrelated to mortality and temporality. To say this, however, is to say that the poem's images and figures have a metonymical reference as well as a metaphorical one.

As another example, take the figure in the poem's penultimate line: "deep as first love." Metaphorically, this suggests that the emotion the speaker is experiencing and trying to articulate is comparable in intensity to that of first love, a one-time only, unrecapturable intensity. But first love may also be taken to be one of the cluster of things "that are no more" that have gathered in the consciousness of the speaker.

This is subtly intimated in The Princess. Immediately following the maid's recital of "Tears," the song is savaged by the progressive Princess Ida, who dismissively refers to its "moans about the retrospect." But the Princess has yet to experience the intensity of first love, as one is later reminded by the repetition of a phrase.

The tear "lost in the bosom" of the singer pings in the memory when one comes to another lyric in The Princess: the superlative love poem "Now sleeps the crimson petal," which ends with its speaker inviting the beloved to "slip/ Into my bosom and be lost in me." The Princess reads this lyric aloud to herself as she sits by the bedside of the wounded Prince in the dawning moments of her first love.

But what about the poem's climactic figure, "Death in Life"? For Miller, the phrase "names the undermining of all presence and possession in this life by a principle of loss." But one could say the same about the words of the Anglican burial service, "In the midst of life we are in death," and thereby entirely misrepresent the service.

Miller and Joseph both think that the end of the poem is unequivocally negative: "In the hermeneutics of Tennyson's melancholy," says the latter, "an 'idle' feeling . . . gradually assumes the apparitional guise of a terrible Deity, Death in Life." I would say that the ending is different in degree but not in kind from what has preceded.

The last line does indeed contain the most desolating equivalent for the emotion that it is the raison d'etre of "Tears, idle tears" to express and communicate. This is aesthetically necessary if the emotional intensity of the poem is to reach a climax and if it is to have the finality needed to make it a totality.

But the last line does not exist independently of the whole of which it is a part. Having reached the end of the poem, instead of asking what its meaning is, one might better ask what is the aesthetic effect of the completed performance. In addressing this question, it is helpful to note that two responses to the maid's performance are adumbrated in The Princess. As we have seen, the attention of Princess Ida is concentrated on the content of the work.

What she finds there is repugnant to her ideology and she consequently dismisses the song. The other response is that of the maid who sings it--who interprets the work in the sense of performing it. She does not confuse the song with its content. As a performer, she is necessarily attuned to its formal and stylistic properties, including the refrain and the rhymelessness. As a result, while she is passionately moved by the work, she does not conclude her recital in a frenzied or despairing state.

The outward sign of her being moved is the shedding of a single tear. Is her tear cognitively void and performatively empty? By no means. Coleridge recognized that tears were arbitrary symbols, but insisted they were symbols nonetheless. They were one of the means through which "in her homely way" the body tried "to interpret . . . the movements of the Soul."

The maid's tear is a sign that through her performance of the poem she has entered into a state of emotional congruence (deeper than ideology or gender) with its speaker. Her tear also signifies that she has had a fulfilling aesthetic experience and, in Coleridge's phrase, rests satisfied.

The subject of "Tears, idle tears" is not perpetual loss and absence, but the abiding in the transient. This double sense is inscribed in the verbal details of the poem and in the interrelation of the parts of this intricate poetic construct and their relation to the totality. It is also present in the binary relationship of the content of the poem to the poem itself. While the former is a transitory emotion, the completed artwork abides.

3

It is not my intention to argue that lyric poetry should be grouped with music as a particular kind of performable artwork, nor to suggest that a performative interpretation of a lyric poem is essentially the same as a critical interpretation. But I hope to have shown that recognition of similarities between the two can be helpful both in clarifying the distinction between aesthetic and interpretative models of literary criticism and in improving the quality of critical discussion of lyric poems.

Of course the meaning of a poem is important; but it is not necessarily the fundamental or the most important critical consideration. It is a question of the relative ranking of the quest for meaning as opposed to attention to other features of the artwork. Any critical account of a poem must respect its aesthetic properties; for many lyric poems, most conspicuously those written "out of a musical impulse," an authentic performance is the sine qua non. "Every work of art," as Gerard Manley Hopkins insisted, "has its own play or performance":

> [The] performance of a stage play is the playing it on the boards: reading it . . . is not its performance . . . books play, perform, or are played and performed when they are read; and ordinarily by one reader, alone, to himself, with his eyes only. [But a "merely mental performance" is counter to] the true nature of poetry, the darling child of speech, of lips and spoken utterance: it must be spoken; till it is spoken it is not performed, it does not perform, it is not itself."

Tennyson wrote poems throughout his adolescence and his first publication was a self-financed volume, Poems by Two

Brothers, published in 1827. In this same year he entered Trinity College, Cambridge, where in 1829 he became friends with Arthur Henry Hallam, a sophisticated, charming and generally admired young man who, after his death in 1833 at the age of 22, would remain in the memory of all who knew him as a person of exceptional promise. He would become the subject of Tennyson's greatest poem, In Memoriam.

Arthur Hallam encouraged Tennyson to write and publish poetry, claiming, in a notorious review of Tennyson's second volume, Poems, Chiefly Lyrical (1830) in the Englishman's Magazine, that Tennyson's poetry represented a new development, the poetry of 'sensation'. In a highly politicised literary society this smacked of radical, republican 'Cockneyism' and the review incurred the wrath of establishment critics like John Wilson of Blackwood's Magazine and, even more damagingly, of J. W. Croker of the Quarterly Review, who viciously attacked Tennyson's third volume, simply called Poems, published in1832.

Hallam was right, however, in recognising the originality in the "vivid, picturesque delineation of objects" in poems like 'Mariana' and 'Recollections of the Arabian Nights', and the peculiar skill with which they are "fused...in a medium of strong emotion". Hallam's death and the harsh criticism of his poems in the Quarterly Review seemed to plunge Tennyson into a period of depression and inactivity.

Certainly, as far as publication was concerned, there was a long 'silence' until Poems in Two Volumes was published ten years later in 1842. During those ten years, however, he was writing new poems, revising poems from 1832, and writing many of the lyrics which would eventually be collected together and published, in 1850, as In Memoriam.

His 1842 Poems was a considerable success. Its new poems included 'Morte d'Arthur', one of his earliest Arthurian poems, 'Locksley Hall', and what he described as 'English Idyls', such as 'Edwin Morris' and 'The Gardener's Daughter'. Equally striking and popular, was the bringing before the public again of earlier poems, sometimes significantly revised.

Alfred Lord Tennyson was born at Somersby Rectory,

Lincolnshire, in 1809. His father was an embittered, almost paranoid clergyman whose wife and 10 children all suffered as a result of his frequent melancholic, sometimes violent, outbursts. Alfred was the third child and his sense of responsibility for the others lay heavily upon him almost all his life though tempered by a strong and abiding affection. His father's death affected him deeply.

Not unusually for the time, family cohesion was fostered through their common interest in poetry. All the children wrote verses continually and read aloud the results, especially Alfred, Charles and Fred who were particularly skilled. Not surprisingly, all were troubled by melancholy: Edward at 18 went mad and spent the rest of his life in an asylum, Arthur became alcoholic and Septimus seriously depressed, while Charles succumbed to laudanum, although he seemed at first to be a more promising poet even than Alfred. Alfred, however, recalled rather their happy comradeship and remained at heart a Lincolnshire countryman, strong accent, 'loud organ-notes' and all. He stood out amongst his peers.

Peter Levi has written a remarkable book. He knows the spirit of the man and sees through many of Tennyson's subterfuges designed to protect it. But he takes the life in conjunction with the poetry, discussing poems without any assertions in connection with specific events. An excellent poet himself, he understands the rarity of such concatenations. Tennyson was an extraordinarily complicated man, far-ranging in his acquaintances, eclectic in artistic matters and overpowering in his enthusiasm.

Of the many biographies, the earliest being his son Hallam's Memoir, this one reads like a continuous conversation with the poet in the midst of his normal social concerns. It enters also into his preoccupations, particularly work in progress. It slides naturally into cogent critical analysis of the most important poems when Levi illuminates details of their quality and their relation to his whole output.

One such impressive discussion is of Morte d'Arthur, a good example of the critic's expertise. 'There had been nothing in English to touch Morte d' Arthur since Milton', he says, and shows how Tennyson, with the backcloth in mind of Malory's narrative in 1485, 'came as close to Homer as Virgil had ever been'.

Tennyson himself had doubts about any attempt to reconstruct chivalric themes in epic form but they do not interfere with his serious intent to develop his own epic repertory in all its varied moods and rhythms, from ballad metre to blank verse.

Matthew Arnold envied him his natural assets; a painterly eye, strong decorative facility and a musical grasp of metre. But Tennyson's poetry also reflects, willy nilly, the familiar mood of intense sadness which only briefly ever left him. 'His inner sense of loss and ruin', says Peter Levi, 'did find an objective correlative in one great narrative poem ... his Morte d'Arthur'.

Again, 'The mysterious fit of quite pure grief with tears is attested in literature and well known in psychology but Tennyson's is one of its classic statements'. So Tennyson even had two separate sources of grief to draw upon. He had published his first book of poems before he went to Cambridge in 1827. Thackeray and Edward FitzGerald were already there, and he made a wide circle of friends.

He met here his closest friend of undergraduate days, Arthur Hallam, whose untimely death five years later inspired In Memoriam, the masterpiece he revised, added to and rearranged for almost 20 years. Levi judges this as perhaps his greatest work although an 'entangled shipwreck, a many time started and incoherent lament ...' in which his deepest emotions were engaged and, most significantly, his many styles are embedded.

All poetic experimentation, it seemed, had compulsively to be hammered out on the touchstone of this, his deepest fount of grief. For 10 years he published nothing, writing incessantly, until at last, in 1850, it was published and he was made the Poet Laureate (probably at Prince Albert's percipient suggestion, for the Prince had read it).

He also felt free to marry Emily Sellwood, who had waited 11 years, never doubting his final word. There followed forty years of happy, if dramatic, domestic life, with two sons and a fine house in the Isle of Wight, where Tennyson was lionised until he could stand no more.

But we owe the brilliant photographs reproduced in this book to one of the more eccentric of his admirers, Julia Cameron, who indulged his taste for drama and extravagant clothes, as well as her own. Emily's diaries came infallibly one pace behind, so that pictorial and verbal accounts justified one another in depicting the lifestyle at Farringford.

This book possesses its own intoxicating quality for it brings to life a major poet whose star has subsequently fallen from a great height. Avid for poetry, the Victorian public made him their idol. The Queen confided in him and Prince Albert recognized his scholarly gifts. Most rewarding are Peter Levi's observations on classical influences, particularly on Tennyson's poetic affinity with the Hellenic Greek bucolic poet, Theocritus.

No other English poet could sustain the Hellenic style and form better, either pastoral or elegiac. Even so, he is ignored in the new Oxford Dictionary of Classical Literature in their entry under Elegy, although Keats, Shelley and Matthew Arnold are there. But Peter Levi has placed Tennyson in his intellectual context, showing where his poetry is overwrought and consisted, as Carlyle said, of 'superlative lollipops', and where it is awe inspiring. His book is full of learning and humour, his references impeccable.

The professed commentators I have not consulted. It appeared better to give one's own impressions of the Poems, unaffected by the impressions of others, except in one or two cases where matters of fact rather than of taste seemed to be in question. Thus on two or three points I have ventured to differ from a distinguished living critic, and have given the reasons for my dissent.

Professor Bradley's Commentary on In Memoriam came out after this sketch was in print. Many of the comments cited by Mr Bradley from his predecessors appear to justify my neglect of these curious inquirers. The "difficulties" which they raise are not likely, as a rule, to present themselves to persons who read poetry "for human pleasure."

Chapter 19

Poems of 1831–1833

By 1832 most of the poems of Tennyson's second volume were circulating in MS. among his friends, and no poet ever had friends more encouraging. Perhaps bards of today do not find an eagerness among their acquaintance for effusions in manuscript, or in proof-sheets. The charmed volume appeared at the end of the year (dated 1833), and Hallam denounced as "infamous" Lockhart's review in the Quarterly. Infamous or not, it is extremely diverting.

How Lockhart could miss the great and abundant poetry remains a marvel. Ten years later the Scorpion repented, and invited Sterling to review any book he pleased, for the purpose of enabling him to praise the two volumes of 1842, which he did gladly. Lockhart hated all affectation and "preciosity," of which the new book was not destitute.

He had been among Wordsworth's most ardent admirers when Wordsworth had few, but the memories of the war with the "Cockney School" clung to him, the war with Leigh Hunt, and now he gave himself up to satire. Probably he thought that the poet was a member of a London clique.

There is really no excuse for Lockhart, except that he DID repent, that much of his banter was amusing, and that, above all, his censures were accepted by the poet, who altered, later, many passages of a fine absurdity criticised by the infamous reviewer. One could name great prose-writers, historians, who never altered the wondrous errors to which their attention was called by critics. Prose-writers have been more sensitively attached to their glaring blunders in verifiable facts than was this very sensitive poet to his occasional lapses in taste.

The Lady of Shalott, even in its early form, was more than enough to give assurance of a poet. In effect it is even more poetical, in a mysterious way, if infinitely less human, than the later treatment of the same or a similar legend in Elaine. It has the charm of Coleridge, and an allegory of the fatal escape from the world of dreams and shadows into that of realities may have been really present to the mind of the young poet, aware that he was "living in phantasy." The alterations are usually for the better. The daffodil is not an aquatic plant, as the poet seems to assert in the first form —

"The yellow-leaved water-lily,
The green sheathed daffodilly,
Tremble in the water chilly,
Round about Shalott."

Nobody can prefer to keep

"Though the squally east wind keenly
Blew, with folded arms serenely
By the water stood the queenly
Lady of Shalott."

However stoical the Lady may have been, the reader is too seriously sympathetic with her inevitable discomfort —

"All raimented in snowy white
That loosely flew,"

as she was. The original conclusion was distressing; we were dropped from the airs of mysterious romance:-

"They crossed themselves, their stars they blest,
Knight, minstrel, abbot, squire, and guest;
There lay a parchment on her breast,
That puzzled more than all the rest
The well-fed wits at Camelot."

Hitherto we have been "puzzled," but as with the sublime incoherences of a dream. Now we meet well-fed wits, who say, "Bless my stars!" as perhaps we should also have done in the circumstances—a dead lady arriving, in a very cold east wind, alone in a boat, for "her blood was frozen slowly," as was natural, granting the weather and the lady's airy costume. It is certainly matter of surprise that the young poet's vision broke up in this humorous manner. And, after all, it is less surprising that the Scorpion, finding such matter in a new little book by a new young man, was more sensitive to the absurdity than to the romance.

But no lover of poetry should have been blind to the almost flawless excellence of Mariana in the South, inspired by the landscape of the Provencal tour with Arthur Hallam. In consequence of Lockhart's censures, or in deference to the maturer taste of the poet, The Miller's Daughter was greatly altered before 1842.

It is one of the earliest, if not the very earliest, of Tennyson's domestic English idylls, poems with conspicuous beauties, but not without sacrifices to that Muse of the home affections on whom Sir Barnes Newcome delivered his famous lecture.

The seventh stanza perhaps hardly deserved to be altered, as it is, so as to bring in "minnows" where "fish" had been the reading, and where "trout" would best recall an English chalk stream. To the angler the rising trout, which left the poet cold, is at least as welcome as the "reflex of a beauteous form." "Every woman seems an angel at the water-side," said "that good old angler, now with God," Thomas Todd Stoddart, and so "the long and listless boy" found it to be. It is no wonder that the mother was "SLOWLY brought to yield consent to my desire." The domestic affections, in fact, do not adapt themselves so well to poetry as the passion, unique in Tennyson, of Fatima. The critics who hunt for parallels or plagiarisms will note –

"O Love, O fire! once he drew
With one long kiss my whole soul thro'
My lips,"
and will observe Mr Browning's
"Once he kissed
My soul out in a fiery mist."

As to OEnone, the scenery of that earliest of the classical idylls is borrowed from the Pyrenees and the tour with Hallam. "It is possible that the poem may have been suggested by Beattie's Judgment of Paris," says Mr Collins; it is also possible that the tale which

"Quintus Calaber
Somewhat lazily handled of old"

may have reached Tennyson's mind from an older writer than Beattie. He is at least as likely to have been familiar with Greek myth as with the lamented "Minstrel." The form of 1833, greatly altered in 1842, contained such unlucky phrases as "cedar shadowy," and "snowycoloured," "marblecold," "violet-eyed"—easy spoils of criticism.

The alterations which converted a beautiful but faulty into a beautiful and flawless poem perhaps obscure the significance of OEnone's "I will not die alone," which in the earlier volume directly refers to the foreseen end of all as narrated in Tennyson's late piece, The Death of OEnone. The whole poem brings to mind the glowing hues of Titian and the famous Homeric lines on the divine wedlock of Zeus and Hera.

The allegory or moral of The Palace of Art does not need explanation. Not many of the poems owe more to revision. The early stanza about Isaiah, with fierce Ezekiel, and "Eastern Confutzee," did undeniably remind the reader, as Lockhart said, of The Groves of Blarney.

"With statues gracing that noble place in,
All haythen goddesses most rare,
Petrarch, Plato, and Nebuchadnezzar,
All standing naked in the open air."

In the early version the Soul, being too much "up to date,"

"Lit white streams of dazzling gas,"

like Sir Walter Scott at Abbotsford.

"Thus her intense, untold delight,
In deep or vivid colour, smell, and sound,
Was flattered day and night."

Lockhart was not fond of Sir Walter's experiments in gas, the "smell" gave him no "deep, untold delight," and his "infamous review" was biassed by these circumstances.

The volume of 1833 was in nothing more remarkable than in its proof of the many-sidedness of the author. He offered mediaeval romance, and classical perfection touched with the romantic spirit, and domestic idyll, of which The May Queen is probably the most popular example. The "mysterious being," conversant with "the spiritual world," might have been expected to disdain topics well within the range of Eliza Cook.

He did not despise but elevated them, and thereby did more to introduce himself to the wide English public than he could have done by a century of Fatimas or Lotos–Eaters. On the other hand, a taste more fastidious, or more perverse, will scarcely be satisfied with pathos which in process of time has come to seem "obvious."

The pathos of early death in the prime of beauty is less obvious in Homer, where Achilles is to be the victim, or in the laments of the Anthology, where we only know that the dead bride or maiden was fair; but the poor May Queen is of her nature rather commonplace.

"That good man, the clergyman, has told me words of peace," strikes a note rather resembling the Tennysonian parody of Wordsworth "A Mr Wilkinson, a clergyman."

The Lotos–Eaters, of course, is at the opposite pole of the poet's genius. A few plain verses of the Odyssey, almost bald in their reticence, are the point de repere of the most magical vision expressed in the most musical verse. Here is the languid charm of Spenser, enriched with many classical memories, and pictures of natural beauty gorgeously yet delicately painted. After the excision of some verses, rather fantastical, in 1842, the poem became a flawless masterpiece,—one of the eternal possessions of song.

On the other hand, the opening of The Dream of Fair Women was marred in 1833 by the grotesque introductory verses about "a man that sails in a balloon." Young as Tennyson was, these freakish passages are a psychological marvel in the work of one who did not lack the saving sense of humour.

The poet, wafted on the wing and "pinion that the Theban eagle bear," cannot conceivably be likened to an aeronaut waving flags out of a balloon—except in a spirit of self-mockery which was not Tennyson's. His remarkable self-discipline in excising the fantastic and superfluous, and reducing his work to its classical perfection of thought and form, is nowhere more remarkable than in this magnificent vision. It is probably by mere accidental coincidence of thought that, in the verses To J. S. (James Spedding), Tennyson reproduces the noble speech on the warrior's death which Sir Walter Scott places in the lips of the great Dundee: "It is the memory which the soldier leaves behind him, like the long train of light that follows the sunken sun, THAT is all that is worth caring for," the light which lingers eternally on the hills of Atholl. Tennyson's lines are a close parallel:-

"His memory long will live alone
In all our hearts, as mournful light
That broods above the fallen sun,
And dwells in heaven half the night."

Though Tennyson disliked the exhibition of "the chips of the workshop," we have commented on them, on the early readings of the early volumes. They may be regarded more properly as the sketches of a master than as "chips," and do more than merely engage the idle curiosity of the fanatics of first editions. They prove that the poet was studious of perfection, and wisely studious, for his alterations, unlike those of some authors, were almost invariably for the better, the saner, the more mature in taste.

The early readings are also worth notice, because they partially explain, by their occasionally fantastic and humourless character, the lack of early and general recognition of the poet's genius. The native prejudice of mankind is not in favour of a new poet. Of new poets there are always so many, most of them bad, that nature has protected mankind by an armour of suspiciousness. The world, and Lockhart, easily found good reasons for distrusting this new claimant of the ivy and the bays: moreover, since about 1814 there had been a reaction against new poetry.

The market was glutted. Scott had set everybody on reading, and too many on writing, novels. The great reaction of the century against all forms of literature except prose fiction had begun. Near the very date of Tennyson's first volume Bulwer Lytton, as we saw, had frankly explained that he wrote novels because nobody would look at anything else.

Tennyson had to overcome this universal, or all but

universal, indifference to new poetry, and, after being silent for ten years, overcome it he did—a remarkable victory of art and of patient courage. Times were even worse for poets than today. Three hundred copies of the new volume were sold! But Tennyson's friends were not puffers in league with pushing publishers.

Meanwhile the poet in 1833 went on quietly and undefeated with his work. He composed The Gardener's Daughter, and was at work on the Morte d'Arthur, suppressed till the ninth year, on the Horatian plan. Many poems were produced (and even written out, which a number of his pieces never were), and were left in manuscript till they appeared in the Biography.

Most of these are so little worthy of the author that the marvel is how he came to write them—in what uninspired hours. Unlike Wordsworth, he could weed the tares from his wheat. His studies were in Greek, German, Italian, history (a little), and chemistry, botany, and electricity—"cross-grained Muses," these last.

It was on September 15, 1833, that Arthur Hallam died. Unheralded by sign or symptom of disease as it was, the news fell like a thunderbolt from a serene sky. Tennyson's and Hallam's love had been "passing the love of women." A blow like this drives a man on the rocks of the ultimate, the insoluble problems of destiny.

"Is this the end?" Nourished as on the milk of lions, on the elevating and strengthening doctrines of popular science, trained from childhood to forego hope and attend evening lectures, the young critics of our generation find Tennyson a weakling because he had hopes and fears concerning the ultimate renewal of what was more than half his life— his friendship.

"That faith I fain would keep,
That hope I'll not forego:
Eternal be the sleep —
Unless to waken so,"

wrote Lockhart, and the verses echoed ceaselessly in the widowed heart of Carlyle. These men, it is part of the duty of critics later born to remember, were not children or cowards, though they dreamed, and hoped, and feared. We ought to make allowance for failings incident to an age not yet fully enlightened by popular science, and still undivorced from spiritual ideas that are as old as the human race, and perhaps not likely to perish while that race exists. Now and then even scientific men have been mistaken, especially when they have declined to examine evidence, as in this problem of the transcendental nature of the human spirit they usually do.

At all events Tennyson was unconvinced that death is the end, and shortly after the fatal tidings arrived from Vienna he began to write fragments in verse preluding to the poem of In Memoriam. He also began, in a mood of great misery, The Two Voices; or, Thoughts of a Suicide. The poem seems to have been partly done by September 1834, when Spedding commented on it, and on the beautiful Sir Galahad, "intended for something of a male counterpart to St Agnes."

The Morte d'Arthur Tennyson then thought "the best thing I have managed lately." Very early in 1835 many stanzas of In Memoriam had taken form. "I do not wish to be dragged forward in any shape before the reading public at present," wrote the poet, when he heard that Mill desired to write on him. His OEnone he had brought to its new perfection, and did not desire comments on work now several years old. He also wrote his Ulysses and his Tithonus.

If ever the term "morbid" could have been applied to Tennyson, it would have been in the years immediately following the death of Arthur Hallam. But the application would have been unjust. True, the poet was living out of the world; he was unhappy, and he was, as people say, "doing nothing." He was so poor that he sold his Chancellor's prize gold medal, and he did not

"Scan his whole horizon
In quest of what he could clap eyes on,"

in the way of money-making, which another poet describes as the normal attitude of all men as well as of pirates. A careless observer would have thought that the poet was dawdling. But he dwelt in no Castle of Indolence; he studied, he composed, he corrected his verses: like Sir Walter in Liddesdale, "he was making himsel' a' the time." He did not neglect the movements of the great world in that dawn of discontent with the philosophy of commercialism. But it was not his vocation to plunge into the fray, and on to platforms.

It is a very rare thing anywhere, especially in England, for a man deliberately to choose poetry as the duty of his life, and to remain loyal, as a consequence, to the bride of St Francis—Poverty. This loyalty Tennyson maintained, even under the temptation to make money in recognised ways presented by his new-born love for his future wife, Miss Emily Sellwood.

They had first met in 1830, when she, a girl of seventeen, seemed to him like "a Dryad or an Oread wandering here." But admiration became the affection of a lifetime when Tennyson met Miss Sellwood as bridesmaid to her sister, the bride of his brother Charles, in 1836. The poet could not afford to marry, and, like the hero of Locksley Hall, he may have asked himself, "What is that which I should do?"

By 1840 he had done nothing tangible and lucrative, and correspondence between the lovers was forbidden. That neither dreamed of Tennyson's deserting poetry for a more normal profession proved of great benefit to the world. The course is one which could only be justified by the absolute certainty of possessing genius.

Bibliography

Ainger, A. The Death of Tennyson. Lectures and Essays. 1905.

Alford, H. The Idylls of the King. The Contemporary Review. Vol. XIII, pp. 104 ff. 1870.

Bagehot, Walter. Literary Studies, 3 vols. 1895.

Baker, Arthur E. A Concordance to the Poetical and Dramatic Works of Alfred, Lord Tennyson, 1914.

Barera, E. A Critical Essay on the works of Alfred, Lord Tennyson. 1896.

Bayne, Peter. Lessons from my masters, Carlyle, Tennyson, and Ruskin. 1879.

Benson, A. C. Alfred Tennyson. Little Biographies. 1904.

Blöndal, S. Alfred Tennyson. 1903.

Bradley, A. C. A Commentary on Tennyson's In Memoriam. 1901. 2nd edn., revised. 1902.

Brimley, George. Alfred Tennyson's Poems. [Cambridge Essays.] 1885.

Brooke, Stopford A. Tennyson: his art and relation to modern life. 1894.

Cary, Elizabeth L. Tennyson. His homes, his friends and his work.... Illustrated. 1898.

Chapman, Elizabeth R. A Companion to In Memoriam. 1888.

Chesterton, G. K. and Garnett, R. Tennyson. [Bookman Biographies, no. 6.] 1903.

Chronological List of the Works of Tennyson. Publ. by the Grolier Club. 1897.

Collins, J. C. Illustrations of Tennyson. 1891.

Cuthbertson, E. J. Tennyson: the story of his life. 1898.

Dennis, John. English Rural Poetry. Studies in English Literature. 1876.

Dhaleine, L. A Study on Tennyson's Idyls of the King. 1905.

Dixon, W. M. A Primer of Tennyson. 1901.

Dowden, E. Mr. Tennyson and Mr. Browning. 1869. Rptd. in Studies in Literature, 1789–1877. 1878.

Dyboski, R. Tennyson's Sprache und Stil. (Wiener Beiträge zur Eng. Philologie.... XXV). Wien und Leipzig. 1907.

Elsdale, H. Studies in the Idylls. 1878.

Elton, O. Tennyson. An inaugural lecture. 1901. Rptd. in Modern Studies. 1907.

Fischer, T. A. Leben und Werke Tennysons. 1899.

Gatty, A. A Key to Tennyson's In Memoriam. 1881. 3rd edn. 1885.

Gilfillan, George. Galleries of Literary Portraits. 2 vols. 1856–7.

[Gladstone, W. E.] Poems, 1842, The Princess, 1847, In Memoriam, 1850, Maud, 1855, Idylls of the King, 1859. The Quarterly Review. Vol. CVI, pp. 454 ff. 1859.

Locksley Hall and the Jubilee. The Nineteenth Century. Vol. XXI, pp. I ff. 1887.

Gordon, William C. The Social Ideals of Alfred Tennyson as related to his time. 1906.

Guiliano, A. Essai sur Locksley Hall et Locksley Hall Sixty Years after d'Alfred Tennyson. Commentaires et comparaisons. 1907.

Gwynn, S. Tennyson, a Study. 1899.

Hallam, A. H. The Poems of A. H. Hallam, together with his Essay on the Lyrical Poems of Alfred Tennyson. 1893.

Harrison, F. Tennyson, Ruskin, Mill and other literary estimates. 1899.

Henley, W. E. Tennyson. View and Reviews. 2nd edn. 1892.

Hutton, R. H. Literary Essays. 1888.

Jacobs, J. Tennyson and "In Memoriam." 1892.

Japp, A. H. Three Great Teachers of our own time: Carlyle, Tennyson and Ruskin. 1865.

Jebb, R. C. On Mr. Tennyson's Lucretius. Macmillan's Magazine. Vol. XVIII, pp. 97 ff. 1868.

Jennings, H. J. Tennyson, a biographical sketch. 1884.

Johnson, R. B. Tennyson and his Poetry. [Poetry and Life series.] 1913.

Jones, Henry. Tennyson [Proceedings of the British Academy, vol. IV.] 1909.

Jurczyk, O. Tennyson. Eine kritische Würdigung zur 100. Wiederkehr seines Geburtstages (6 Aug., 1909). Englische Studien. Bd. XLI, pp. 28–69. 1910.

Ker, W. P. Tennyson: the Leslie Stephen lecture. 1909. [See The Modern Language Review, vol. v, pp. 530–1, 1910.]

Koeppel, E. Tennyson. Berlin, 1899.

Lang, Andrew. Alfred Tennyson. (Modern English Writers.) 1901.

Lauvrière, E. Repetition and Parallelism in Tennyson. 1910.

Layard, G. S. Tennyson and his pre-Raphaelite Illustrators. 1894.

Littledale, H. Essays on Lord Tennyson's Idylls of the King. 1893.

Lockhart, J. G. Poems (1833). The Quarterly Review. Vol. XLIX, pp. 81 ff. 1833.

Lockyer, Sir N. and W. L. Tennyson as a Student and Poet of Nature. 1910.

Lounsbury, T. R. The Life and Times of Tennyson, from 1809 to 1850. In preparation.

Luce, M. A Handbook to the Works of Alfred, Lord Tennyson. 1895.

Nature in Tennyson. The British Review. Sept. and Oct. 1915.

Lyall, Sir Alfred. Tennyson. (English Men of Letters.) 1902.

MacCabe, W. G. Personal Recollections of Tennyson. 1902.

Maccallum, M. W. Tennyson's Idylls and Arthurian Story from the sixteenth century. 1894.

MacCrie, G. The religion of our Literature: essays upon Carlyle, Tennyson, Browning, etc. 1875.

MacEwen, V. Knights of the Holy Eucharist. [Thoughts on the spiritual teaching of Tennyson's The Holy Grail.] [1912].

Mann, R. J. Maud vindicated. 1856.

Masterman, C. F. G. Tennyson as a religious Teacher. 1900.

Matthews, C. E. Earlier and less known poems of Tennyson. 1883.

[Mill, J. S.] Tennyson's Poems. The London and Westminster Review. Vol. XXX, pp. 402 ff. 1835.

Myers, F. W. H. Tennyson as Prophet. The Nineteenth Century. Vol. XXV, pp. 381 ff. 1889.

Modern Poets and the Meaning of Life. The Nineteenth Century. Vol. XXXIII, pp. 93 ff. 1893.

Napier, G. G. Homes and Haunts of Tennyson. 1892.

Nicoll, W. R. and Wise, T. J. Literary Anecdotes of the Nineteenth Century. 2 vols. 1895. [See the various articles connected with Tennyson contained in both vols.]

Noel, Roden B. W. Essays on Poetry and Poets. 1886.

Pallen, Condé B. The Meaning of the Idylls of the King. 1904.

Paul, H. W. The Classical Poems of Tennyson. (Men and Letters.) 1901.

Rawnsley, W. F. Tennyson, 1809–1909. A lecture. 1909.

Robertson, John M. New Essays towards a Critical Method. 1897.

Roz, F. Tennyson. Paris, 1911.

Saintsbury, George. Corrected Impressions. 1895.

The Later Nineteenth Century. Edinburgh, 1907.

Salt, H. S. Tennyson as a Thinker. [1893].

Silvestri-Falconieri, F. di. Lord Tennyson. 1911.

Sneath, E. H. The Mind of Tennyson. 1900.

Stephen, Sir Leslie. Studies of a Biographer. Vol. II. 1898.

Stirling, J. H. Jerrold, Tennyson and Macaulay: Critical Essays. 1868.

Swinburne, A. C. Tennyson and Musset. Miscellanies. 1886.

Tainsh, E. C. A Study of the Works of Alfred Tennyson. 1868.

Tennyson, Hallam, lord. Alfred, Lord Tennyson: a memoir. 2 vols. 1897.

(ed.). Tennyson and his friends. 1911.

A. T.'s Works. Edns. 1898–9, 1907 and 1913.

Thackeray, afterwards Ritchie, Anne I. Records of Tennyson, Ruskin and the Brownings. 1892.

Traill, H. D. Tennyson and Vergil. The New Lucian: being a series of dialogues of the dead. New edn. revised and enlarged. 1900.

Van Dyke, H. J. The Poetry of Tennyson. [With a bibliography.] 1898.

Walters, J. C. In Tennyson's land. 1890.

Tennyson: Studies. 1893.

Warren, T. H. The Centenary of Tennyson. A lecture. 1909.

Waugh, Arthur, Alfred, Lord Tennyson. A study of his life and work. 1892. 2nd edn. 1893.

Way, A. S. Tennyson and Quintus Calaber. The Journal of English Studies. Vol. I, no. 2. Sept., 1912–Jan., 1913.

Weld, A. G. Glimpses of Tennyson. 1903.

Wilson, John (Christopher North). Tennyson's Poems. Essays critical and imaginative. Vol. II, pp. 109 ff. 4 vols. 1866.

